Ted Parrish's

ECHOES OF OLD WATFORD, BUSHEY & OXHEY

A complete collection of nostalgic local history articles
first published in
the Watford edition of the 'Evening Post-Echo'
between January 1982 and November 1983

entitled

'Ted Parrish Remembers'

Edited by Lesley Dunlop

467 415 22 9

First published 2013

British Library Cataloguing in Publication Data
A catalogue record for this book is available from the British Library

ISBN 978 0 9576738 0 9

Published by Past Days Publishing
The Knoll, Higher Sea Lane, Charmouth, Dorset DT6 6BD
www.pastdayspublishing.com

Illustrations scanned by Bob Dunlop

Page layout and printing by Metro Commercial Printing Ltd
Sandown Road, Watford WD24 7UY

Dedicated to Ted's grandchildren,
Robert, Laura and James Dunlop

Acknowledgements

Thomson Regional Newspapers
for permission to reproduce the articles

'Ted Parrish Remembers'

in book form

Maps and related notes reproduced by kind permission of Stephen Castle

Archive photographs courtesy of

Denise Mangles (née Leader)
George Lorimer
Joan Cousins
Frederick Hocker
The Honourable Mrs Jennifer Brown (née Bethell)
1st Watford Boys' Brigade
Bushey Museum
LEGO Group, Denmark
National Portrait Gallery, London

My husband Bob for his help, encouragement and support

All illustrations, except those credited elsewhere, are from the Editor's own collection

Photographs marked with an asterisk are from glass plate negatives by Watford photographer
Harry Cull

Front cover illustrations: Frederick Lewis' Omnibus Company's open-topped motor buses, Market Place, 1920s*
Attenborough's fields and Haydon Hill, photo by Ted Parrish

Rear cover illustrations: Ted Parrish, 1944
Cassiobury Park Gates, 1912

CONTENTS

Author's Biography

Reginald Edward Humphrey (Ted) Parrish was born in Watford in 1920, the only child of Reginald and Agnes Parrish. He spent his early years in Watford Fields and was a pupil at Watford Field Junior School. In 1927, after the family moved to Haydon Road, Oxhey, he attended London Road School in Bushey, later completing his education at Watford Grammar School for Boys.

During the Second World War, Ted served with 113 Squadron of the RAF in India and Burma. He concluded his war service as Technical Sergeant at the de Havilland Aircraft Company, Hatfield, lecturing on the multi-role combat Mosquito aircraft. At the end of the war he resumed employment at the Bank of Nova Scotia in London and was the bank's Regional Executive when he retired in 1980.

In the late 1950s Ted joined Watford & District RAFA, then an ailing branch. Serving tirelessly as welfare officer, chairman and finally president, he organised fundraising events, Wings Week collections and Battle of Britain commemoration services, receiving a 50-year service badge before his death in 1997.

A founder member of the Liberal party in post-war Watford and one of the 'First Eleven' who contested every seat in 1960, Ted stood twice for Kings Ward and Oxhey Ward, losing by only 45 votes after a recount. In the same year he formed the King's Jazz Club at Oakley Studios in Clarendon Road to raise funds for the Liberals. A move to the Compasses on the corner of Watford High Street and Market Street followed. By the late 1960s the club's increasing popularity necessitated a move to The Hertfordshire Arms in St Albans Road and in 1972 the club made a final move to Durrants, becoming known as Croxley Jazz Club.

In August 1960, after Ted successfully convinced the town's Parks Entertainment Committee that the youth of Watford needed entertainment in line with the times, the Saratoga Jazz Band played in the bandstand in Cassiobury Park, entertaining more than 350 fans; the first of three successive summers of jazz in the park. Ted organised a canal boat shuffle in 1960 with the band on board 'Water Kelpie'. In 1961 he hired a double-decker bus and ran a highly successful jazz session at Woburn Abbey with the Maryland Stompers. Over the years, Ted was responsible for numerous decorated floats for the jazz club, RAFA and Watford Cine Society in Watford's Whitsun carnival processions.

Ted assisted the Watford Council of Youth, compering Johnny Kidd and the Pirates at the 'small' Town Hall (Watford Colosseum) and the Temperance Seven at Watford Technical College (West Hertfordshire College). In the early 1960s he famously rejected the offer of a performance from an unknown group called the Rolling Stones; even then, their fee was exorbitant for the WCY!

Ted joined Watford Cine society in 1966. An accomplished and enthusiastic filmmaker, he made numerous award-winning films in a variety of genre: ambitious fictional films based on his scripts, overseas travelogues and evocative documentaries relating to Watford, Bushey and Oxhey, e.g. 'Memories of Watford' (1975-1980), 'Bushey in the Early '70s' and 'Oxhey Village' (1976-1979). During 1974-1975 he made 'Time to Think' in objection to the demolition of 195-197 High Street, Watford. It was screened at the Public Enquiry.

Ted was a founder member of the Friends of the Chiltern Open Air Museum, where he and his wife Peggy regularly helped as stewards. He recorded the museum's first 10 years on film. He was also an active member of Watford & South West Hertfordshire Archaeological Society for many years.

A staunch committee member of Oxhey Village Environment Group, Ted organised the Oxhey Village Fayre for nine years with Peggy's support. Under OVEG's banner, he vigorously campaigned to raise funds for the replacement of the wooden memorial cross on Watford Heath. Since the new cross was dedicated in 1994, it has become a focal point for local annual Remembrance Sunday services.

An avid local history researcher and writer, Ted's letters and articles appeared regularly in the 'Watford Observer' newspaper and 'Hertfordshire Countryside' magazine. In 1986 Bob Nunn invited him to write the foreword to his reprint of W R Saunders' 'History of Watford' and in 1987 he was the main textual contributor to Bob's 'Book of Watford'. He contributed to Bob's 'Book of Watford II' (1996).

In 1997 Oli Phillips, former deputy editor of the 'Watford Observer', wrote a tribute to Ted headed 'Remembering the True Son of Watford'. He said: "I knew Ted for some 37 years. He was my first contact; the first telephone number in my book when I was a fledgling journalist. He was a gentleman in the old sense: kindly, polite and attentive." Oli noted that the description of Ted as a 'true son of Watford' had been coined by "one of Ted's many admirers, the late John Ausden".

Waiting at Harebreaks before the Whitsun Carnival procession, 1960. Ted is standing, second on left.

Wreath-laying at Battle of Britain Commemoration Service, Langleybury, 1966. Canon Ron Martin officiating, Ted is front right; Peggy with hat to right of Canon Martin.

Ted, Peggy and grandson James at Watford Heath memorial cross before its dedication in May 1994.

Preface

As a matter of priority I must express my thanks to Thomson Regional Newspapers Ltd, to which company I am indebted for permitting the reproduction of a series of weekly articles that I wrote for the Watford edition of the 'Evening Post-Echo' over a span of nearly two years, until its demise in November 1983. However, space constraints exercised by the Editor and his staff frequently caused the reduction of words, if not paragraphs, to comply with available column inches. As a result, a number of my articles were not reproduced in their entirety. To remedy the situation, they are now presented in their unexpurgated form and with my original titles.

It is necessary to remind the reader that the series first appeared between January 1982 and November 1983 and, in the intervening years, Watford and especially the High Street has changed almost beyond recognition. The town about which I lovingly wrote is now a treasured memory. Its major industries have been lost and Watford is no longer a manufacturing base of any consequence. The social structure has adjusted itself to meet the demands of economic changes, but parochial resistance to environmental changes has increased with the emergence of numerous organisations to counter the dictates of local authorities.

Perhaps the so-called 'market forces', which appear to direct the course of events, will stabilise and the old values return. Please, then, bear in mind these factors as you read of other eras that reflect the collective memories of older generations; memories which may invoke a smile or, conversely, touch a raw nerve. If they so much as prompt symptoms of nostalgia, they will have served their purpose well.

I hope you enjoy my articles and the early photographs, which together make this book a unique record of people, places and events in Watford, Bushey and Oxhey in past days.

Ted Parrish
Watford Heath
1995

Editor's Foreword

On 27 January 1982, the Editor of the Watford edition of the 'Evening Post-Echo' introduced my father to his newspaper's readers as follows: "Ted Parrish has been part of Watford life for more than 60 years. His love for the town and his unrivalled recollections of the 'good old days' make him the perfect man to write a column looking back over the years. That is why I have asked him to produce a series on life in the area as it used to be."

Since my father handwrote the 96 manuscripts on which this book is based (no doubt there would have been many more had the newspaper survived), significant changes to the area have continued apace. In order, therefore, to help the 21st century reader identify locations of buildings or places that my father remembered from his boyhood in the 1920s or his teenage years in the 1930s, or which were standing proud when he wrote his articles in the early 1980s but are now confined to memory, I have added explanatory footnotes. Where practical, premises are cross-referenced with their current trading names and/or street numbers.

To add a further dimension, I have included a selection of letters that my father received from interested readers, whose own memories were rekindled by his articles.

A significant number of illustrations in this book are appearing in print for the first time.

Lesley Dunlop
Charmouth
2013

Note: Pre-decimal pounds, shillings and pence have been left unaltered.
As a reference, one pound comprised 20 shillings (20s) and one shilling comprised 12 pence (12d).
'Half-a-crown' was two shillings and sixpence, and a 'guinea' was 21 shillings (£1 1s).

BUILDINGS OF ARCHITECTURAL & HISTORIC INTEREST IN WATFORD TOWN CENTRE – IN 1950 AND 1975

"It is ironical that 1975, European Architectural Heritage Year, should have been a year of wholesale destruction. In 1950 there were 121 buildings of historic interest surviving in Watford's town centre (Fig 1). By January 1975 there were only 40 (Fig 2) and in January 1976, 35." Stephen Castle.

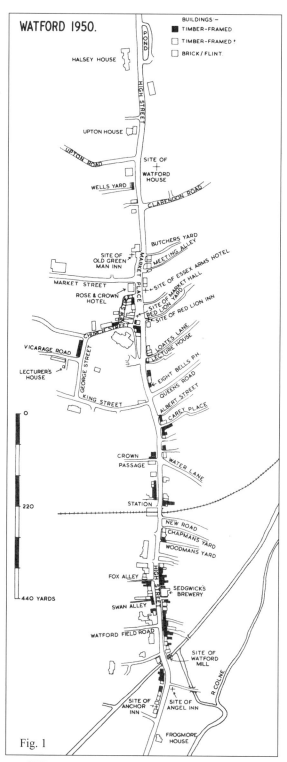

Fig. 1

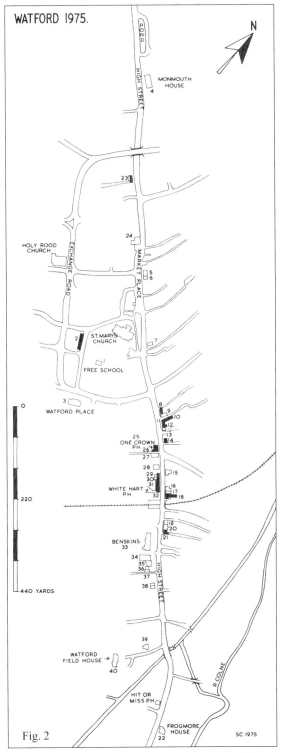

WATFORD 1975.

Fig. 2

SC 1975

Fig. 2 Buildings of architectural and historic interest in Watford town centre as at 1975

1. Free School 1704; **2.** Bedford Almshouses 1580; **3.** Watford Place, King Street, c1790, much rebuilt c1825; **4.** Monmouth House, High Street, c1626-1639; **5.** 63-65 High Street, 1889; **6.** 67 High Street, late 18th/early 19th C; **7.** 97 High Street, 18th C; **8.** 129-131 High Street, 17th C; **9.** 133-135 High Street, 19th C; **10.** 1a Carey Place, 16th C; **11.** 137-139 High Street, c1614; **12.** 141 High Street, 16th C; **13.** 145 High Street, 1780; **14.** 149-151 High Street, 17th C or earlier; **15.** 167-167a High Street*, 18th C; **16.** 173 High Street*, c1800; **17.** 175 High Street*, c1850 or earlier; **18.** 177-179 High Street*, rearward wing 15th C, frontage/middle range 16th C; **19.** 189-191 High Street*, late 18th/early 19th C; **20.** 193 High Street*, 19th C but partly 15th C; **21.** 195 High Street*, 15th C; **22.** Frogmore House c1716; **23.** 22-26a High Street early 16th C; **24.** 58 High Street, early 19th C; **25.** The One Crown PH, 156 High Street, 16th C; **26.** 158 High Street, 17th C; **27.** 160 High Street (formerly Three Crowns PH), early 19th C; **28.** 166-168 High Street, 18th C; **29.** 172 High Street, 17th C; **30.** 172a High Street, late 17th/early 18th C; **31.** 174-178 High Street*, 17th C; **32.** The White Hart PH, 180 High Street*, early 17th C; **33.** Benskins Brewery residence, 1775; **34.** Benskins Brewery outbuilding, 18th C; **35.** 202 High Street, c1800; **36.** 202a High Street 18th C; **37.** 204 High Street, early 19th C; **38.** 212-214 High Street 19th C. Rear of 214 ?17th C; **39.** 250 High Street (formerly Brookside House), early 19th C; **40.** Watford Field House*, ?early 19th C.

NB By 1977 buildings marked with an asterisk were either demolished or threatened with demolition.

Stephen Castle's maps and related notes from his publication 'Timber-Framed Buildings in Watford' (1977) are particularly relevant to this book. They are reproduced with his kind permission.

WATFORD THROUGH THE DECADES

1907

1911

1920

1935

X

BUSHEY & BUSHEY HEATH IN PAST DAYS

High Street, Bushey, 1901

High Street, Bushey, 1907

Black Cottage, Bushey, 1907

Windmill, Bushey Heath, 1907

BUSHEY & BUSHEY HEATH IN PAST DAYS

High Road, Bushey Heath, 1908

High Road, Bushey Heath, 1911

London Road, Bushey, 1913

Elstree Road, Bushey Heath, Caldecote Towers behind wall on left, 1913

OXHEY IN PAST DAYS

Lower Paddock Road, Oxhey, 1933

Mrs Holdsworth, Haydon Villa, 137 Lower Paddock Road, Oxhey, early 1900s

Avenue Terrace, Oxhey, 1970s, photo by Ted Parrish

Oxhey Infants' School, 1978; demolished later that year

OXHEY IN PAST DAYS

Capel Road, 1979

Miss A Horwood's shop, 90 Villiers Road, 1980

Jazz at the Haydon Arms, 1980

Oxhey Village Environment Group (OVEG) visit to Moor Park Mansion, 1980.
Ted Parrish is second from right, front row. Also in group: Peggy Parrish,
George Lorimer & Godfrey Cornwall, Rickmansworth historian

EARLY 20th CENTURY PHOTOGRAPHS OF BUCKS AVENUE, FORMERLY BEGGAR'S LANE, AND PINNER ROAD, OXHEY, BY FREDERICK HOCKER

1   In the Beginning

On taking pen to paper, for no better reason than I am less than dexterous on the keyboard, I heed the words of one Lucretius which, if I remember correctly, went something like this: 'But nothing is so easy that it may at first seem difficult'. That is exactly how I feel about introductions, but there is no alternative to this simple formality. So may I firstly introduce a brand new feature about the area's past and, secondly, introduce myself, of which I suppose I count as part.

We are too easily inclined to talk about the 'good old days' when recalling Watford as a market town surrounded by villages and open country, albeit in the form of large estates. I must confess, in a historical context, that the town has always fascinated me and my researches into its past have been an enjoyable and rewarding pursuit. Perhaps I am less familiar with the present as it so rapidly recedes into the past. Change is often so gradual that it can even pass unnoticed. There are few sources of information to remind us of our childhood; this period is a largely unexplored area, as so much is committed to memory rather than paper.

Lucretius was right. Now the formalities have been observed, who knows what stories, observations and anecdotes will emerge as we set our time machine in motion and journey back half a century or more. There is a wealth of material which has lain dormant in the mind, just waiting for someone to press the memory recall button. I see nostalgia and memorabilia as the warp and weft of a delicate fabric, now a little faded and even frayed at the edges, but still worth taking out of the bottom drawer.

I made reference to the 'good old days' but we know that in terms of deprivation they were not. However, in terms of human compassion, understanding and helping our neighbour, they were good, very good days. The Welfare State offers no substitute for such graces. I can remember the General Strike of 1926, the unemployment problems of the 1930s, the war years of the 1940s, the shortages of the 1950s and the relative prosperity of the following two decades. These events were some of the major social milestones of which there is now little material evidence, except the contrast of dated architectural standards in Watford High Street and nearby residential areas. The bad times have been tempered by the good and we of an earlier era are surely richer for the experience, if not poorer by monetary standards.

In retrospect, Watford's agrarian character irreversibly changed when, in the 1830s and 1840s, the London and Birmingham Railway opened its stations at Watford Junction and Bushey. In the same decade, the gas works were built on the banks of the River Colne at the southern end of the old High Street. The combined effect of the new embankment at Bushey Arches and the heightening of the ground level above the river at the gas works caused periodic flooding which, as a legacy of the past, is still with us. Local government changes and policies accelerated the decline of the market town when, in 1922, Watford's status was raised to that of a borough. Agriculture continued to wane, as the demands of industry and housing absorbed the barley fields and apple and cherry orchards for which the town was once famous.

We are told the origin and meaning of Watford may be found in the ancient word 'wao' meaning 'hunting' or, in other words, 'a ford used by hunters'. It was here, in the Lower High Street, that the town's origins may be traced from the 12th century. Traditionally, expansion took place along the main road towards Aylesbury, which explains why we have a mile-long High Street.

In medieval times, wagonways gave access to yards (Woodman's Yard, for example) on each side of the highway. It was not until the 19th century that new roads such as King Street, Queens Road, Market Street and Clarendon Road were built to give access to the east and west. But that was a long time ago. We are more concerned with people, places and events from the 1920s to the early 1980s. I remember what it was like going shopping in Watford in the '30s. No sooner had you stepped off the bus someone would say "Hello, I thought I'd see you today". Perhaps half-a-dozen chance meetings would occur in one afternoon, but that is just how it was. Everyone seemed to know everyone else. At each encounter we did not edge away and excuse ourselves in haste because if we missed the bus there would be an hour to wait. In those days there were buses galore.

Service and pleasantries were part of the age. No supermarkets to contend with, we enjoyed personal service. Hardly anything was packaged. Each butcher had his own slaughter house behind the shop and fresh fish was collected daily from the train at Watford Junction in the early hours of the morning. After all, everything had to be fresh because there were no freezers or fridges; just ice supplied by the ice factory in Wiggenhall Road.

The kitchen of pre-war years offered little or no convenience. The 'range' ovens or the cast-iron gas stoves were less than sophisticated, with no thermostat to protect the contents from burning. Cooking really was a culinary art under those conditions. The 'washing machine' was still a coal-fired 'copper' or gas-fired boiler tucked away in the corner of the scullery.

More fortunate families could avail themselves of the Silverdale or the Watford Steam Laundry. The washing was collected with clockwork regularity and returned in large fibre boxes in which the laundry was meticulously ironed and folded. It was a service the customer expected and received. Anything less would have been quite unacceptable. We still suffered the Victorian upstairs downstairs syndrome that perfection was only just good enough.

Watford Steam Laundry advertisement, 1915.

The paintwork of the milk carts and covered vans gleamed, the horses were groomed until their coats sparkled, the brasses glistened and the black polished leather harnesses glowed a rich subtle black. The drivers were dressed according to their trade, just as the bowler hat distinguished those who received salaries rather than wages. There was little envy; we were too well disciplined. Napoleon's statement still held true. We were a nation of shopkeepers and the retail price code was strictly observed. Competition was eliminated and the local corner shop thrived. Whatever the pros and cons of this strange practice, it did provide a stability that was reflected in the economy and in our daily lives.

2   The Mill's on Fire

The glare in the sky and the noise of fire bells aroused the curiosity of the residents of Watford Fields. Those who had not gone to bed put on their coats and hats and crossed the dark fields in the direction of the High Street. Some thoughtfully roused their neighbours who hurriedly dressed to join the steady flow of people. They were all speculating as to which building was involved, until word got back to the stragglers: "The mill's on fire".

Watford Mill in centre, 1903.

It was Wednesday 3 December 1924 when Mr Edward Putnam, one of the directors of the Watford Flour Mill, returned to his home in the late hours. He lived almost opposite the mill and always gave a customary glance at the huge building before entering his house. That night he thought he could see a flickering light through the windows of the third floor and there was a sound he could not identify. Fortunately there was a police constable on his beat who accompanied Mr Putnam to investigate the mysterious light. Together they entered the mill and found the third floor on fire. The Watford Fire Brigade was called and soon six hoses were playing streams of water on both the back and front of the building. The stacked flour bags, wheat, oats and animal feeding stuffs contributed to the rapid spread of the flames. Mr Putnam had arrived home at 11.15pm. At midnight, in a shower of sparks and bricks, the roof collapsed.

Ever-vigilant Chief Officer Ryder of Bushey Fire Brigade observed the effects of the conflagration, rallied his firemen and arrived on the scene soon after midnight to help fight the blaze. The local police arrived to divert the traffic and control the increasing crowd that gathered to watch the fire. By 1.00am it was reckoned to be under control, but the old mill was a brick shell with steam and smoke rising from the ruins. I knew nothing of the excitement of that night, at least not until the following morning when I was taken to witness the scene of devastation by my mother. She, like a number of her contemporaries, had left the comparatively quiet Cotswold village of Bourton-on-the-Water to seek work, if not her fortune, in Watford. She went into service with Dr Wimble, whose home and practice was on Chalk Hill in what was then New Bushey, now Oxhey. He was a man of Victorian demeanour, kindly but strict and a pillar of respectability. He was also a man who commanded, rather than demanded, respect.

After her marriage in 1919, my mother's first home was in Watford Fields and we joined that compact and stolid community living in the shadow and aroma of Benskins Brewery. All things were permanent and all people immortal. Why should I have thought otherwise in those early and innocent years? The burning of the mill was my first exposure to the ever-changing environment.

The mill, like Charter Place, was not a structure that could be admired for its beauty, line or form. It was a functional four-storey brick building almost bordering the road. There had always been a mill on the site since monastic times, when it was held by the Abbot of St Albans as part of the Manor of Cashio. The 'new' mill was built in 1826. It was equipped with two water wheels and seven pans of stones and was said to be the envy of the county. The machinery was updated in 1921 and continued to operate as a flour mill until the fire. It is believed that the mile-long mill stream was created by the monks.

After the fire, the ruins were put up for sale and the business was transferred to the mills at Hemel Hempstead. Watford's heritage was beginning to be whittled away. Nothing remains, except the stream which turned the water wheels. Now a car sales operation extends over much of this historic site. The stream still crosses under the High Street and alongside the Pump House, Watford's home of amateur drama and music, and back into the Colne[1].

In the days of the old 'pea-souper' fogs, when it really was difficult to see a hand in front of you, one could almost be guided by the various smells emanating from the industrial premises in Lower High Street. Combating the exhilarating smell of hops and other ingredients being brewed at Benskins was the smell of the corn products at the mill and then the gas works. Oh, the gas works! The coke ovens and distilling units thrust a perpetual cloud of fumes into the atmosphere. The smell was revolting. Add to that the sparks, steam and smoke of the passing steam locomotives across Bushey Arches. Not surprisingly, Watford's residents were complaining about Watford's gas in the '70s – and I mean the 1870s! I ask for your indulgence in quoting a few of many lines written in anger by a local author, which appeared in the 'County Chronicle' of 4 March 1871. The verse was prompted by the gas company giving notice of its intention to apply to Parliament for 'extension of powers'.

> "Five shillings per thousand (cubic feet) is charged for light
> That brings out more clearly the darkness of night.
> And emits such a smoke! It fact, is so spurious
> That to health there's no doubt it is very injurious.
> This company thinks people are so benighted
> As not to care much in what way they are lighted..."

The full verse may be found in Henry Williams' 'History of Watford' published in 1884 and reprinted in 1976.

Whatever we may think about North Sea gas, we should be grateful that coal is no longer the source of our gas supply. I am.

3   "Coming to the Flicks?"

I recall four cinemas in or near Watford town centre in the mid-'20s: the Super, Coliseum, Empire and Central Hall[2]. The days of the travelling showmen who hired the Agricultural Hall (also known over the years as the Clarendon Hall and the Drill Hall)[3] for one night stands and Frederick Downer's Electric Theatre had long since passed.

"Coming to the flicks?" was a common expression with youngsters and parents alike. We were seldom able to jingle enough coppers in our pockets to go to the flicks and share the filmic delights of an illusory world. The term was a derivative of the old word 'flickers', used to describe the flickering effect created by the combination of hand-cranked cameras and equally primitive projection equipment. The word, like so many contemporary expressions, has receded into obscurity although we are frequently reminded of those days when BBC2 screens some of the vintage comedies. Chester Conklin, Harold Lloyd, Buster Keaton and Charlie Chaplin, the great purveyors of comedy, immediately spring to mind.

The films we saved so earnestly to see were still silent. We were quite content to read the dialogue after the words had been silently mouthed. We were weaned on such epics as Conan Doyle's 'Lost World' with Bessie Love and Lewis Stone; 'The Arab' starring Ramon Novarro, the idol of mothers and daughters; 'Rupert of Hentzan' (so often remade as 'The Prisoner of Zenda'), featuring the now-forgotten Bert Lytell; and 'The Thief of Baghdad' with the legendary Douglas Fairbanks Snr. We thrilled to the swashbuckling adventures, hardly conscious of the middle-aged bespectacled lady pianist's improvised music accompanying the changing scenes as she gazed at the screen with an expression of detached boredom.

The Super, once Watford's roller skating rink, was later renamed the Carlton. Its doors have been closed to patrons for over a year and it is now (1982) a furniture emporium until such time as its designated fate meets Borough Council approval[4]. Before the advent of costly renovations in the late '60s or early '70s which effectively changed its shape, I recall the little wooden balcony at the back of the stalls. It was raised just 2-3 feet above the audience, with room for only two rows of seats; a favourite rendezvous of courting couples.

Electric Coliseum, October 1912. Films advertised include 'Lieutenant Rose and the Train Wreckers' and Mary Pickford's 'The Inner Circle'.

Central Hall, a Siegmund Lubin film is advertised, 1914.

The Coliseum, or the 'flea pit' by which title it was more readily identified, occupied a commanding position on St Albans Road between the road bridge at Watford Junction and Leavesden Road. The weathered exterior suggested a building of warehouse proportions and its entrance doors were at right angles to the road facing the railway line. It had reached the end of its viable life and went into a rapid decline. The building was demolished in the late '50s and a garage now stands on the old site[5].

The Central Hall in King Street, later renamed the Regal and subsequently the Essoldo, became another victim of the drift away from the cinema. It was converted into a bingo hall in the '70s, with little change to the familiar front elevation[6]. The sole survivor of the four picture houses is the Empire. Despite two major alterations, which included its recent conversion to two theatres, it is still my favourite cinema. Perhaps it is a bad case of nostalgia. I have vivid memories of its less prosperous days when the distempered walls were stained by the archaic gas-fired radiators generously spaced along the walls which gave out both a generous heat and distinctive smell. I still warm to the thought that on the coldest day a seat nearest the radiator made the Empire the cosiest cinema in Watford[7].

Perhaps we share the same vintage heroes. I can think of Richard Dix, Jack Holt, Ralph Graves, Tom Mix and his horse Tony, as well as that famous canine, Rin-Tin-Tin. It was in later years that Bebe Daniels, Jean Harlow, Jessie Matthews and Madge Evans became the subject of my increasing youthful attention. My treasured photographs, signed by some of yesteryear's stars, attest to my sublimation to their celluloid charms.

We must not forget the pianist. How I envied her exalted position and her good fortune in seeing the films not just once, but nearly 20 times a week. Perhaps I spoke of my enthusiasm indiscreetly. My mother, I regret to say, misconstrued the reasons for my envy and in 1927 condemned me to seven years of musical tuition on the pianoforte. My tutor was Miss Snelling, a mature spinster with particularly good qualifications. She was tolerant but strict in both manner and tempo as the metronome invariably lulled me into a hypnotic trance. Against all odds, I passed a number of examinations at Watford School of Music in Queens Road. But the musical training was in direct conflict with my vowed endeavours to become an engine driver.

We were not to know that the days of the silent films were numbered. As if in anticipation of the coming of the 'talkies', a site was cleared on the east side of the Pond and in 1929 a brand new picture house was opened. Originally called the Plaza, the name was changed to the Odeon in 1936. Its alien architecture contrasted boldly with the timbered buildings bordering The Parade[8]. Large off-white ceramic tiles embellished the front elevation, as did a miniature dome. The foyer was made a feature, with two short flights of terrazzo steps, wrought iron balustrades and gleaming brass handrails. This luxurious environment promised the optimum in escapism. The polished mahogany box office boasted two pay desks: 6d and 1s to the left; 1s 9d and 3s 6d to the right. The corridor to the front stalls seemed endless, before emerging halfway down the auditorium through heavy velour curtains. A curved wooden barrier divided the front stalls from the back stalls. Just below stage level and in the centre was a massive wooden-cased Compton organ console with three keyboards and an infinite number of stops.

Plaza's pillared entrance on extreme left. A Conrad Nagel film is advertised. Early 1930s.

The Pond in the early days; Darby's Nursery made way for the Plaza, 1907.

The house would invariably be packed; the films still silent. In 1929, Al Jolson's 'The Jazz Singer' took London by storm. In Watford, the first 'talkie' received no less acclaim. The golden era of a revitalised film industry was about to begin and, commensurate with this breakthrough, two more cinemas were yet to be built to meet Watford's insatiable demand for entertainment.

4   The 'General'

The London and Birmingham Railway opened the first section of its iron road as far as Boxmoor in 1831 and Watford has been well served by railway networks ever since. Of the many improvements made to the London and North Western Railway system, one of the most significant occurred when an electric railway, started before the First World War, was completed and the Bakerloo underground service was extended to Watford via Queens Park in 1917. It was a weekday service and did not run on Sundays until 1919.

Watford Junction and a Milnes-Daimler motor omnibus, 1906. In 1920 the London General Omnibus Company operated General omnibuses from the station; by 1934, 22 bus routes operated in the Watford area.

A spur from the main Metropolitan line via Croxley Green through to Watford was not completed until 1925. The railway terminates on the border of Cassiobury Park, but it was planned to take the line into Watford High Street and connect with Watford Junction. However, the link was never made and the building was converted into shop premises. For many years, and until after the First World War, it was occupied by up-market furnishers called Cedars. It was then acquired by Grange Furnishings and within the last year (1981) became a shoe shop. A close look above the shop front will suggest its Metropolitan origins[9]. What a pity the concept never materialised.

We were well served by railways, but what of our public motor transport? We know Watford never enjoyed a tramway system. In all probability, the unassailable Clay Hill at Bushey protected us from the intrusion of London's tramcars into the High Street. In fact we have always been dependent on buses for our urban journeys.

Horse-drawn buses were a familiar sight at the beginning of the 20th century and it was not until after the First World War that the motor bus appeared on our streets. A bus service was found to be a lucrative operation and private enterprise, not slow to jump on the bandwagon, formed new companies and established limited services. In the '20s, the London General Omnibus Company began acquiring local operating licences and their 'NS-type' buses with solid tyres and open tops became a familiar sight from 1924 through to the '30s. On the side was emblazoned the single word 'General'. The driver was all but exposed to the elements and the conductor stood bravely, if not firmly, at the rear of the lower deck, equally exposed to the weather. The passengers fared little better. Those who could not be accommodated inside were obliged to take seats on the upper deck with umbrellas and heads well down, sitting on slatted seats that were less than comfortable on long journeys. It was not until 1920 that the 'General' vehicles stopped at prescribed places. Before that, it required only a hand signal to stop the bus at any point on the route!

I am almost sure that the cheapest fare was 1d for a ride which, to a child, seemed endless. Pennies did not come easily. One penny was the sum earned for any number of errands on a Saturday morning, which included a long shopping list, with the Watford Co-operative 'divi' number carefully written at the top. Families were obliged to be as thrifty as the Scots in those days.

During the school holidays or on a Saturday afternoon my income would be subsidised to go to the flicks and I would be given an extra penny to "come back on the bus and then you won't be late for tea". Honour bound to return on the bus, I was only too pleased to oblige. Tom Mix must have had a more comfortable ride on his horse Tony than I ever enjoyed on those solid tyres, but all kids are gluttons for punishment. Whatever the weather, we would choose the open top and, if it happened to be raining, we would crawl under the heavy covers which were stretched across the wooden seats. They provided excellent protection from the rain and when the conductor, whose head and shoulders would appear at deck level, saw no passengers in view, he duly returned to the lower deck. Fortunately we would not have to press that large mushroom-shaped brass knob at the top of the stairs that by some mysterious linkage system sounded a bell in the driver's cab. The bus stop was a popular one and we would join the alighting passengers!

No self-respecting schoolboy would allow a penny to wear out his trouser pocket and, in accordance with the best monetary practice, it would be invested at the first opportunity. A Barratt's sherbet with a hollow liquorice tube to suck out its powdered contents would still leave enough money to buy some tiger nuts. What better investment could be made when, with reasonable discipline, the delectable purchases could be made to last for hours?

In 1925 the 'General' introduced buses with covered tops to combat, I suppose, the growing menace of children hiding under the canvas covers. A further tragedy occurred in 1928 when double-deckers were fitted with pneumatic tyres and the ride became so smooth that it was just not fun anymore. But there were some compensations when the legal speed limit was increased to 20 mph in the same year.

A few private operators still plied their vehicles throughout the '20s, but the Road Traffic Act of 1930 forced many firms out of business. Perhaps this was the fate of the single-decker Lewis buses with their bus station and depot in Market Street. In the same year, Green Line coaches were introduced with a completely new operating schedule and fare structure.

In those days, we were all dependent on public transport and very few people could afford cars. The bus and train services were good and, by today's reduced standards, phenomenal. Politeness, cleanliness, pride and service were all taken for granted. Bus followed bus and train followed train, which negated the use of a timetable. Progress, it seems, has its price. I quote a few words which appeared in a London Transport publication of 1934 concerning the training of its staff: "… Safety, comfort and convenience of the public are borne in mind throughout (the training). And there is that little extra of personal service – courtesy to the passenger…" Maybe they were the good old days.

5   Please May We Have Our Fountain Back?

A century ago Henry Williams described Watford Heath as "a picturesque and very healthy part of the Parish of Watford. It is reached by Watford Fields, Tommy Deacon's Hill, a field beyond and over the railway bridge from which there is a nice view of the surrounding neighbourhood, or from the bottom of the High Street along Pinner Road". Except for the field, which must be Oxhey Road, his directions may just as easily be followed today, although the landscape has suffered many changes in the interim years. In Williams' time, there were no roads, just cart tracks and footpaths and a rickety wooden bridge over the River Colne. The area was then part of the Manor of Wiggenhall, the family seat of the Deacons.

Crossing the bridge and to his right, Henry Williams would have seen the derelict three-storied Silk Mill in the process of being converted into a steam laundry, before taking the narrow path up the hill within a thickly wooded area and crossing the road (Eastbury Road) into a field which gave access to the bridge at Watford Heath. The story goes that the Deacon after whom the hill is still named has never been identified, since the eldest son of each generation was christened Thomas! The view from the bridge to which Williams referred had not changed until just a few years ago when a much-needed independent pedestrian bridge was built. Sadly, the panoramic view of St Albans and its Abbey can no longer be enjoyed.

Watford Heath Farm House, demolished in the late 1950s, now flats. Photo courtesy of Joan Cousins.

Despite the inevitable changes with the passage of time, Williams' terse description of Watford Heath is just as true today – but he omitted one salient historical feature. The Heath is a unique legacy of manorial wasteland and, for that reason, has become one of the few beauty spots left within the borough boundaries. It still retains a rural identity, despite in-roads made by Victorian, Edwardian and modern developments.

Watford Heath was once primarily an agricultural community with many more cottages and residents than are apparent today. It was a compact hamlet with the proverbial pond, a National School and a 'workmen's club room'. The club had its own cricket team and played their matches on the green. Watford Heath Farm House, its fields long since developed for housing, and a solitary barn, survived the centuries until they were demolished to make way for a modern apartment block in the '60s. The National School, closed towards the end of the 19th century, was converted to cottage accommodation and has remained unchanged ever since. A number of old cottages and the pond disappeared, probably as a result of the arrival of the Ely family who acquired an estate encompassing Watford Heath in the mid-1800s when they established Oxhey Grange as their new home.

Watford Heath National School (Nos 3 & 4). Rev Newton Price, Oxhey's first vicar, built the Watford Heath National Cookery School for girls at the rear in 1873 (No 5), 1908.

Mr W T Ely was largely responsible for the many improvements made to the cottages for the benefit of his tenants. He died in 1881 and in his memory a drinking fountain was erected on an island site which, many years later, became the terminus of the old 302 country bus route. Due to the difficulty of turning double-decker buses, the island was reduced in size and, as a consequence, the drinking fountain disappeared in the late '50s. Of polished granite and Victorian design, the following inscription appeared on one of the panels: "William Thomas Ely of Oxhey Grange, born 1821 died 1881. This fountain, erected by his sisters in loving memory of a good brother, is here offered for public use, 1883".

The 302, or rather its current equivalent, no longer terminates its route at this point and now, local residents argue, the fountain should be reinstated in its original

Watford Heath memorial drinking fountain.

position. It is said that some years ago an enquiry was made of Watford Town Hall as to the fountain's deposition, with the reply that it could not be found.

Another mystery is the old wooden cross, 8-9 feet tall, which once graced a plot of no more than 12-square feet, contained within iron railings and accessed by a gate. The site may be found on the southern perimeter road on a sharp bend between the bowling green and the Royal Oak. I cannot recall any plaque or notice that ever gave a clue to its origin, although there is a natural temptation to assume its presence suggested the commemoration of the death of local residents during the First World War. The cross disappeared many years ago, but the little plot remains[10].

Royal Oak on left. Medieval cottages in foreground were demolished in the 1920s and replaced by semi-detached houses, photo 1908.

There are two pubs on the Heath: the Load of Hay c1840 and the Royal Oak, built a decade or two later. They are still an integral part of the rural scene, but it is Rose Cottage that is more inclined to stir latent memories. Mr and Mrs Roy Baker's little general store and sweet shop, like the pubs, catered for residents and visitors alike. A particular attraction and a rendezvous for cycling clubs before the First World War was their Rose Tea Garden. In the best topiarian tradition, a privet hedge bordering the road was lovingly topped with four large capital letters – T E A S.

A very close inspection of Rose Cottage reveals its origin as a modest cottage. It was later given a full cosmetic treatment of oak timbers and carvings, perhaps during Mr Ely's campaign to improve his tenants' housing. An extension was built which later became tea-rooms and, after the Second World War, a meeting house for many local organisations. In more recent years Mr Baker has dedicated himself to the restoration of Rose Cottage as a residence. During a conversation with him last year (1981) he told me he had discovered old stone railway sleepers which had been used as a foundation beneath internal walls he had demolished.

Why not take a walk to Watford Heath following one of the routes suggested by Mr Henry Williams a century ago. You will see 18th and 19th century cottages and 20th century houses, all somehow blending into a landscape that represents 300 years of domestic architecture. Unfortunately you will not be able to enjoy a cup of tea at the Rose Tea Gardens, but you will be well received at the Load of Hay or the Royal Oak.

6   The Band of Hope

A century ago in the area administered by the Watford Local Board there were no fewer than 70 public and beer houses. The hostelries were so well supported that their presence was claimed to promote "drunkenness from time to time and consequently much poverty and misery". In an attempt to contain what was popularly known as the "great national curse", the Watford and Bushey Temperance Society was formed in 1869. Whatever may be said of well-meaning Victorian philanthropists, when they adopted a particular cause, none was more dedicated. That was certainly true of Mr Henry Kingham of Henry Kingham & Sons, wholesale and retail grocers of the High Street, who was the Society's president and one of the leading figures in the local temperance movement. In the company's 13th annual report published in 1882, his death was noted in the following terms: "When temperance workers were few in Watford and the cause very low, Mr Kingham was devoting a large amount of his time and influence to the interests of total abstinence, and for some considerable time conducted the only Band of Hope there was in the town almost entirely unaided".

The Society also promoted the Blue Ribbon movement, which required an abstainer to demonstrate his promise by wearing a piece of blue ribbon on his coat, thereby proclaiming his allegiance to the cause. In 1883 a nine-day Temperance Mission was conducted in the Agricultural Hall when it was claimed that a total of 3,000 people attended the meetings wearing blue ribbons.

A national call to control intemperance by closing pubs on Sundays also received the Society's support. Among its many members who signed a national petition were such names as Herkomer, Capel, Puddefoot and Chater. The petition was presented to Parliament and contained nearly 600,000 names in two columns on a continuous roll of paper 12 feet in diameter, 2¾ miles long and weighing over 3 hundredweight. The Victorians knew the value of good presentation and publicity stories; monologues, ditties and jokes about workhouses are legion. Forgive me if I add just one more to the collection.

In autumn 1883 a handbill was printed and circulated in Hemel Hempstead bringing certain facts to the notice of local ratepayers. It presented an analysis of a return called for by the House of Commons of the quantity and cost of alcohol consumed in every workhouse in England and Wales for the year ending 31 December 1881. The militant temperance workers used this information for their own ends by comparing the returns of a number of local towns including Watford and Hemel Hempstead. For convenience, the annual figures have been rounded off to the nearest pint and pound.

	Spirits	Wines	Beer	Inmates
Watford	195 pints/£35	44 pints/£4	320 pints/£12	229
Hemel Hempstead	292 pints/£25	21 pints/£1	1325 pints/£55	71

When Hemel Hempstead was spending ratepayers' money at £1 2s 11d per head, Watford held the figure down to 4s 6d. The national figure was 7s per inmate. The costs beg analysis, but the point was made. Compared with Watford, Hemel Hempstead was operating a five star workhouse. The pressures brought to bear by Watford's Blue Ribbon gang were having a sobering effect on both the accounts and the inmates, but at least Watford was enjoying better quality drinks!

Unfortunately little information is currently available concerning the activities of the society in Watford and Bushey in later years. One could argue that its success brought about its downfall. With certainty, I can say that the Bushey branch of the society was still operating in the late '20s; I am not so sure about the early '30s. In the best tradition, I think it just faded away.

The Band of Hope, of which I was a member, met weekly in the corrugated iron-clad 'school room' of the Wesleyan Chapel, near the corner of King Edward Road and the main road to Bushey. Although now in Oxhey, its address was once New Bushey. With a number of my young contemporaries I regularly attended the meetings at a cost, I seem to remember, of ½d a week. I would take with me a little yellow card, on the face of which was printed a square for each week of the year. Having paid the entrance fee, a neat hole would be punched in the appropriate square. A mixed audience would noisily settle itself down on long wooden forms, which offered only marginally more comfort than standing.

The small bespectacled figure of the local organiser would hesitantly remind us of the evil of drink and our commitment to total abstinence. I was not a little bemused by any reference to alcohol when my favourite drinks were lemonade and ginger beer. There would be a short prayer and then a formal introduction of the speaker. If we were very lucky, we would be treated to a magic lantern show. The lantern, a massive black metal contraption with a decorated chimney and huge brass-mounted lens sticking out the front, was mounted on a large elevated wooden stand. The projectionist stood with boxes of large glass slides close at hand. The lecturer, with his inevitable pointer, would take his position by the screen and signal for the lights to go out. A murmur of expectation from the audience was clearly audible. The image of the first slide appeared on the screen in black and white. The speaker's voice droned in our ears, but we were soon enthralled by the excitement of being conducted to some mysterious unknown country. Forgotten toffees remained in pockets, consolidating with the inevitable fluff that gathered there.

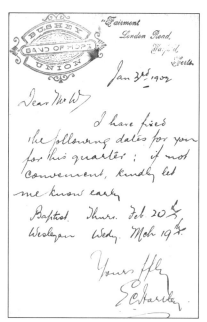

Former Methodist Chapel in Villiers Road before its move to King Edward Road in 1904, when it became the Bushey & Oxhey Methodist Church 'school room'.

1902 Band of Hope postcard from Mr E Hartley to Mr Worsfold.

The cue to the projectionist to change a slide or wake him up – I was never sure – was a thump on the floor with the thick end of the pointer; the picture on the screen obediently changed. The uncomfortable forms were no impediment to our enjoyment of such simple pleasures. The young element in the audience was reasonably well behaved, content and happy that the continuing campaign against the demon drink was bringing a little entertainment into our otherwise disciplined and mundane lives.

7   Things That Go Bump in the Night

When Watford was just one long street, the majority of the town's residents were of country stock. Technological progress in the Victorian era necessitated a rapid change of skills and personal adjustment to the needs of an industrial environment. They coped relatively well with the changes forced upon them and, over a reasonable period of time, adapted to the demands of a new era.

They were less successful in discarding their country style superstitions: the product of illiteracy and village life which fostered a fear of the unknown. In the early 19th century one of the most notorious districts believed to harbour illusive ghosts was Feather Bed Lane, a pretty bridle path that once started at the bottom of Clarendon Road. The path was well below the level of the adjacent fields. Elms and oaks cast their dark shadows on the well-trodden track before it emerged alongside the road bridge at Watford Junction. A little is left of the old path, although the immediate environment has suffered considerable change. The Bridle Path, by which name it is now known, was then regarded as the favourite rendezvous of troubled spirits. Many tales were told of ghostly sightings, strange noises and inexplicable happenings which naturally occurred after dark.

The tale is told of a young man who doubted the sincerity, if not the virtue, of his lover and on some pretext arranged to meet her late at night in Feather Bed Lane. The girl arrived at the agreed place and waited for the young man. Fortunately he was late and the impatient girl wandered around the fields to pass the time. She discovered a newly-dug grave and realised the purpose of the meeting. Without a second bidding, she ran away and so saved her life. But that was not the end of the story, as sometime later a man hanged himself on a tree in the lane. It was not established whether it was the boyfriend.

Watford Tunnel was believed to be haunted as a result, no doubt, of a tragic incident which entombed a number of men digging inside the tunnel during its construction. Several houses were also claimed to be haunted, including a certain residence in Hagden Lane. For a long time, 97 High Street remained untenanted because the premises were said to be haunted by the spirit of a lady who had previously resided there. Mr David Downer, a stationer by trade and a stoic by nature, chose to ignore its reputation and acquired the property for a very modest rental. During the many years he lived and traded there, he was never troubled by even one unearthly visitation of the deceased lady.

The body snatchers of fiction were not necessarily the product of an author's fertile imagination. The body snatchers of Watford were notorious. When circumstances create a sellers' market and, provided the financial reward is commensurate with the risk, there is usually someone prepared to trade – whatever the commodity. In this case, bodies were in demand. They were required by surgeons in the course of training their students, so body snatching became a remunerative growth industry.

In the early 19th century near the junction of Water Lane with the High Street, there was a beer house of doubtful reputation called the Nag's Head. At that address lived a man who many believed to be one of the organisers of body snatching in Watford. To support their argument, they claimed such nefarious crimes ceased on his departure from the town. Although the evidence was circumstantial, stories of his activities were rife. The recovered bodies were said to have been placed in the cellar of the beer house until a coach was found to transport the remains, packed in coarse wrappers, to London.

One day a package was left at the Eight Bells Inn for collection by the evening coach to London. Mr Kemp, landlord of the Nag's Head, visited the inn and recognised the nature and contents of the package. He conveyed his suspicions to Mr Kilby, the landlord, who failed to act on the information and allowed the package to be duly collected! On another occasion, a parcel was left at the Rose & Crown for collection by the evening coach. Dogs in the hotel picked up the scent and the police were called. The parcel was opened and there was found to be a girl who had been buried only a few hours earlier.

Eight Bells on extreme left; Queens Road just beyond, 1906.

The package was repacked and placed on the coach, accompanied by two policemen. They waited at the address to which it had been consigned and two men arrived to collect the parcel. One man escaped, but the other was apprehended and brought back to Watford the following day.

The source of supply was the churchyard of St Mary's Parish Church. At night or in the early hours of the morning the body snatchers moved in. They searched for evidence of fresh earth mounds and promptly exhumed bodies for speedy despatch to the metropolis. How they could avoid detection for so many years is difficult to understand, but it is quite feasible that stories of the haunting of the churchyard were told in the public and beer houses in the knowledge they would be embellished by the telling.

So great was the fear of the bereaved that those who could afford the extra cost arranged for an oak board to be placed above the coffin with crosspieces set into the sides of the grave. The poor people of the parish were obliged to maintain day and night vigils over the graves until the bodies had sufficiently decomposed. When Mr Ewer of Chalk Hill Lane died in 1845, his relatives took the precaution of first having three family coffins removed before the deceased was laid to rest at the bottom, with the security of the old coffins placed on top before the grave was filled. The desecrations continued until 1850 and by that time Watford had achieved an unenviable reputation as a result of the activities of the body snatchers.

Hauntings and apparitions are by no means confined to the past. There was an incident at Odhams reported in the 'Evening Post-Echo' of 20 December 1979. Employee Jim Dinwoodie claimed to have seen on at least 15 occasions the head and shoulders of a man wearing navy blue overalls. Odhams printing plant, a relatively modern building, seems an unlikely place to experience close encounters of a ghostly kind.

We are conditioned to expect the atmospheric environment of ruined castles, eccentric Victorians and family tragedies to be conducive to supernatural activities. And so they are, for those very ingredients are present in Bushey village and the number of hauntings reported within Herkomer's old 'castle' and its complex suggest that the area may well be the most haunted in Hertfordshire. But that's another ghost story.

8   The Watford Brewery

As I live on the fringe of Oxhey village, a walk into Watford takes less than 20 minutes. More often than not, walking is quicker than taking public transport. During the relatively few minutes to reach Queens Road, I choose to ignore the grotesque southern entrance to the town, preferring to remember the Wheatsheaf onwards; this is where Watford has its roots.

The High Street begins immediately beyond the bridge over the Colne where, not so long ago, an old-established and thriving community existed. For me, the most outstanding buildings in a now-barren stretch of the road were the premises and residence once occupied by Sedgwick's. I find the image of the frontage on the High Street so easy to recall. The three-storied Georgian building bordered the pavement. Its central front door and fanlight was further embellished by fluted ionic columns supporting a canopy; the neat white-painted sash windows were set in red bricks. Brick-built carriageways each side of the building gave access to the brewery buildings at the rear, including the family residence.

SEDGWICK'S WATFORD BREWERY STEAM FIRE ENGINE TURNING OUT.

Sedgwick's Brewery advertisement, 1915.

The complex was listed by the Department of the Environment but, notwithstanding its historical association and architectural value, the demolition contractors soon reduced the residence to rubble in 1964. As I pass the site of Sedgwick's, or rather the Watford Brewery, I secretly mourn its loss and scorn those responsible for the desecration of Watford's heritage[11]. The brewery once rivalled the almighty Benskins. Its origin may be traced to the middle of the 17th century but it still did not qualify as the first brewery in Watford. That honour must be given to one John Day who was a brewer in 1619. In 1635 the Swan Inn operated its own malt house and brew house and served, in all probability, a good pint.

The Watford Brewery belonged to the Smith family, until they sold it to George Whittingstall in 1792. In 1824 he bequeathed it to a distant cousin by the name of Edmund Fearnley (provided that he changed

The Swan Inn, late 1920s.

his name to Edmund Fearnley Whittingstall), after whom Fearnley Street was no doubt named. Young Edmund's good fortune continued. Two years later, another relation left him three properties, one of which was the Swan Inn[12].

Mr F W Sedgwick acquired the brewery in 1862 and then it passed to Mr F J Sedgwick, whose name was to become synonymous with Watford's growth and development in the Victorian era. The Sedgwick family retained an interest in the brewery for 62 years. Benskins, in the process of buying out its rivals, acquired Sedgwick's Watford Brewery in 1924. Production continued and in 1932 new maltings were built to increase output.

Ironically, Ind Coope took over Benskins in 1957 and, as all beer drinkers will know, brewing in Watford was phased out. After four centuries of brewing ale and beer with Colne spring water, Watford's historical connection with the industry was finally severed. Some of the maltings backing onto the river remain, but sadly they are of no particular architectural merit or age. Now they only serve to cast melancholy shadows on the river, reminding us of the town's once unsurpassed reputation for brewing. If you are sufficiently interested to see what remains of the Watford Brewery, take the old cobbled yard between Stapleton's and Jewell's. Turn left at the bottom and you will pass the maltings before arriving at the bridge of Water Lane. The chances are you will see no one in the course of the short walk[13].

For some unaccountable reason we have lost our interest in the Colne – the river upon which the old mills of Watford were dependent until the arrival of steam power. In the early 19th century, before the arrival of the railway, the river abounded with fish. The largest quantity of eels caught in one day at Watford Mill was claimed to be 3 hundredweight. Trout, perch and pike attracted anglers from all over the town. As late as 1883, Mr C H Thomas landed a trout said to weigh 9¾ lbs. Stopping on the bridge in Lower High Street and looking at the murky water, without the obnoxious presence of the gas works, soon conveys the reason for the absence of fish except the hardy tiddlers.

Fishing by the bridge, Water Lane; Fighting Cocks in background, 1909.

Alongside the river bridge at Water Lane some 130 years ago was a public house called the Fighting Cocks. The name revealed the once popular but cruel sport of cock-fighting that was carried on there in earlier years. Before the pub finally closed, the proprietor operated a 'pleasure boat station' which became a very popular venue for the young lads and reckless lassies of Watford. A rowing boat could be hired for 1s an hour, with half-a-crown deposit to cover Mrs Lucy Deacon against "any loss she may sustain by damage to the boat". With the hire boat service in juxtaposition with the pub, little imagination is required to foresee many wettings and duckings by the more irresponsible and less sober members of Watford's society. The most popular day was Sunday, when both premises would be crowded to near capacity in the afternoon and evening. Those sufficiently fit or adventurous could row as far as the bridge at Bushey Mill. Which closed first I cannot say, but the pub was converted into residential premises.

Surprisingly, that was not the end of boating on the Colne. I recall a little wooden boathouse run by Mr Andrewartha on the Watford side of the bridge crossing the river at Oxhey Park. At weekends and during school holidays his boats were tied to an equally small landing stage. The boats were beautifully maintained. The sun sparkled on the newly-applied varnish; even the mooring ropes looked as if they had been bleached. The level of the water was substantially higher in those days.

Oxhey Park has always been an attractive and well maintained area of steep wooded and grassy slopes right down to the river. Swans once regularly nested in the quieter reaches of the mill stream or less accessible parts of the river. Young men took their young ladies on the river for the afternoon. Married couples walked their children along the bank or picnicked under the trees. Weeping willows traced a line in the slow-moving water, restrained voices and occasional laughter of children playing with a ball and the noise of oars in row locks epitomised the lazy, hazy days of summer and innocence in the '20s and '30s.

Today, the Borough of Watford is keen to establish a linear park in the Colne Valley expressly for walkers. It is a commendable decision, as far as it goes[14]. Paths are for walking, rivers are for boating. Old-fashioned pastimes have a habit of coming back.

9 The Pyramid Puzzle

Of the many buildings in Lower High Street systematically whittled away by successive councils, Benskins mansion somehow survived. Now it stands out in near isolation. If its conversion into Watford Museum saved it from demolition, I am well content. It is one of the most exciting museums in Hertfordshire and many of the exhibits evidence the town's industrial and domestic connections with the past.

Watford-born Terry Scott meets retired WGSB teacher Herbert Lister at Watford Museum opening, 14 March 1981.

After the first snowfall, just before Christmas, I was tempted to call in yet again to admire the exhibits and the manner of their presentation. On entering the reception area, I overheard a conversation between an attendant and a visitor. The subject matter was a 'tunnel' in the High Street. On some quite inadequate pretext, I joined in the conversation. The visitor described an incident in 1934, when he was 12 years old that obviously left an indelible impression on his mind. "It was somewhere at the back of W H Smith, the stationers; there were some steps and an arch with a skull, or skull and crossbones above the arch. Beyond was a tunnel with turnings and it seemed to me then as if it was a ½ mile in length".

Making due allowances for the usual exaggerated impressions made on a child's mind, I was convinced that he was recalling his descent into the mausoleum erected in 1781 to commemorate the death of Mr Thomas Meadows of Watford House, former owner of the Watford House Estate. As far as I can determine, the estate extended on the east side of the High Street from either Meeting Alley or Butcher's Yard, beyond Clements[15]; in depth, it went back as far as Watford Junction. In 1864 the estate was divided by a new road called Clarendon Road that gave access to the station.

Where the High Street meets Clarendon Road, which we still know as Dudley's Corner, was Chestnut House. It was converted from maltings into the Conservative Club in 1885 and rebuilt in 1889. That same building is there today if you look above the level of John Collier's shop front[16] The club moved to The Parade, 8 High Street in 1921. Next door at Dudley's Corner was a tiny cottage, now Evans, and beyond that the old Lime Tree Commercial Temperance Hotel, so named because of the row of lime trees that once fronted the original house. The mausoleum

Dudley's Corner, Watford High Street/ Clarendon Road, 1979.

was at the back of these properties although from early maps and before development it appears access to the gardens in which it was built was via Clarendon Road.

Following the building of the Agricultural Hall, the Palace Theatre and the skating rink (later the Carlton), the mausoleum still survived. Henry Williams described it in his 'History of Watford' published in 1884. "The entrance to this vault is wide, with circular head, on the keystone of which is carved a skull, and the sides are covered with a kind of clinker set in cement.... The roof is pyramidal in shape having 25 steps, each of which diminishes until the top is reached, which is pointed... the (interior) height from the floor to the roof is about 25 feet. There is a second vault or chamber... entered by descending a flight of steps from a doorway cut in the wall of the principal vault and this terminates with an immense icehouse which, with the second vault, appears to have been added to the mausoleum after the latter was erected".

A MAUSOLEUM IN A GARDEN.

This quaint and interesting relic of old Watford stands in the grounds of the Lime Tree Hotel, in High Street. These grounds, prior to the cutting of Clarendon Road, formed part of the Watford House Estate, which was at that time owned by Mr. Thomas Meadows, and this Mausoleum was erected to his memory in 1781. It is built of brick, coated with cement, and stands 25 ft. high; there are two vaults or chambers, the principal one being about 10 ft. square. The other is entered by descending a flight of steps from a doorway cut in the wall of the first vault, and this terminates with a large icehouse. As will be seen in the photo, a skull is carved over the entrance, and on the inner wall facing the same, is fixed a marble tablet bearing the following inscription : This Mausoleum was erected to the memory of THOMAS MEADOWS, Esq., Anno MDCCLXXXI.

Pyramidal mausoleum to Thomas Meadows.

It may not be apparent from this abbreviated description that the vault was subterranean and the top of the vault, looking like a brick pyramid, projected above ground some 25 feet. The description given by the museum visitor was sufficiently accurate to convince me that he had entered the mausoleum that day in 1934. The distance from the entrance through the vault to the icehouse was only 60 feet, according to drawings available for inspection at the Central Library. But that short distance does not constitute a tunnel "a ½ mile long", so I was back to square one. Or so it seemed until a chance conversation with my daughter.

She recalled a conversation with an old resident of Watford who told her that highwaymen were particularly active in the Hamper Mill area and, after a successful hold-up, would gallop into Watford via 'Tommy' Deacon's Hill. Once on the hill they could be seen with a telescope from the Green Man, as the view was unobstructed in those days. We can only guess what precautions were taken at the Green Man, which was a coaching inn. Perhaps fresh getaway horses were prepared. On their arrival they entered the inn, took the tunnel to the mausoleum and duly made their escape. It was a perfect escape route on the other side of the High Street.

I have been unable to find any reference to such a tunnel in locally-published books, but since it was necessarily a secret known only to a few, it is not surprising there is no record of its existence. The thought occurred to me that the building of the ice house as an extension to the mausoleum could have been a cover for the additional work involved in building a fairly long tunnel. Was this the tunnel that seemed "a ½ mile long" to our young explorer? Could he have discovered the secret passage between the Green Man and the mausoleum? The original Green Man was demolished in the 20th century and rebuilt, only to be demolished again in the last few years and rebuilt as a showroom for Eastern Electricity[17].

When Mr Aubyn Fairhead lived at 1b Dudley's Corner in 1948 the mausoleum had virtually disappeared, although he remembers something that looked like an air raid shelter on or near the site. It is now too late to continue investigations because the site was excavated to make way for Charter Place.

The Green Man, 1973. Photo by George Lorimer.

The boy's adventure certainly bears out the legend and it is strange to think it would not have come to light but for that chance meeting at Watford Museum.

10   "Coming for a Swim?"

In the '20s the sporting finger could be pointed at Water Lane as the centre of Watford's outdoor activities. The whole area could be called a latter day Woodside. The Bushey Grove Bowling Club complemented the tennis courts of Wren's, the polish manufacturers. Cricket and football, as the seasons dictated, were played with equal enthusiasm. Boating had long since been abandoned, but now the river was being used as a swimming bath. Upstream the Colne was still clean, untainted by the gas works as it flowed round Munden, past Aldenham Church and through Otterspool before entering Bushey and Watford. The point at which the Five Arches viaduct crossed the Colne would not have appeared to be an ideal site for a swimming bath, but the Victorians thought otherwise. They adapted the river by altering its course and reinforcing the bank[18].

Changing rooms were built on each side in the shadow of the viaduct and a wooden bridge was constructed to span the river. In later years Mr West occupied the ticket office at the end of the bridge. At a cost of 1d, or was it 'tuppence' (2d), one could cross the bridge and enjoy the delights of well-maintained dressing rooms and a long concrete section, from which the first jump could be made into the shallow end. For another penny, Mr West would dispense a gigantic round oatmeal biscuit with a ginger flavour, a challenge to any young lad's appetite. For the kids without coppers in their pockets, a few changing rooms were available free of charge near Mr West's office. In those days I could not swim and was destined to acquire the knowledge elsewhere.

In earlier days the sundeck above attracted many visitors, but latterly it was relegated to the accommodation of wet, bedraggled boys drying off in the sun. One tradition was still more or less observed. The Victorian dogma of respectability cast its shadow on our generation. On six days a week bathing was confined to either ladies or gentlemen. Only on Friday were the sexes permitted to mix. I suspect Friday was the most popular day of the week at the old Watford baths. But the days of the baths were numbered. After Watford mill was destroyed by fire at the end of 1924 the sluice gates, of which remnants may still be seen behind the site of Sedgwick's Watford Brewery, were neglected and allowed to deteriorate[19]. In the course of time, the gates were no longer capable of retaining the head of water necessary to maintain an adequate depth back at the baths.

Swimming gala, Bushey 'Rec', 1930s.

Commentator with megaphone, Bushey 'Rec', 1930s.

Fortunately the swimming baths at King George V Recreation Ground in Bushey offered an alternative but less adventurous prospect. By way of compensation, the tea shop sold the very same biscuits so the appetites of ravenous schoolboys were whetted, if not satisfied. My introduction to Bushey Swimming Baths was not voluntary. As a pupil of the old and now demolished London Road School[20], I was one of the less enthusiastic members of a large class that was regularly conducted to the baths at the 'Rec'. The reluctant shuffling party equipped with towels, costumes and school caps already knew the means by which they would be taught to swim. Bad news travelled fast. We knew the adage 'sink or swim' could be translated literally. The method of teaching was not unique – but very effective.

"Your turn", Mr Goose shouted in a voice possessed only by a mature schoolmaster. There was no escape. A ring was placed around the waist, to which was attached a line fixed to a long bamboo pole. "Down to the shallow end" he yelled, as if there was an option. The water was icy cold. Supported like a fish at the end of the rod, I performed the 'dog paddle' in accordance with instructions. Perhaps I should have said I went through the motions. Theory and practice were diametrically opposed. Dog paddling a foot under the surface, I quickly learned, could not be sustained indefinitely. A heave on the rod and, with relief, I saw blue skies and breathed fresh air. Words of encouragement were hurled at me. Suddenly I found myself still, but only just, afloat without support. I could swim. Not many boys left London Road School unable to swim.

Hamper Mill, 1908.

The thirst for new adventures was now insatiable. At half-past-six in the morning during school holidays we would ride on our cycles to Hamper Mill. Those without a means of transport were accommodated on handlebars or astride the rear wheel. The trips were reasonably well planned. Towels, bread, frying pan, fat, beef sausages, knives and forks, mugs, tea and sugar were collectively brought along to support the expedition; milk presented a transportation problem. Someone could always produce matches and paper.

We crawled with our machines under a barbed wire fence in Sandy Lane and, with heads still down, made our way to a flooded gravel pit. There we stopped and dived into clear cold water, daring each other to swim to little islands of only a few feet in diameter, which the day before had been beyond our endurance. We usually came out of the water exhausted, but always hungry. We were all Cubs, so the process of making fires was our business. In no time dead wood was burning. The tantalising smell of beef sausages swimming in fat was more than we could bear. As we devoured the sausages and bread, a billy can was filled with water from the pit and brought to the boil. I forget by what primitive process we made tea, but it tasted like the nectar of the gods. By eight o'clock we were back home, more than ready to run errands for a few pennies to keep us in sweets for the rest of the week.

I was never bored. Boredom was not symptomatic of our age. We amused ourselves; our imaginations were fertile. There was no television to neuter young minds. If anything, radio encouraged imagination. They were happy, inconsequential days of fun, inventiveness and laughter. Our parents would not necessarily have argued with our simple philosophy; our youthful antics probably drove them to distraction. We acquired our worldly knowledge from the 'Childrens' Newspaper' and Arthur Mee's encyclopaedias. It was a genteel age, except when the village bobby gave one a cuff across the ear for scrumping, or rather for bring stupid enough to be caught.

11   The Sales 1927 Style

The year 1927 is of personal rather than historical significance. It marked the year my parents moved from a rented house in Watford Fields to a new freehold housing development in Haydon Road, built by Percy Jaggard of Bushey. My impression of the immediate area, in terms of adventure, left me in no doubt of its tremendous potential. Behind the house, like a Norman keep, the old London Road School cast a sombre shadow across the garden, as well as in the heart of the young beholder.

Beyond the junction of Haydon Road and Cross Roads were ancient grazing lands, a footpath, a spinney, stream, pond and 'moat'. The prospect of exploring alien territory tempted me like Africa tempted Rhodes. The fields are still called Attenborough's after the family that owned the estate and lived at Haydon Hill, the large early Victorian house bordering Merry Hill Road.

It was the era of the 'Ovaltinies', parchment tulip-shaped light shades with 60-watt bulbs hanging from the centre of distempered ceilings, floral wallpaper, floral curtains, floral carpet squares, linoleum and brown painted woodwork. The dining furniture was elaborately carved dark oak with high-backed chairs which were sufficiently uncomfortable as to be anti-social. The massive turned table legs always managed to get in the way of children's swinging feet. The exposed floor boards between the carpet and the woodwork were invariably treated with a combined stain and varnish.

A black leatherette-covered portable gramophone, a gift from Sunripe Cigarettes for collecting hundreds of packet fronts, stood on a small table with a pile of brown paper-sleeved 78 rpm records, but the three-valve radio and new Blue Spot cone speaker demanded and received our increasing attention. The picture would not be complete without a nostalgic reference to the roaring coal fire and, of course, the draught under the door. In retrospect it could be regarded as a romantic era, but wages probably amounted to £4 a week and, in many cases, a lot less. So what did we buy in those days and for how much?

Let us go shopping in Watford during the January sales of 1927. Jay's, the furnishers at the top of the High Street, were selling an iron and brass decorated bedstead at 32s 6d, a six-piece dark oak dining suite at 14 guineas, a three-piece sitting room suite in silk damask at £22 and a mahogany bedroom suite at £22 10s. If you were looking for a bargain in china, Lawley's offered a 76-piece breakfast, tea and dining set at 55s, or you may have been tempted by a five-piece cut-glass cruet set including a tray at 11s 3d. For the ladies, Pearkes sold fancy doe skin gloves at 4s 11½d and art silk hose at 1s 6½d. Trewins in Queens Road stocked 9 feet by 10½ feet carpet squares at 6 guineas, a leather-lined coach-built pram at 3 guineas, jumpers and handbags at 4s and teacloths at 8d each.

Even 55 years ago, householders were doing it themselves. Langrish was selling six rolls of wallpaper for 2s and a pint of paint for 3s. Wireless retailer Leonard J Ive of Clarendon Road would have shown you the popular GEC Gecophone, a three-valve job excluding speaker, which sold for £18 5s 0d. Or should you have been one of the very few who could afford a car, A Christmas & Co had on offer a solid-tyred four-seater Trojan Chummy at £125.

Bushey Hall, 1911.

Commuters could buy a weekly season ticket from Watford Junction to Oxford Circus for 9s 9d and, if they wished to celebrate a birthday, they could enjoy a Saturday evening out at Bushey Hall Hotel. A dinner dance – evening dress only – was 8s 6d or, if you just chose to dance, 3s 6d.

During the course of exploring some of Watford's shops, we may have noticed that for the first time for many years the east side of St Mary's Church was open to view from the High Street. A site had been cleared to make way for Lilley & Skinner's new shop[21] and, for a short time, shoppers had their first opportunity of seeing the church from an entirely new angle.

Monmouth House and The Platts prior to reconstruction, 1900.

Building activity was not confined to this part of the High Street. At the same time, old Monmouth House and The Platts were being reconstructed in the form by which we know the building today. Few people realise that the original house dates back to the 17th century when a mansion was built on the site as a dower house of Moor Park Mansion for the widow of the Earl of Monmouth who retreated there after the death of her husband in 1639. The dowager lived there for only two years before she died and the mansion was sold to William Carpender who came to Watford in 1640. In 1771 the mansion was divided into two residences. A Mr Woodcock purchased the northern section and spent £2,000 on alterations. He could well afford the extensive changes as he was the inventor of a red dye used for soldiers' uniforms.

In 1837 the Carpenders repurchased the house but they could not find a buyer when they put it up for sale in 1884. During that period the northern end was called Monmouth House and the southern end The Platts. As the shopping centre extended towards the Pond, many old residences were demolished to make way for new shops and offices. The rebuilding of Monmouth House was a notable exception. Great care was taken by the architect to restore the original building and it is to his credit that internally and externally much of the old house was preserved. It is a pity Watford Borough did not, by example, adopt the same attitude towards the town's other old and treasured properties.

To round off the day in 1927 we could have gone to the Palace Theatre to see 'Dick Whittington and his Cat' with Florence Guest, Gus Elton and Teddy Williams. On the other hand, what about a cup of tea at Lyons, a bus back home and then a warm by the open fire. Who could resist such a temptation after doing the rounds of the sales on a cold winter's day in Watford?

12   What Might Have Been...

I cannot walk by the Carlton cinema and the newly refurbished Palace Theatre without recalling a situation which developed in February 1927 that could so easily have changed the face of Watford. At that time it was said the respective owners discussed the foreseeable problems of accommodating audiences as the town's population continued to increase. It is possible they may have anticipated the advent of the 'talkies', although it is more likely they were concerned with the inevitable impact the new Plaza and its Compton organ would have on their own audiences. Whatever the true reason for bringing them together, their plans for the future had one thing in common: the demolition of the cinema and the theatre. On the site would be built something quite new in concept and appearance. Today I suppose we would call it a leisure centre as it included a restaurant, dance hall and auditorium with intended use as a cinema and theatre, accommodating an audience of between 2,000 and 3,000.

The proposed amalgamation and development never came to fruition, but imagine how the town's entertainments industry would have been affected between the 1930s and 1950s. With the invasion of television into our homes in the lean years of the '60s and '70s, we can only guess the fate of such a complex. One thing is certain, the Palace Theatre would not be playing to full houses today if the amalgamation had taken place. It is doubtful if the Regal (formerly the Central Hall) or the Empire would have survived the competition of a cinema of even greater capacity than the Plaza.

Ye Corner; the cinema entrance was just past the dairy, on Aldenham Road, 1908.

We may well marvel at the tremendous support given to picture houses by the public, even though movies were in their infancy. By the same token, such enterprises attracted the attention of the speculators since profits seemed assured. Perhaps this was why even Oxhey almost had its own cinema. When the corner site of Aldenham Road and Chalk Hill was developed as a Swiss-inspired complex of flats and shops now known as Ye Corner, the architect incorporated an entrance to a proposed picture house in Aldenham Road. The auditorium was to be built at the rear of the new premises, but it was never completed. Over 60 years ago the entrance became the workshop of a clockmaker, Mr Forward. He retired after 40 years at the age of 78 and the business was continued by Edsall & Davies for another 20 years before they moved to new premises in the same development. It is now occupied by Ken Rivers, a tattoo artist[22]. The inner entrance may still be recognised by ornate ceramic tiles and what may have been the pay box now projects as a window into the old foyer.

You may remember the report in 1980 that Watford Borough Council, or at least some of its members, once again proposed that the Metropolitan line, at a point between Croxley Green and Watford, should be joined with the British Railways' line at Croxley and so create a new railway access to Watford Junction. The same proposals had been made in the early post-war years and, as far as I know, detailed plans were completed at the time. As I mentioned in one of my earlier articles, it had always been intended to bring the 'Met' into the heart of Watford and it is ironic that even today the concept has not been entirely abandoned[23]. The choice of another direct line to Baker Street would surely cause many passengers to change their commuting habits – but that is only part of the story.

When you walk along the canal or drive over Cassio Bridge, have you ever wondered why the embankments and the viaduct are so high as the 'Met' line passes over Baldwins Lane or why BR's Croxley Station is nearly a mile from the area which it is supposed to serve? Believe it or not, these two odd features are related.

The London and North Western Railway naturally opposed the incursion of a second railway system into Watford since they had the monopoly of all goods and passenger traffic. The fact that in 1904 Watford had sent a high level deputation to the Metropolitan Railway, followed by a petition in 1906 to plead for a spur to be built from Rickmansworth into the town, was of no consequence to the LNWR. In a last ditch attempt to delay, if not stop the project, the LNWR claimed that the line at Croxley would be extended along the Chess Valley to the north. The projected line would have crossed the road at Cassio Bridge in the direction of Baldwins Lane. The Metropolitan was accordingly forced, at great expense, to raise the height of their viaduct to allow the phantom LNWR bridge carrying their line to pass underneath! The extension was never built, but the extra cost involved nearly stopped the 'Met' coming to Watford.

I can think of one other instance of what might have been. Towards the end of the last century, Mr F J Sedgwick was not only a successful brewer, but also a highly respected citizen and public figure. He owned Watford Brewery which occupied a site on the east side of Lower High Street backing onto the River Colne between Water Lane and the old Watford Mill. He came up with the idea of creating a new arm to the canal at Rickmansworth by utilising the river as far as his brewery. There he could load his beer destined for London and bring back the raw materials required for his brewing operation on the return journey. Unfortunately illness intervened and his scheme did not progress beyond the planning stage, but just imagine the changes that may have been prompted by Watford being connected to the Grand Union Canal. There could well have been a large marina alongside George Stephenson College[24], a boat repair yard, cruisers for sale and hire, a chandler's shop and so on. Because of Mr Sedgwick's illness, Watford was denied a completely new leisure industry only a few yards from the very centre of the town.

13   War Games (Playing Soldiers)

The architect of the stone fortress was well satisfied with its functional design and competent construction. Built on top of the highest hill, it commanded an unrestricted view across the vast plain. In the middle distance a train puffed its way in the direction of the fortress, sometimes disappearing in the dense forest bordering the line. Farmhands waved to the driver of the engine from the fields and farmyards. The statuesque herd of cows ignored the clatter and hissing of the slow moving goods train. Things are never what they seem. The apparent serenity of this pastoral scene would have deceived even Constable. Then the first shell exploded just below the castellated tower breaching the near-impregnable walls. The shattered, falling masonry indicated battle had commenced. The commander of the fortress retaliated with every gun at his disposal.

We were not even aware in those early days that we were engaged in war games, now the prerogative of retired generals and disenchanted first lieutenants. Notwithstanding our inexperience, our tactics were reasonably sophisticated if not original. Our enthusiasm was unbounded. There were no restrictions; the rules of the game were determined only by the parameters of our imagination.

The fortress was constructed of Lott's Bricks, once made in a small factory in Vale Road, Bushey; hard, dense miniature bricks of all shapes and sizes; lintels, arches, cardboard roofs, almost everything with which to build modest cottages or Norman keeps. The goods train comprised the cheapest Hornby tinplate engine with a four-wheeled tender and three wagons of doubtful pedigree. The attacking army ranged from First World War soldiers in khaki of no particular regiment throwing hand grenades or charging with fixed bayonets to the Black Watch in ceremonial uniform. The artillery back-up was represented by two field guns firing wood dowling and percussion caps and one naval gun mounted on wheels. The latter was a near-lethal weapon.

Such was a child's imagination, without limit or inhibition. The battle had just begun to warm up when a detached alien voice disturbed our concentration. "Are you two coming down for something to eat?" An hour of preliminary skirmishes had given us an appetite. Even amateur generals get hungry. A truce was called as we descended the stairs trying to guess the nature of the meal by the appetising aroma rising from the kitchen.

Ted (centre) and friends, 1927.

Each week during the winter months we would play our war games in an empty room heated by a round black paraffin stove standing perilously on three splayed legs. The linoleum floor covering was our battle field. At the end of the afternoon and before tea, the carefully prepared stage set was dismantled stone by stone, gun by gun and soldier by soldier, each piece lovingly returned to its allotted box. Toys did not come easily and breakages could not be replaced. Apart from birthdays and Christmas, we did not expect presents. When a kindly aunt or uncle silently slipped a silver coin into a grubby little hand accompanied by a knowing wink, the gratitude was genuine. Perhaps the economic pressures rubbed off on small shoulders. Small family incomes would not stretch to occasional, let alone frequent treats to which the new generation is accustomed. Our young expectations were directly related to our parents' capacity to give. No wonder we looked after our toys.

At the first opportunity I would present myself at my favourite toyshop, Mayfield's. It was next door to Steabben's the outfitters, just above High Street station. The shop changed hands many years ago, although it remained essentially a toy shop. It was called Cramers and continued in business until 1963 when a disastrous fire gutted the shop and the rooms above. I remember it as a veritable Aladdin's cave. Open shelves were stacked with farm animals, shepherds and their dogs, shire horses, hay carts, fencing and hay stacks. Packed in long cardboard boxes and neatly tied into place by their necks and feet were hand-painted lead soldiers of all regiments, marching, charging, kneeling, firing. Cavalry officers in full dress uniform were mounted on brown painted horses. The final choice was dictated by the money in my pocket.

The other toyshop, long since disappeared, was Goodson's – full almost to the brim with soft toys, teddy bears, prams, dolls, dolls' houses and clockwork motor cars. In later years came the natural progression to Meccano and Hornby trains, usually purchased from Clements, although I could never pass the window of Wren's without envying those who could afford a real methylated spirit-fired steam engine for just 50s.

In 1937 the rumble of war drums could be heard in the far distance. Watford showed few visible signs of preparation for war but in 1938 the scene changed. Air raid sirens, like elongated metal mushrooms, began to appear at street corners. Sirens were mounted on double poles, trimmed at the base with barbed wire. The batteries of the 79th Heavy Anti-Aircraft Regiment were established, although not fully mobilised until July 1939.

A recruiting drive by the Hertfordshire Regiment Territorial Army attracted many volunteers. The Auxiliary Fire Service with their trailer pumps attached to private cars and vans were to be seen training at the old Fire Station nearly opposite Monmouth House. Air Raid Wardens were recruited and trained. Volunteers filled sandbags, which were placed around the lower stories of the Peace Memorial Hospital and other key operational centres.

Watford's youth looked on bemused, incapable of realising the impact and consequences of war. Preparations, now more apparent, went ahead at an increasing pace: black-out precautions, Anderson shelters and, finally, identity cards and gas masks. Our elders, used to the privations of the First World War, knew the priorities in both short and long term. There was no panic. They were accustomed to alternating war and peace. We listened to the BBC news reports and watched the Pathé, British Movietone or Gaumont British newsreels at the cinemas. The straws were in the wind, but what they portended was beyond the ken of schoolboys and those seeking jobs after leaving school. We had not travelled beyond our shores. Our knowledge of Europe and elsewhere was confined to text books and glamorised films.

It is true we were familiar with technical developments in the air, having frequently cycled along the A41 and, finding a vantage point, watched the Royal Air Force demonstrate its capabilities at the Hendon Air Display. Some were familiar with the changing Army techniques of mobility, seen at the annual Aldershot Tattoo.

The atmosphere was charged with uncertainty, the mind with confusion. Youth had no reference by which to identify itself in a society preparing for war. Carnivals, flower shows and bazaars remained part of the social calendar; it was as if peace and war were running in parallel. But soon our war games would be for real. Ironically, my companion of those early days of lead soldiers joined the Army and was killed during the war.

14   The Open Road

The open road promised adventure; the fulfilment of some long-forgotten boyhood dream. There was a certain mystique about country lanes and villages that would otherwise be inaccessible. Those were the feelings in the '20s and the '30s when cycling, motor cycling and motoring offered us the freedom of the open road. The possession of a push bike, motor bike or car made available highways and byways denied our forbears. The prospect of exploring rural England generated a new excitement without parallel. There was no driving test until the mid-'30s, but as the traffic was relatively light and speeds of 40mph were considered fast, an unidentified learner driver was not a particular hazard.

At the end of the '20s, a lady's bicycle could be purchased for £4 17s 6d at Trewins in Queens Road. The model was traditional in every respect except for one special feature; it was guaranteed for 50 years! Come to think of it, if some of those machines are still around, they have only recently come out of the guarantee period! One of the most popular shops was Gray's, also in Queens Road. There one had the choice of Rudge, Humber and Raleigh cycles. Almost next door was Lloyd Cooper, which shop is still there today, selling New Hudson and Sunbeam bikes. There were other shops which spring to mind such as Hitchings & Son at Dudley's Corner, which offered BSA, New Imperial and James cycles. The average price was around £5 and a Sturmey-Archer three-speed, purchased as an extra, was an additional £1. A saddle bag, bell and oil lamp would bring the price to nearly £7.

Young rips with a job and no girlfriend aspired to something much more exiting. A BSA solo machine sold at £29 15s and with a sidecar at £56 10s, or you could buy an upmarket Ariel. Both makes were available at Lloyd Cooper, while Gray's offered Triumphs, Enfields and the expensive Rudge. For nearly £140 you could acquire a Rudge, a box sidecar and a small touring caravan big enough to accommodate two people. I must admit never having seen one, but perhaps a reader has fond memories of his caravan towed by a combination!

Traditionally, the three-wheeler has always claimed a road tax advantage. In 1928 Morgan marketed a 'convertible' trades vehicle for £112. If you are wondering how a trades vehicle can be converted, let me explain. The rear container section could be detached revealing a full four-seater car. The road tax was just £4 a year. I have mentioned Trojan cars in an earlier article, but who of mature years will have forgotten the Brooke Bond vans with their solid tyres? Trojan's advertising slogan in 1928 was wholly topical: 'Keep your money in this country by buying British goods'. It could have been written today with equal, if not greater meaning. The car was guaranteed for 5,000 miles, without any time limit.

In those days I lived near Vale Garage, on the corner of Haydon Road and London Road. A solitary petrol pump projected from the pavement outside the glass doors of the showrooms. Large resplendent black or dark blue Austin saloons were invariably on display. It was the occasional red Austin Swallow with miniature ships' ventilators protruding from the leather-strapped bonnet which made my pulse race. I knew that one day it would be the car of my choice. As it was, I had to be content with a Sunbeam sports bike with a two-speed fixed wheel. Two or three years later I left it outside a friend's house on the Cassiobury estate one Sunday morning. That was the last I saw of my prized Sunbeam with its chromium-plated forks.

The call of the open road was irresistible and, if a lorry happened to pass, we just grabbed any available projection at the rear and held on for dear life. It never occurred to us that lorry drivers had mirrors but, since they never remonstrated, perhaps they were accustomed to hangers-on. The practice was common enough but, in retrospect, their speed was only in the region of 15 or 20 mph so the risk was minimal. But the police would have taken quite a different view and the time came to cast off on arrival at a road junction where a policeman was on point duty. Otherwise we respected the police and avoided the relatively hard justice meted out to offenders.

Clay Hill, Bushey 1910.

To be caught riding a bike at night without a light in 1928 prompted a fine of 2s 6d and cycling on a path, a major offence in those days, could cost 5s. The theft of a machine was more serious: a fine in the region of £5. Out of 32 cases at the Watford Police Court, 22 were summonses against motorists: 15 for not having a current Road Fund Licence and seven for failing to illuminate their rear number plates. A driver of a car who exceeded 10 mph in Bushey was fined £3 and another who drove down Clay Hill at a speed exceeding 12 mph was fined 10s. Either police were more vigilant in those days or there was so little crime that motorists were fair game.

The volume of traffic inevitably increased; it doubled between 1922 and 1925 and the Automobile Association thought fit to issue a warning to motorists in general and their members in particular that in certain areas the police would prosecute in cases where motorists failed to keep to the white lines. "Every motorist" warned the AA "when approaching corners and driving around road junctions should look out for the white lines and keep well within them". It was, of course, the thin end of the wedge. Motorists could park almost anywhere in Watford High Street and, by the late '30s, traffic problems, especially on market days, became an increasing concern. With the arrival of traffic lights, and when the Town Hall was completed in 1938-1939 with a large car park at the rear, it was obvious to all road users that was the shape of things to come.

I cannot recall those days without a tinge of nostalgia; petrol 1s 2d a gallon, a decoke for £5 and cars that seemed to last forever. They were the golden days for motorists when we were content to take a trip on a Sunday afternoon with a picnic hamper to Chipperfield or Commonwood Common. Only last year I stopped at Commonwood on a Sunday afternoon. It was deserted.

15   Listen to the Band

We are often guilty of claiming, if not swearing, that the summers of our childhood were so much warmer than the summers of more recent years. Personally I am not convinced we enjoyed constant sunshine or that it hardly ever rained. I am open to correction but it is my belief our memories are at fault, not the weather. In retrospect, we were a pretty hardy race. Our buses had open tops, there was no central heating in our homes and no electric blankets; only draughty houses that allowed the smoke from open fires to go straight up the chimney. We tolerated chilblains as we retreated to bed and warmed cold feet on a 'stone' hot water bottle. Electric and gas fires were expensive to run, so they were used only occasionally and not at the slightest provocation. They were the days of Boots' cod liver oil and malt, Scott's emulsion and chapped hands.

Spring promised warmth and summer more or less kept that promise. More than the blossom appeared in May. It was also the month the Borough of Watford began its season of entertainment in Cassiobury Park. The cast-iron bandstand, resplendent in a new coat of paint, was contained within a privet hedge, sufficiently high to spoil the enjoyment of those on the outside. Music in the park was a seasonal event, a cultural session, invariably anticipated with relish by Watford's residents. I recall a choice of a green painted slatted chair, upright and uncomfortable, or the luxury of a deckchair for a few more pennies. Uniformed attendants, as smartly dressed as the instrumentalists in the band, arranged the chairs for the hundreds of people who regularly attended the Sunday concerts. Tickets were available to citizens for the season, but the majority bought their tickets at the entrance. The military bands of the Coldstream, Welsh, Irish, Scots and Royal Horse Guards appeared frequently in Cassiobury Park. The bands of the Royal Air Force, the 17th/21st Lancers (the Death and Glory Boys) and even the 10th and 11th Hussars enthralled large audiences. The music of the period included excerpts from 'The Desert Song', Gounod's 'Faust' and Rossini's 'William Tell'; selections from Rodgers & Hammerstein's 'The Girl Friend' and Puccini's 'La Boheme'; and stirring marches of Sousa and variations on favourite themes such as 'The Old Folks at Home'.

The bandstand in Cassiobury Park and Saratoga Jazz Band, early 1960s.

The applause was thunderous, the scene colourful. Colourful, that is, with the bright military uniforms in the bandstand and the dresses of the ladies in the audience. Men were dressed in their Sunday best: a dark suit, white stiff collar and shirt, a sombre tie and black shoes. Their sons were dressed in equally dull clothes, with short trousers and grey woollen stockings. Some young men threw caution to the wind and sported open-necked shirts. Old and young displayed their 'Alberts', with anything from an Ingersoll to a silver Waltham pocket watch neatly tucked into their top jacket pockets. The first performance started in the afternoon at 3.00pm; the second performance was timed for 7.00pm. The late audience usually comprised courting couples who appreciated the opportunity of holding hands as much as listening to the music.

Teas and refreshments could be obtained at the pretty red brick pavilion by the Shepherds Road entrance to the park. The shining floor, spotless windows, sparkling glasses and glistening shine almost dazzled the eye. There was waitress service for those who took their tea in the pavilion or a counter service for those who chose to eat off the tables on the lawn outside. To complement the choice, a colourful Grillo's ice cream handcart was always near at hand.

Cassiobury Park Tea Pavilion and fountain, 1930s.

The season ended in August, although I cannot recall the date of the last official concert at the bandstand. I write 'concert' advisedly because, in true J B Priestly style, occasional concert parties appeared during the summer. I recall Murray Ashford's Westcliffe Entertainers and the Bubbles Concert Party. Laughter and song echoed across the park in the cool of a summer's evening. It is a memory I treasure; a memory of a past age of grace that somehow ended with the war.

There were many other things to do on a Sunday. No doubt British Railways have a fancy name for it, but in the '20s we just called them day excursions. Many people took advantage of travelling at low fares and here is an example. From the Metropolitan Station at Watford a day trip to Rugby cost 4s 6d and Leicester or Nottingham 5s. We will not see those days again. It is true there were few passenger facilities, so hampers were prepared to take on the journey. Sandwiches, cakes, flasks of tea all came out during the trip. From a child's point of view it was part of the adventure of travelling. The best aspect was, of course, being hauled by a green-liveried steam engine belching a varying mixture of smoke, steam and soot. The former filled the carriage with a smell like bad eggs and the latter, sooner or later, was sure to go into the eye of every little boy looking out the window.

We looked up at the mysterious chain which appeared to have no end and wondered what would happen if someone pulled it. The experience of travelling by steam is one which will never be forgotten. It was more than just having a steam engine in front of the train. We forget the man in the signal box hand-operating all the signals, the porter who opened the door of the carriage as if he was pleased to be of service, the bookstalls on almost every station, the Nestlé chocolate machines which offered a flat red-packaged, silver paper-covered slab of rich chocolate and the scales that indicated your weight on a large dial and could be seen by almost everyone on the station.

There was the stationmaster with his gold-braided cap, as proud of the railway as he was of his uniform. He had both power and authority, which he exercised at the appropriate time. The train would not leave until the guard's flag was waved from the rear and that was only when all the doors had been checked. The station clock would not only be working but also showing the right time, although sometimes allowed to run two or three minutes fast. Now that was the age of the train.

16   The Tragedy of the Park Gates

Fifty years ago (early 1930s), Cassiobury Park reached the height of its popularity. There were weekly music recitals at the bandstand, sports activities such as tennis and bowls and, for those who enjoyed walking, the fascination of watching the diesel-powered and horse-drawn working boats negotiating the lock before they took the towpath or entered the woods via the famous avenue of limes. Local artists paid their tribute to the medieval watermill near the bridge in charcoal, oils or watercolour, while others chose to stroll beside the watercress beds where the shallow bubbling water was pure and clean. The rich green leaves of the watercress thrived in these idyllic surroundings.

The much-lamented Cassiobury Park Gates 1910.*

The promise of all these good things was epitomised by the old red brick and stucco lodge and green-painted park gates bordering Rickmansworth Road, which had once given access to Cassiobury House. Beyond the gates were beautifully tended gardens where the highly colourful flower beds were the envy of every amateur gardener. The park had its own character and was as much an integral part of the town as the High Street. From the turn of the century to the early '60s, more picture postcards were sold featuring the park gates than any other beauty spots in Watford. The lodge complemented the market town image.

MANY HAPPY RETURNS OF YOUR BIRTHDAY.

Almshouses erected in Rickmansworth Road by Louisa,
Countess of Essex, Birthday greetings card, 1886.

Alongside were the almshouses, erected in 1876 by Louisa, Countess of Essex; a row of timbered cottages with diamond-paned leaded windows separated from the pavement by a single chain suspended between low oak posts. The walk from the Cross Roads with its drinking trough and AA box or, in the late '30s, from the newly-created roundabout with its flower beds rivalling those in Cassiobury Park, was attractive and inviting. We would pass the Peace Memorial Hospital, in front of which Mary Pownall Bromet's inspiring bronze statues reminded us of those who gave their lives in the First World War. Immediately beyond the hospital, trees lined the way to the Park Gates.

Who, in their right mind, could have envisaged that man, or rather local government, would have even considered the destruction of what was once Watford's most attractive road. When, in 1970, the lodge and gates were demolished, the residents of the town suddenly became aware that their environment was in jeopardy. The bureaucratic machinery, ignoring the protests, got into top gear and systematically destroyed the majority of Watford's architectural and historical connections with the past.

Carved clock panel from Cassiobury House, on permanent loan from the Royal Cornwall Museum. Displayed in the Cassiobury Gallery, Watford Museum.

Cassiobury House 1910.*

Few will remember Cassiobury House when the Essex family lived there. More will remember the years when it stood empty, a memorial to the past that had no place in a modern building estate. There is little doubt that Queen Elizabeth I once slept there in the 16th century. Queen Adelaide, widow of William IV, lived there between 1846 and 1848. Queen Victoria and Edward VII visited the house. The mansion was worthy in material terms of royal patronage. It had been rebuilt by the second Lord Capel who was created Earl of Essex by a grateful Charles II. The gardens were said to have been inspired by Versailles. The elaborate décor included wood carvings by Grinling Gibbons. Some of the many pictures were painted by Vandyke, Reynolds and Turner. Family heirlooms were abundant. The estate extended from Grove Mill to Callowland and Cassiobridge and beyond. Daniel Defoe wrote in 1778 "the whole spot is one of the finest places near London" and he was not given to exaggeration.

George Devereux de Vere Capel, 7th Earl of Essex, and Adele, Countess of Essex, Cassiobury Park 1910.*

35

The Earl of Essex allowed the public access to Cassiobury Park as far as the canal and along the towpath to Grove Mill or Cassio Bridge and tickets were issued to those taking advantage of this facility. Near the turn of the 20th century the Earl started selling off his land: 35 acres of Callowland Farm, 50 acres of Harwoods Farm and 208 acres of Cassiobridge Farm. The buyers were two men who, it could be claimed, were the founders of late Victorian and Edwardian Watford. Their names were Ashby and Brightman. They turned the town from a leasehold to a freehold area and made properties available at the lowest prices.

They were highly successful speculators and, when they purchased 180 acres of Cassiobury Park, they offered 60 acres to the then Urban District Council at cost to preserve the park. By the same token, it would enhance the property values of their houses built on its perimeter. This seemingly magnanimous gesture provoked a storm of protest on the one hand and elated support on the other. It split Watford right down the middle in the best political tradition. Nearly a year passed before a qualified acceptance of the offer was announced. The final terms included the purchase of 60 acres at £16,500, equal to a penny on the rates, and an option to acquire a further 25 acres five years later.

As the Cassiobury Estate was whittled away to provide housing, accommodation for the Watford Grammar School for Boys and a sewerage farm, it was inevitable that sooner or later the mansion and the remaining land would be put up for sale. It happened in 1922. The land was sold, but who wanted a historic and costly house with only a few acres of land at a time when the country was suffering a recession? In 1927 the old and deteriorating house was pulled down. Its fixtures and fittings were sold by auction and Gibbons' staircase went to a wealthy American who incorporated it into his house in Florida. In later years it was loaned to the Metropolitan Museum of Art in New York, where it may still be seen. Job lots of bricks, timber, beams, lead guttering, doors, window frames and the like went under the auctioneer's hammer.

Much of the building material was acquired by local builders and may now be found incorporated into houses of that period built at Watford Heath and elsewhere in Watford. Only last year I was shown a small wrought iron gate, possibly of Italian origin, erected in a garden in Bushey that was acquired at the auction. There is a carved panel in Watford Museum on which a clock was once mounted. The remains of Cassiobury House are scattered far and wide.

When the lodge and the Park Gates were demolished in 1970, the Town Hall was surprised at the adverse public reaction. But it was too late; Watford's 'trade mark' had been reduced to rubble. Our citizens have long memories and have never forgiven this deliberate act of vandalism. You may well question my claim but Watford Cine Society, in its infinite wisdom, recorded the demolition on movie film and, I can assure you, the audience reaction is something to be heard to be believed.

The Cloisters, Cassiobury House 1906.

36

17   The Peace

Each time I take my wife to do Red Cross duty at the Peace I realise it has an affectionate place in my heart. Its correct title is the Peace Memorial Wing of Watford General Hospital but to me, to us I am sure, it is still the Peace[25]. Now it is obscured by wide roads, junctions and underpasses as well as by diesel and petrol fumes. Once upon a time it was accessible from Rickmansworth Road via a sweeping drive bordered by lawns and flower beds. The frontage was dominated by Mary Bromet's three bronze statues mounted on a plinth of Portland stone. The setting was a credit to the traditional Hertfordshire style of architecture of earlier years, exemplified by Watford Grammar Schools for Girls and Boys – red brick and white sash windows; an ageless design which has dignity and charm.

Watford Cottage Hospital Saturday Fund appeal, 1908.

We are inclined to take hospitals in general and the Peace in particular for granted, but a century ago there was little that could be identified or would qualify as a hospital. It is true there was an infirmary and an infections hospital at the rear of the old workhouse in Church Street. Then the new workhouse was built in Vicarage Road and also Watford Isolation Hospital in Tolpits Lane, well within range of the sewerage farm, spreading over many acres of old farmland just beyond Scammell's factory. About the same time, in 1885, a new Cottage Hospital was built at the Bedford Almshouses end of Vicarage Road to serve Watford and district. This was the time when the town's population was beginning to increase due to the attraction of cheap residences being built by Ashby and Brightman. But the small and attractive hospital was soon found to be inadequate and, over the years, two new wings were added. After war was declared in 1914, thousands of casualties were brought back to England for treatment and Watford suffered the embarrassment of having insufficient accommodation to accept wounded soldiers into the Cottage Hospital. In fact Voluntary Aid Detachment units were set up in alternative buildings offered by patriotic citizens and the Council. Watford's inability to provide hospital care for the military left its mark on the conscience of its residents. In the immediate post-war years these shortcomings prompted action. In the event of another war, Watford needed to be able to meet the demands of a nation in conflict. A new hospital was a necessity and a fitting memorial to Watford's many war dead.

The promotion of a public appeal to raise £90,000 was headed by a committee, of which the Earl of Clarendon was chairman; Mr C H Peacock, secretary; and Mr H Brown, treasurer. Its members included most of Watford's prominent citizens. To raise this sort of money at a time of economic depression was a tremendous undertaking but, undaunted, the committee set about its task. By 1923 sufficient funds were available to prepare plans and the foundations of the new hospital. In that year the Countess of Clarendon laid the foundation stone.

In another two years the new building was completed, £90,000 having been raised in its entirety. King George V and Queen Mary were invited to perform the opening ceremony. They declined on the grounds

Peace Memorial Hospital, late 1930s.

of pressing engagements. The Duke and Duchess of York were also approached, but they declined for the same reason. However the Princess Royal, Princess Mary, accepted. She arrived in Watford on a wet June day in 1925 to officially open the Peace Memorial Hospital. School children, who were given the day off, were only too pleased to line the route to greet Her Royal Highness. Bunting and flags adorned the High Street to celebrate the occasion. Shopkeepers dressed their windows and residents their houses. Even the weather failed to dampen onlookers' enthusiasm.

The Mayor, Alderman Thorpe, aldermen, councillors and local government officers greeted the Princess Royal on her arrival in the Market Place. There the Town Clerk, Mr W Hudson, read an address of welcome which was then presented to Princess Mary. Arriving at the hospital, she was handed a gold key by the architect, Mr Wallace Marchment, with which to open the main door and so formally opened the new hospital. A Service of Dedication was conducted by the Bishop of St Albans before the Earl of Clarendon proposed a vote of thanks. As a final gesture, the Princess planted a cedar tree in the hospital grounds.

Despite the adverse weather conditions, the ceremony went smoothly and efficiently. The result of years of ceaseless work raising money, planning and building had given Watford a hospital modern in both design and equipment. It was of sufficient proportion to meet parochial and national emergencies. Although the project had cost £90,000, money was still needed to provide more sophisticated equipment and, in 1929, an anonymous donor gave £12,000 to equip an x-ray unit. No doubt there were many similar examples of generosity, but none quite so touching as a £60 cheque presented to the chairman by John Dickinson's, whose employees had contributed to a Penny Fund.

But such was the growth of Watford in the '30s that in a decade the hospital's accommodation was once more inadequate. The continuing increase in population necessitated yet another appeal, this time to raise £70,000 to provide further extensions to the hospital. Once again, money was forthcoming.

Historically, Watford seems to have countered past and present recessions. Perhaps the diversification of local industries helped ward off the cold wind of depression which then, as now (1982), affected so many other parts of the country. Watford was never a mean town. Even in 1929 the Council, ignoring the crisis, had purchased The Elms, on the site of which it planned to build a new complex intended to accommodate a town hall, offices, fire station and swimming baths. It was put out to competition and, with a number of amendments, the plans came to fruition in 1938-1939. If the project had suffered any significant delay, it would never have been completed in pre-war years. We can count ourselves lucky that our Town Hall is not a facsimile of Charter Place, but it was a very near thing.

18   Musical Evenings

If the occasion demanded music, there was always someone who could play an instrument of some kind. Nearly every home had a piano. The 'upright' as it was called and the music stool, under the seat of which sheet music could be stored, were as much part of the furnishings as a television set is today. There the comparison ends. Little skill is needed to press a button or turn a knob and settle in a chair expecting to be entertained. To be able to play the piano was no mean accomplishment. It required a long apprenticeship on the part of the learner and prolonged stamina on the part of the listener. Sons and daughters, like their parents, were expected to reach a reasonable degree of proficiency on a musical instrument. It was the way things were in Victorian and Edwardian times and, from the parents' point of view, there was no valid reason why the old order should ever change. The ability to entertain was second only to academic qualifications and something of a social necessity.

The gramophone, so long as the clockwork motor had to be rewound after each record, had not taken over. We were growing out of the crystal set and headphone era, but the valve wireless was still too expensive to make an impact on family life. In these circumstances, a musical evening was not a special event. The guests usually arrived on a Sunday evening. Rosie Chilton, an accomplished pianist, Lil Allitt with her viola and a bespectacled man, whose name escapes me, with his oboe and sometimes a lady with a cello. My father, an adept musician, doubled on violin and clarinet. Sometimes Henry Cummings would come to charm us with his rich baritone voice or Gertrude Leader, a well-known local singer from Cross Road, Oxhey.

It seemed to me the first hour was taken up tuning their instruments before launching themselves into harmonious pieces such as 'Humouresque' or 'Danny Boy'. At an appropriate time, my mother

Reginald Parrish (author's father) with his violin, 1910.

appeared with trays of sandwiches, cakes and steaming cups of tea, the only occasion the dedicated players would permit an interruption. The neglected fire was refuelled with coal from a black scuttle and poked to induce the ash to filter through the grate into the tray beneath. This was my cue to go to bed without protestation. I could hear the music just as well from my bedroom, until sleep muted the strains of the quintet playing a sea shanty.

Our upright piano was a Crowley, a name which may not be familiar. The make had a good reputation and, needless to say, was a little more expensive than most. There is, of course, a very good reason for mentioning the name of the manufacturer because Crowley pianos were made in Watford. The factory was in Riverside Road, better known in those days as the Rookery. There, a relatively small work force produced pianos with a first class reputation which were dispatched all over the country. By the early '30s, the days of the piano were numbered and gradually the wireless took over as a focus for family entertainment. In an effort to increase sales, Mr Crowley decided to create his own retail outlet and purchased premises opposite the old Plaza cinema. The same shop is now (1982) a restaurant called The Chef[26]. Along the expansive side windows, a selection of pianos was displayed and often prospective purchasers could be seen and heard playing. The showroom was spotless. The floors were as highly polished as the popular rosewood veneer on the pianos. To promote more business, Mr Crowley decided to sell records, but such was his dedication to classical music he refused to market records that we could now describe as being in the 'top 20'. If it was Bing Crosby's latest recording you were looking for, then it was necessary to go to Bailey's in the High Street or Elliott's in Queens Road. Mr Crowley stuck to his principles and eventually the business and the factory were forced to close.

In those days there were few active local charities in Watford concerned with looking after the aged. I confess I do not know the origin or history of Mr Gosling's Home for Aged Women in Cassio Road, but I do know it received the help and support of local residents[27]. Friends of the home had made it possible for the aged residents to enjoy an annual New Year's dinner, a feature of which was a gift for each of those attending. No meal was ever complete without a diversion and Lil Allitt, an employee of Crowley's, always made herself responsible for the entertainment. In later years, Lil Allitt became secretary of Watford School of Music. She was a character in her own right; a personality loved and respected by all who knew her.

In early January 1929 the residents enjoyed a concert that was typical of the period: a pianoforte solo by Miss Chilton called 'Shepherd's Hey', songs by Miss Leader and Miss Malin, which included 'The Little Dutch Garden' and 'Butterfly Wings'; 'Quanto sei bella', a violin solo by my father; a recitation 'How Jimmy Treated the Baby' by Mr Batchelor; and 'Erbert A B', a monologue by Mr Keable. It sounds like an old-fashioned music hall programme, but the elderly people really enjoyed those evenings.

On other occasions Mr Barker would bring his specialised brand of entertainment: a puppet show. He lived in Mill End, in a little terrace cottage decorated like a gypsy caravan. His face bore the deep lines of an actor whose career may have been less than successful. Then he found a new interest. He made a large portable puppet theatre with scenery and puppets. I suspect the little jointed wooden figures with their painted faces and colourful costumes were as real to him as the two boys he adopted. Mr Barker was a master of his craft and a natural entertainer who found the right niche in the entertainment business. His puppets were one of the most popular shows presented at Mr Gosling's Home.

My father formed his own dance band called the Sylvanians and frequently played in Watford and the surrounding villages. Only one of the band members made the big time – Henry Cummings. In later years he made frequent BBC broadcasts and became one of the country's top concert singers. He regularly returned to Watford Town Hall in the late '40s to sing with the Watford Philharmonic orchestra and choir.

19   Watford's Vanished Industries

In my last article I mentioned the demise of a piano manufacturing industry which once flourished in Watford. I was reminded of another product no longer made in the town, namely chocolate. Since the beginning of the 20th century, perhaps even earlier, cocoa was processed on a site bordering Bushey Mill Lane and Sandown Road, but in the early years two major fires occurred causing extensive damage to the factory buildings. I am not sure, from this doubtful beginning, when Delecta Chocolates came to Watford, but the company established itself in the same spot and thrived in the area that became known as Delactaland. A whole range of chocolate products was produced. Either their packing department was not a popular place of work or their rapid expansion necessitated more staff, but in 1929 the company were frequently advertising for new staff.

There is nothing new under the sun, or at least very little. I am sure this story will have a familiar ring. With a fair amount of publicity, Delecta announced a national competition. A lid from a box of chocolates or a wrapper from a bar was sufficient to evidence purchase. Competitors were required to state the order of popularity of some dozen lines – hard centres, soft centres, milk or plain slab, with or without nuts and so on. The first prize was £500, or the price of a new semi-detached house; the second prize, £250, was almost enough to furnish a house and buy a new car; the third, £100. In current terms (1982), the first prize would be worth something in the region of £35,000 or more. By any standard, they were generous prizes. Delecta was succeeded by De Beukelers, then famous for their chocolate wafer biscuits and liqueur chocolates. It is a name with which we are not now familiar, but the memory of their delicious wafer biscuits lingers on. I think the firm ceased production in the late '50s or early '60s, but the name Delectaland survived the demise of chocolate production.

It was in 1929 when the Borough Council had to go cap in hand to the County Council to secure a small strip of Beechen Grove School playground so that Red Lion Yard could be widened in connection with a proposal for a new borough market. Red Lion Yard was expected to become the main entrance for delivery vehicles and so keep the High Street access points for shoppers only. The proposal was received with mixed feelings by Hertfordshire Education Committee which, in a position to call the tune, required the corporation to improve the whole length of road from Red Lion Yard to the new market. It is not often the Town Hall is told what to do!

Although it was a time of recession, the council was considering the purchase of the old mill in Cassiobury Park, beside which was a wharf. Apparently the Earl of Essex, who allowed the canal to be built through his estate, was provided with his own private wharf so that the long boats and 'butties' (towed craft) could unload coal for use at Cassiobury House. Coal, once the mainstay of the Industrial Revolution, was no longer in demand. Heavy industry, dependent on its use, was running down and coal stocks accumulated until pits were forced to close. In this regard, Watford was fortunate; its industries were diversified and light rather than specific and heavy. The town was not directly involved in mass unemployment. The only major coal consumer was the gas works in Lower High Street. The areas, in national terms, with the highest concentration of unemployment were called 'distressed areas' and coal mining was one of the most badly hit industries at the end of the '20s. National campaigns were organised to help the miners. The Lord Mayor's Fund, to which Watford Borough Council generously contributed frequent cheques for £100, was one of them. On a parochial level, door-to-door collections of clothing for the miners and their families were organised. To give you some idea of local responses to the appeal, an estimated 5 tons were collected from just Oxhey, Cassiobury and St Andrew's wards. Deprivation and generosity often go hand in hand. The Watford Rotary Club arranged transportation of the clothing. Whatever may be said about the town of those days, its residents were most generous.

Despite the hard times, the Cobra Polish Company in Greatham Road really had something to celebrate. The chairman and directors invited their staff to Bucks Restaurant to celebrate the New Year. At dinner an announcement was made that the company had received a world record order for boot polish! I recall that a large proportion of their production was exported, especially to South American countries. Having survived the war, not long afterwards the Cobra factory was gutted by fire but the premises were never restored. Production ceased and Watford lost yet another unique industry.

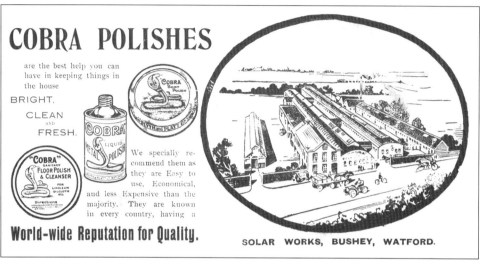

Cobra Polish advertisement, 1915.

Perhaps the healthy state of Watford's industries in the early years inspired Messrs A B Cox[28] and J J Stirling Hill to write a new comic opera for the Watford Operatic Society in the style of Gilbert and Sullivan. The plot was described as "a satire on this commercial age". The new work was called 'The Merchant Prince'. Although everything went wrong that could go wrong on the first night, the critics were kind, if not sympathetic to this home-made product. Despite all the headaches associated with a brand new musical, it was a success.

Even in the days of March 1928, the prices of the seats were by no means inexpensive: stalls were 4s 9d, circle 5s 9d and 4s, pit 2s 6d, and the gods 1s 3d. A seat in a box was relatively modest at 5s 9d. At the end of that momentous week, Mr Stirling Hill surprised members of the society when he announced the show was being transferred to the Scala in London the following May. If the show had such merit as to warrant a date in the metropolis, perhaps Watford Operatic Society may have cause to think in terms of giving it another airing. It would make a change from the traditional and safe American musical. With the current wave of nostalgia for the '20s, its success should be assured. I suspect the satire would be as potent today as it was then.

The economic conditions prevailing in past and present eras are not that dissimilar. There must be exceptions, of course, and one of them is the workhouse. Many unemployed had taken to the road in search of jobs. Watford's workhouse, like our coaching inns, was the last stop to London. In 1929 the Board of Guardians' attention was drawn to the overcrowded conditions existing at the infirmary in Vicarage Road where inmates were sleeping on the floor between the beds.

20   Watford on a Sunday

I have already made reference to Watford's oldest cinemas, as well as the entertainment provided by the borough in Cassiobury Park during the summer months. On this occasion, I am mindful of the entertainment available to the public when cinemas closed on Saturday night and did not open their doors until Monday afternoon.

Younger generations, through no fault of their own, are generally left with the impression that in those days only pubs and churches opened their doors on a Sunday evening. The impression is accurate, but only up to a point. It was certainly true that there was no dancing on a Sunday, but there was musical entertainment at three-weekly intervals during the '20s and '30s at Watford Palace Theatre. Seats could be reserved at 2s 4d and 1s 10d or, if you joined the queue, unreserved seats could be acquired at 1s 6d. The concerts started promptly at seven o'clock, timed, no doubt, to avoid clashing with evening church services. The presentation and content of the concerts maintained a strict decorum which distinguished them from weekday variety shows. By the same token, they were far removed from the classical concerts. They could be described as taking a middle-of-the-road approach, offering nothing too serious or offensive. The majority of the audience was invariably adult and dressed in their Sunday best. Well-creased trousers of shapeless cut, waistcoats and single-breasted jackets, stiff collars and unimaginative ties. Ladies, in contrast, wore colourful dresses with hemlines below the knee and dainty, slightly pointed high-heeled shoes. Men removed their trilby hats and ladies kept their close-fitting, narrow-brimmed hats firmly over their bobbed hairstyles.

They were advertised as National Sunday League Concerts and, as the title suggests, every effort was made not to attract criticism that audiences were enjoying themselves too much. It was all very conventional. A band always headed the bill, such as Ernest Rutterford and his Band, Hamilton Spencer and the New Plaza Band or Bainbridge Robinson and his Band. The band leaders and their orchestras probably comprised musicians who had once accompanied silent films. The programme generally avoided the popular tunes of the day and confined itself to what we once termed 'light music'. The repertoire usually included vocalists and I can recall Olive Goff singing 'Lass with a Delicate Air' and 'Nightingale in June', while Glyn Dowell charmed with 'For You Alone' and 'Here in the Quiet Hills'; popular ballads with a Victorian flavour. The audience was not quite so restrained in showing appreciation. Many encores were demanded and the singers duly responded with a verse and chorus.

Few will have forgotten Harry Hemsley, one of the first child impressionists. He made at least one appearance at the Palace with the National Sunday League in 1929. At that time his name was not a household word. Fame came to him in later years when he endeared himself to the nation through the medium of radio during and after the war. No wonder the audience enjoyed his act so much. Little did they know he was to become one of the most popular voices on the air, or rather those of the children he created.

Not even the BBC played other than light music on Sundays, so we had to wind up our gramophone to hear the latest tunes. Some have survived the half-century; others have fallen by the wayside. Do you remember 'All by Yourself in the Moonlight'? It took the country by storm. The tune was hummed and sung by millions and whistled by errand boys riding their bikes. Now it is just a memory; one of the records the BBC never retrieves from its archival library. 'Ah, Sweet Mystery of Life' was quite another matter. It seems to have come through almost unscathed by time or taste. Do you remember Helen Kane? She recorded for Zonophone and two of her hits were 'That's my Weakness Now' and 'Get out get under the Moon'. Then there was the wonderful duo of Layton and Johnstone. Remember their 'Bluebird Sing me a Song' or 'Was it a Dream?' In those days, the words and the tunes were simple and the tempo strict; we danced together, not 6 feet apart!

With diamond stylii coursing over our LPs we are inclined to forget the little flat tin box, always difficult to open, that contained 100 short shiny needles and the warning notice recommending a new needle for every record played. It was about this time that gramophones could be fitted with an electric pick-up in place of the old mica diaphragm sound box and plugged into the amplifier circuit on the wireless. The day of the radiogram was nigh.

For the adventurous or those seeking real life thrills, there was a welcome alternative. Although the visit of the Flying Circus only lasted for 10 days, the period included two Sundays and more than qualified as Sunday entertainment. The aircraft – rickety old string bags of doubtful vintage – used one of the fields of Leggatt's Farm adjacent to the 'arterial' road. The grazing land was adequate for cattle, but a little bumpy for landing.

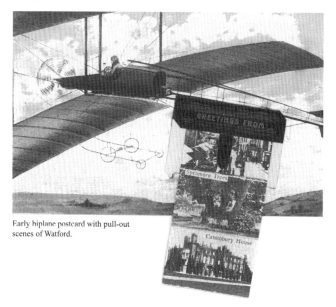

Early biplane postcard with pull-out scenes of Watford.

For 5s you could take your life in your hands and climb into an open cockpit and then take a trip around Watford. The old bi-plane with a radial engine rattled across the uneven turf into the wind at near maximum revs. Sooner or later the wheels hit up, bump, and the plane was literally launched into the air. The bracing wires whistled and the fuselage shuddered as it staggered to keep flying speed and turn at the same time. The goggled pilot looked confident enough, but little else contributed to one's peace of mind.

If that was not exciting enough, there was the aerobatic show in which loops, rolls and stalls became the norm. The excited audience did not so much admire the stunts as the aircraft for staying in one piece. Apart from the noise of the engine, the crowd suddenly became motionless and quiet as the stunt man casually climbed out of the cockpit and walked, if that is the right word, along the lower wing, weaving in and out of the struts and bracing wires. It was the thrill of all time; something one only expected to see at the flicks and there it was, all happening for real. Our hearts were in our mouths until he finally climbed back into the aircraft and it landed safely on the grass. We need not have worried. He probably wore a parachute, although in retrospect the plane was flying at only a few hundred feet and it may not have had time to open. As for the aircraft, the advertising posters assured us that "all our machines are inspected every 24 hours under Air Ministry regulations". A comforting thought.

21   Watford's Ancient Market

Watford was once described as a market town consisting of "one street and two or three dirty lanes". This unkind observation was made many years ago. Even in medieval times, Watford had its own Tuesday market operating under a charter believed to have been granted by Henry I. Another charter, for two fairs to be held annually, was granted by Edward IV. We still have a market, so whatever happened to the fairs? It appears they were 'abolished' by the old Local Board of Health in 1873 for the reasons, so it is claimed, that they had "degenerated into gatherings principally for drunkenness and immoral practices". I can only assume the fairs used to be held in the Market Place, which was the centre of the town's commercial activities. If you have ever been to Pinner Fair, you will have some idea of the impact it makes on the village for just one day a year. Who knows – perhaps some day the legality of that significant, if not momentous, decision will be successfully challenged and the fairs will be reinstated.

Watford Market, 1927.

Architecturally speaking, little is left of the old Market Place as it was at the turn of the 20th century. Gone are the Essex Arms and the Corn Exchange, strongholds of commerce and politics. They stood on a site occupied by Timothy Whites and Cawdells, the latter store having been demolished in 1973 to create an entrance to Charter Place. This was once the stopping place of the old London and North Western buses which served Watford, Bushey and Harrow. On the other side of the road was the Rose & Crown Hotel with its daily coach service to Hatchett's Hotel in London. I believe the last coach to run to the metropolis was in 1886, some 50 years after the arrival of the railway. The Rose & Crown was demolished in the late '60s to make way for Boots' new store on the corner of Market Street. Gone too is the Green Man, the Compasses and Fisher's although the latter building remains, still recognisable, on the corner of New Street[29]. The Spread Eagle, which occupied a site in the vicinity of Millets store, has long since disappeared[30].

As early as 1927 the borough was seeking ways in which to acquire the market rights in anticipation of transferring the market from the Market Place to a new site in Red Lion Yard. At that time market days were Tuesdays and Saturdays. The last market to be held in the High Street was on Saturday 22 September 1928. It was the end of an era. There were good reasons for wanting to change the venue. The volume of traffic through the High Street was continually on the increase and our local authority was concerned with the risk to shoppers of passing vehicles.

There was a double row of stalls; one facing the pavement and the other facing the road. The stalls were made up of converted barrows or temporary wooden structures, each protected by a canvas or tarpaulin slung over a primitive framework to protect stallholders and their wares from the rain. The awnings were angled in such a way as to allow water to drain between the back-to-back stalls. There was little order or conformity in the line of stalls stretching the whole length of Market Place. Some of the stall holders would shout in throaty voices to advertise their goods, especially the butchers, fishmongers and greengrocers. The noise, litter and colour were not very different in medieval times. Then, bare-footed children ran among the stalls, smocked peasants bartered and blue-coated apprentices sought bargains.

The stall holders could be readily distinguished from the customers by their regulation dress of hose, breeches, doublets and flat caps. Only the absence of the stocks and whipping post as a means of meting out instant justice distinguished 500 years of market trading in Watford.

The whereabouts of the charter is a mystery. It originally granted the Abbots of St Albans a market in Watford; that seems fairly certain. In all probability it has been lost, so we will never know why the rights were given to Watford and not Cassio, to which reference was made in the Domesday survey. That one factor undoubtedly contributed to the prosperity of the town, which had established itself near the River Colne and spread to the north as far as Cassio Hamlet.

The new market in Red Lion Yard got off to a bad start. Many will remember it as a compact area, dirty underfoot and covered by a metal and glass roof to protect everything and everyone from inclement weather. The borough, without too much thought, had replaced one open area with another. After all, it had survived five or more centuries in the open air. The new market was paved and drained as it would have been in the street. That was the theory of it, but in practice all sorts of problems occurred when it rained. Water drained from the awnings onto the stallholders, their wares and the public. In due course, the council relented and provided a roof spanning the whole market area. It seemed as if the new Watford Market would continue to operate from Red Lion Yard for the next 500 years. But it was not to be.

Beechen Grove School as demolition begins; Red Lion Yard on left, 1973. Photo by George Lorimer.

In the post-war years traffic in the High Street again became a problem with the advent of private rather than public transport. Increasing numbers of cars forced the planners to extend their interests from new roads to new developments. Every local authority was at it and Watford was no exception. It was rather like keeping up with the Joneses. As part of the grandiose scheme of the mid-'60s, demolition started in the central area and, in the '70s, Cawdells was one of the first casualties. The market, too, was temporarily transferred to the ground floor of the Shrubbery Car Park to clear the rear of the old site for development. The Drill Hall and Beechen Grove School were also demolished. In a short time, the whole area was laid waste.

The move to The Parade was both unsuccessful and unpopular. The low ceilings and narrow passageways between the stalls was neither good for access nor trade. With clinical fluorescent lighting, the excitement of the old market had gone. We missed the smell and roar of the old Tilley lamps burning paraffin; we missed the stallholders wrapped up in overcoats, scarves and mittens, stamping their feet on the ground and swinging their arms to keep warm. In the cold their breath could be seen as it condensed in the ice-cold air. The shouting and chatter added to the noise of shuffling feet and the cries of children. The floor was always dirty and when it rained a thin slime of sticky black mud splattered everywhere. Old people picked up broken boxes to light their fires. There was an atmosphere which can never be recaptured. Now, the market is almost back on its old site, although in a very different environment.

We would catch a bus home; there was no waiting. Perhaps there was a traffic jam in the High Street, but the policeman on point duty at the junction of King Street and Queens Road usually sorted out the problem. The bus conductor had a sense of humour, smiling eyes and a happy face, despite standing on the open platform. We arrived home exhausted. Invariably, a disembodied voice said "Can someone put the kettle on?" Someone always had, as shoes came off and felt slippers relieved tired feet. In the '20s, everything stopped for tea.

22   Watford's Forgotten War Memorial

Ask any resident of Watford of any age the whereabouts of the town's war memorial and you will almost certainly be told that it used to be outside the Peace Memorial Hospital. Then there will be an explanation that, due to the road scheme (Phase 3), it was moved to the side of the Town Hall opposite the Central Library. Some will further qualify their directions by telling you that it was originally erected to commemorate those Watford's citizens who died in the First World War. There seems little doubt in the minds of many local people that it is indeed the town's official war memorial and this belief is perpetuated on the occasion of Watford's Civic Service held annually on Remembrance Sunday when wreaths are laid by the Mayor, veterans' associations and many other organisations.

The cost of Mary Bromet's 'Peace Memorial' – three bronze statues and the plinth on which they stand – was originally paid for by public subscription amounting to some £1,000 back in the late '20s after the hospital was opened. However, it is not Watford's war memorial. Even our local authority subscribes to the myth that it is. In fact, the official war memorial, by virtue of ignorance or design, is all but forgotten. It is not neglected for reasons which will become apparent, but why is it ignored by the Borough of Watford, which makes no effort to recognise its presence?

It is a long story, but worth the telling. We have to go back to 24 February 1929. At Vicarage Road Cemetery on that Sunday, where 55 servicemen were buried, a memorial cross erected by the Imperial War Graves Commission was unveiled by the Mayor, Alderman F J B Hemming in the presence of 1,000 people who attended the ceremony. The design of the cross was similar to crosses in Flanders and other war cemeteries in France. It was erected close to the main entrance gate.

The Service of Dedication was conducted by the Rev Henry Edwards, Vicar of Watford; the Rev J Parton Milum; and the Rev G H Ruffell Laslett in the presence of members of the Borough Council, territorials of the Hertfordshire Artillery and representatives of the British Legion, including Watford branch, the Toc H and bereaved parents. The hymns 'O God Our Help in Ages Past' and 'O Valiant Heart' were sung, not without tears, accompanied by the Salvation Army Band. The Vicar of Watford and the Mayor together mounted the steps of the plinth and dedicated the memorial. The 'Last Post' and 'Reveille' were played by Mr S Simmons. After the National Anthem, both the service and ex-servicemen paraded in Vicarage Road as the mayoral party, ministers and guests departed in sadness, but reconciled in the knowledge that the men and lads of Watford who gave their lives would never be forgotten. None could ever have envisaged that 50 years later there would be no commemoration service at the war memorial.

Watford branch Royal Air Forces Association march past Watford Town Hall, late 1940s.

I cannot speak for the interim years of 1929 to 1939, but I am quite sure that members of the British Legion, if not mayoral parties, made their annual pilgrimage to Vicarage Road. I was on active duty during the war years, but I am qualified to tell you what happened in the post-war years of the mid-'50s and '60s. Each Remembrance Sunday morning, active members of the British Legion and the Royal Air Forces Association met at the Watford United Ex-Serviceman's Club in St Albans Road, together with Watford's Silver Prize Band. It was a long-standing arrangement with, I suspect, its roots deep in the past. From there we marched to Vicarage Road Cemetery.

The dedication was spoken by one of the Legion members, our wreaths were laid on the memorial and we paid silent tribute to the dead, then marched back to St Albans Road. Year after year we remembered them. Our numbers diminished and one Remembrance Sunday morning the Silver Prize Band failed to appear but, undeterred, we marched to the memorial in silence and returned disillusioned. There were six, perhaps eight, of us. The end of that unpublicised, unsupported annual event was in sight. Concurrently, the Watford branch of the British Legion was rapidly losing support and it was reluctantly agreed to abandon the march to the memorial. The civic remembrance service in the afternoon was still well attended and wreaths were duly laid at the 'Peace Memorial'. As far as I am aware, and I would dearly love to be proved wrong, no veteran wreaths have since been laid on the war memorial. What went wrong?

I cannot say when the Watford branch of the British Legion was inaugurated, but I assume it was in the early '20s. What town or village throughout the country did not have a Legion hall? Well, Watford was one and perhaps that was its downfall. Regimental standards are, and always have been, a traditional part of the Army's historical past. It was well after the First World War that Legion branches were granted their own standards. Watford had to wait until March 1929.

Clarendon Hall was then traditionally associated with the military. In the same tradition and in the presence of the Mayor and corporation, representatives of local organisations including Legion branches and the women's sections of Harrow, Hemel Hempstead, Harpenden, Croxley Green, Rickmansworth and St Albans, the Earl of Clarendon received the new standard from the flag party of the 343rd (Watford) Battery Royal Artillery (TA). The Earl then presented the branch with the new standard and concluded his speech by saying that it would be one of the branch's most sacred possessions and that they would regard it as an emblem which "may never be unfurled save in the cause of justice and righteousness".

The standard was proudly carried by the bearer as the parade of hundreds marched to St Mary's Church via the High Street and King Street headed by the Silver Prize Band. At the church, the standard was dedicated and consecrated by the Vicar of Watford. The service over, the parade regrouped in Church Street and marched back to Clarendon Road. The occasion was only marred by the deaths of Earl Haig and Marshall Foch.

Tea followed at Gibbons' Restaurant. It was an august gathering. Mr Tomkins, chairman of Watford branch; the Deputy Mayor; Mr Hudson, the Town Clerk; Lord Clarendon; Lord Stopford; Sir Dennis and Lady Herbert. Also present was Mr E Terrell, Liberal candidate for Watford, whose words were prophetic. "As time went on those who took part in the war (1914-1918) would naturally lessen in numbers, but the spirit of those years will always be carried on by the Legion". Watford branch finally closed at the end of the '60s. The overwhelming support it deserved was never forthcoming. Watford's war memorial now stands in silence, only because of the distance separating Vicarage Road Cemetery and the Town Hall.

23   The Wind of Change

The weather that Sunday evening, 12 January 1930, was seasonally cloudy and windy. It was already dark when the sky cleared, peppered with stars and blotted with scudding luminous cotton wool clouds. The moon was particularly bright, shedding sufficient light to negate the street lights. The atmosphere was clear as crystal; cold, but not frosty. Families settled by their fires listening to the wireless broadcasts, reading their Sunday newspapers, playing cards or thinking in terms of putting the children to bed.

Imperceptibly, the wind veered round from southwest to northwest and in no time householders were telling themselves it was going to be a rough night. Their innocent prediction proved the understatement of the year. Windows and doors began to rattle and dustbin lids could be heard rolling down garden paths. The wind through the telegraph wires assumed its traditional hum but, like a violin out of control, the low frequency vibrations increased into a whine and later a scream. Fences started to rattle and shake as gusts reached 50 or 60 mph. Ominous cracks could be heard coming from the direction of our garden as trellis work disintegrated and the loose boards in the fence began to fling themselves in all directions. The roar was deafening as tiles and slates started to flap in empathy.

Husbands placated their wives and wives assured their children as gusts reached 80 mph – and occasionally touched 100 mph. Hoardings swayed until they finally collapsed in a mass of flying timbers and torn paper; tiles and slates were whipped off roofs and even telephone poles snapped, trailing wires across roads and depositing broken insulators like snow into the gutters. Trees resisted the pressure of the wind until their clinging roots were forced out of the ground. Tree after tree, invariably the mature elm, keeled over beyond the point of no return. Chimney stacks and gutters could no longer resist the fluctuating pressures as bricks and chimney pots brought down what was left of stripped roofs. There were many calls made upon the Peace Memorial Hospital ambulance service that night. Some ambulances got through to the injured and some never made it, trapped between or damaged by falling trees. Many compared the storm with the one they remembered in March 1916.

Great Storm, 28 March 1916, Grove Mill Lane. Driver and lady passengers escaped as a tree fell across the car.

At last the wind abated and next morning Watford, local towns, villages and farmers counted the cost. Two people had died from injuries and many recounted miraculous escapes. Debris was everywhere, although the town had all but escaped the ferocity of the storm. A tree had been uprooted in Upton Road and a number of pedestrians escaped injury. Areas outside the town had not been as fortunate. Some of the roads out of Watford were completely blocked. In a northerly direction, the road to Hemel Hempstead was made impassable when five mature elms crashed on the road between Hunton Bridge and Kings Langley near the footpath to the station. A bus had stopped just inches from the first tree. None of the passengers were hurt, although a number suffered from shock. Watford's ambulances had battled their way to Chenies and Maple Cross to pick up the injured. The high red brick wall bordering Bushey High Street and part of Lord Bethell's estate suffered severe damage.

Watford has experienced many storms since the beginning of the 20th century, but none had been quite as devastating or costly in the way of damage as that Sunday night. With the advantage of hindsight, the decade came in like a lion and, for that matter, went out like one too. How could we know that the '30s was to be the end of an era in historic and social terms? There were straws in the wind which we failed to recognise at the time as the precursor of things to come; the need, for example, of keeping in touch with hospital patients.

In the form of an open letter, the Hon Arthur Holland-Hibbert proposed the formation of an Old Patients' Club, open to all those who had benefited from the medical and nursing skills given to patients of the Peace Memorial Hospital who otherwise "may not be alive or might not be in good health". There was an "intense gratitude", particularly among Peace patients, which had not gone unrecognised by the Hon Holland-Hibbert. He devised a means by which their gratitude could be physically expressed and fostered with positive results.

An open meeting followed his proposal and it was agreed the subscription should be 2s 6d a year and would go partly towards the work of the hospital and, as a target, the ultimate endowment of a hospital bed. He further suggested an annual social gathering at Christmas when one of the wards was generally empty, thereby giving the club the opportunity to discuss ways and means of raising funds such as whist drives, bazaars, concerts and flag days "in good fellowship for what the hospital had done".

The meeting duly adopted the title Old Patients' Club, despite attempts by the Rev Frank J Gould to call it the Ex-Patients' Club. I admit not knowing the fate of the club formed in 1930 but understanding the charitable attitude of mind of those days, I expect it went from strength to strength until the halcyon days of social security when our contributions were made compulsory and the need to run hospitals on a charitable basis no longer became necessary. Perhaps the League of Friends is a direct descendant of the old club.

Another factor which suggested fundamental change was the end of the old order of the Board of Guardians which for so long had managed the workhouse and directed the fate of its inmates. In 1930, ultimate responsibility for its operation passed to Hertfordshire County Council, with a local Public Assistance Committee appointed as a representative directing policies. Not that Watford's workhouse was badly run. Quite the contrary; it was rated as a model institution with which others were compared. The changes accounted for the loss of two workhouses in Hertfordshire, including one at Berkhamsted. For the first time, the guardians' hands were tied. In themselves, the changes were not significant, but the transfer of part of the primitive 'social security' system to county control was the precursor of what was to follow in the post-war years. The wind of change was blowing, but would not reach storm force for many years.

24   Titania's Palace

The adage 'little things please little minds' was a phrase, I seem to remember, often used by disillusioned parents whose children apparently aspired to no more than inconsequential heights of learning and who blatantly refused to show any sign of repentance. In retrospect, I can think of one instance when the old saying held true, especially in the context of the second line, 'little trousers fit little behinds'.

The Victorians revered embellishment and detail and it has taken us just 100 years to appreciate their talent, skill and near-faultless workmanship. Now, Victoriana is seen in a different perspective and due appreciation is being shown for their creative abilities. However, these qualities did not suddenly disappear with the death of Queen Victoria; rather they phased themselves out as each new industry turned its attention to mass production in later years. Old skills were forgotten, but not irrevocably lost.

Amongst those who resisted change by action rather than deed was an architect by the name of Major Sir Neville Wilkinson KCVO. His name was once a household word, for who had not heard of or seen Titania's Palace? The palace was formally opened, or rather unveiled, by Queen Mary at Olympia on 6 July 1922, the date of her wedding anniversary. The building was quite unique and became a source of admiration for the exquisite workmanship and infinite detail which its many specialist contributors had lovingly added with their individual skills. Its only peculiarity was that the fully furnished palace measured 9 feet by 7 feet. On the other hand, it weighed 3¼ tons and was insured for £20,000 or, in today's terms (1982), an equivalent of £850,000.

Titania's Palace at Egeskov Castle, Denmark. Photo courtesy of LEGO Group, Denmark.

Titania's Palace consisted of 16 rooms surrounding an open courtyard. Dismantled, it could be stacked into 12 packing cases. By the time the model came to Watford it had been on the road for over seven years, including three years in the United States. The management of the Peace Memorial Hospital was instrumental in arranging for this gigantic miniature palace to go on exhibition at Clements, where Mr Edmunds made the necessary arrangements. During the years it had been on display, £30,000 had been raised in aid of children's charities. In Watford the proceeds went to the Peace.

Sir Neville was also a philanthropist. He had created the palace in his spare time over a period of 16 years and conceived the idea of using it as a means to raise funds for charitable purposes. Lord and Lady Clarendon, Mr Kingham and, of course, Mr Edmunds attended the opening ceremony. The occasion was significant in another respect; Lord Clarendon was making one of his last public appearances before taking up his appointment of Governor General of South Africa. Sir Neville, something of a national figure, also attended the opening ceremony, ostensibly to explain the intricacies of his fairy palace. He even toured our local schools to publicise the exhibition and explain his unique hobby to fascinated pupils. In consequence, parents had little option but to concede to their children's wishes to see the palace. My demands, I am sure, were no less insistent.

I forget on which floor at Clements the palace was placed on display, but I do remember the price of admission: 1s for adults and the more acceptable charge of 4d for children. It was worth every penny of my mother's money as far as I was concerned! The windows of the palace were open and each room was illuminated by electricity. Everything was made to a minute scale, even the clocks on the mantle shelves. Beautifully carved furniture graced each room and I have vivid memories of the liberal use of gold and silver. The Queen's throne, shaped like a peacock and encrusted with pearls, was just 2½ inches high. In her boudoir was an inlaid satinwood grand piano, perfect in every detail. It was said that Sir Hubert Parry had played the National Anthem on the tiny keyboard with a sharpened matchstick. There was the Hall of the Guilds, as ornate as any fairy could have desired, and the morning room where a game of chess could be played with tweezers.

The Palace surpassed anything a child's fertile mind could have imagined, lacking only the presence of Titania herself although, who knows, she may have been in residence all the time. It became the talking point of the town's children and the envy of most. At the appropriate time the exhibition piece was dismantled, returned to the packing cases and loaded onto the specially-equipped lorry bound for another venue[31].

In the last 50 years, so many changes have taken place. Watford was then still a market town surrounded by villages, farms and estates, although the danger signals were ever present at the end of the agrarian order. The demands for land for development continued at a tremendous pace. Leggatt's Farm was one of the early casualties when part of the old spinney was acquired in 1930 by the borough for Watford's second municipal cemetery. For the benefit of passing motorists or perhaps as an inspired warning, do you remember the two notices placed side by side which caused comment if not merriment? One announced the new site was acquired as a cemetery and the other was equally uncompromising: 'Choose your own site now'. The majority, I suspect, deprived themselves of taking advantage of such a down-to-earth offer.

25   The Heyday of the Wheatsheaf

A century-and-a-half ago, Watford was sufficiently rural to attract day trippers from London. They would arrive late Sunday mornings or early in the afternoon and spend the rest of the day walking along the banks of the River Colne around Wiggenhall, but always making their way back to the Wheatsheaf Inn. Today, the thought of visiting the pub in the shadow of Bushey Arches would be for reasons other than the scenic beauty of our Lower High Street. All that time ago, the Wheatsheaf was reckoned to be one of Watford's principal inns due, it was said, to the large number of local tradesmen who frequently spent their evenings concluding business deals or appreciating the excellent quality of its ale, or both.

At weekends the inn became the forerunner of the '30s 'road house' when couples and parties descended on the house for pleasure and entertainment. At the side of the building was a well-tended orchard and, at the back, gardens and a variety of trees. In their shade, the landlord set out tables and chairs for the benefit of customers and his trade. On hot summer afternoons, a lone fiddler often played to the crowds that frequented the gardens. No doubt the relatively sober afternoons degenerated into boisterous evenings, despite the law which prohibited such conduct on Sundays.

Old Toll House and gate.

Another reason for its importance was the presence of the Toll House, which once stood a few yards to the south on the same side of the road as the Wheatsheaf. It has been described as a "square building of two floors, hanging from the front of which was a lantern that before the introduction of gas (1834) contained a small oil lamp, the flickering light from which made the darkness of the night more visible". The author, who must surely have visited the inn before writing his impressions, went on to describe the clock fixed to the front wall adjacent to the lantern and the heavy gate that was always kept in a closed position until "the utmost farthing had been paid". There was one solitary chimney which emerged from the apex of the roof.

The toll gate keeper slept there overnight, if not permanently, and was expected to gather tolls 24 hours a day. It was a busy road junction, as the gate commanded entry into Watford from London and Hamper Mill. The turnpike through Bushey, operated by the Sparrows Herne Trust, was a busy thoroughfare and the toll gate keeper's lot, like the policeman, was not a happy one. In all probability he consoled himself at the inn, from which he could keep an eye on passing traffic. Between 1756 when Mr Joseph Casmore kept the inn and 1851 when Mr John Spencer took over, a theatre was built at the rear of the yard. It was a wooden barn-like structure and crudely equipped but nevertheless it was the town's first theatre, attracting many touring companies and, no doubt, a few wandering minstrels. It is reported that Henry Irving appeared there as a comparatively young man as a member of Holloway's Portable Theatre. Some time later, Wilson Barrett made an appearance with another touring company.

At the turn of the 20th century, the Wheatsheaf was a Salter house and by the '20s ale and stout were supplied by the Cannon Brewery which was founded by the second Mr John Dyson near Fox Alley. The brewery and maltings were sold to Joseph Benskin in 1867. By 1872, Mr Benskin had added a new brew house and had achieved an output of 250 barrels a week. The courtesy title 'Cannon Brewery' continued in use for many years.

As main roads were taken over by local authorities, Sparrows Herne Trust ceased to operate and in 1872 the Toll House was demolished. All that is left is an iron marker post embedded in a traditional flint wall. Traffic now had the free range of the roads and the importance of Lower High Street declined with the arrival of the gas works and the railway, which together destroyed the beauty it once enjoyed. Walking through the area today, it is difficult to remember the time when shops, pubs, houses and merchants bordered the road right into Watford. Even as late as 1930, the road in the vicinity of Bushey Arches was only 30 feet wide; more than adequate for the stage coaches, horses and carts and pack horses of a century ago.

Sparrows Herne Trust turnpike marker, 1990. Photo by Ted Parrish.

By a twist of fate, the Cannon Brewery Company in Watford had resolved to improve the old-fashioned Wheatsheaf, which had seen better days. The inn had lost its charisma and, unfortunately, its customers. The pub was too far gone for a face-lift and the decision was made to pull it down and rebuild. In the meantime, the Borough of Watford was planning to improve the Lower High Street by widening the road between the river bridge and the Arches. As soon as they became aware of the brewery's intentions, the corporation approached them to discuss their road scheme in the context of the rebuilding programme. Benskins offered the land on which the old Wheatsheaf stood in return for a drive in from the main road, to be built at the Council's expense. Negotiations commenced with the other land owners affected and, on completion, the old inn was pulled down. The level of the surrounding land was raised because of frequent flooding and the rebuilding of the Wheatsheaf started in 1930 at the rear of this historic site. Today the road at this point is 60 feet wide and the new Wheatsheaf still serves its customers with drinks and lunches[32]. The orchard has disappeared and the site of the old theatre could well be part of the large car park. The only

The Wheatsheaf through the Arches, early 1990s. Photo by Ted Parrish.

extraneous noise emanates from the inter-city trains passing over the Arches and the ever-increasing traffic. Gone is the beauty for which the Colne was famous. I would be only too delighted to tell you that the ghost of the fiddler may still be seen on Sunday afternoons, but I have to disappoint you; there is nothing left of the old inn that even a phantom fiddler would recognise, except perhaps the Sparrows Herne Trust turnpike marker across the road.

I have dwelt on the past, but not to the exclusion of the present. The Wheatsheaf, as I have said, continues to flourish under the auspices of Neville Griffin who surely follows in the tradition of those earlier landlords for whom the word hospitality had a special meaning. Until the night of 16 February 1980, apart from his regulars, few people were aware of those latent qualities. With a grinding of metal, the London to Manchester inter-city train left the track at Bushey Station, travelling north at 80

Derailed carriage at Bushey Station after accident, 16 February 1980.

mph. Carriages were scattered along the line, even north of the viaduct. That Saturday night, 47 passengers were taken to hospital and the remainder were taken to the Wheatsheaf where Mr Griffin immediately placed a number of rooms at the disposal of the police. Warm drinks were prepared for those who had escaped the accident and were suffering from shock. The Wheatsheaf became a temporary control centre with Neville Griffin's assistance. No publican could have given greater service to those who arrived so unexpectedly on that tragic night.

26   Full Circle

We are inclined to believe that we saw our first talkie at the Plaza in 1929, but it has been claimed that the honour for showing the first sound film in Watford should go to the Super. I gather it was of an experimental nature. Be that as it may, there is no question that those of us who had been brought up on silent films regarded the introduction of the talkie as a technological revolution. It was something more than not having to read the captions in the middle of every scene. It was a touch of magic.

The new Plaza was adapted to show talkies without too many problems. The old silent cinemas – the Coliseum, Super and Central – presented obvious difficulties. They had all been operating a number of years and, as well as becoming old-fashioned, they were also a little run down. With the prospect of even greater audiences, the respective owners took the opportunity to close their picture houses for conversion to sound in the summer of 1930 and also refurbished and modernised the interiors to Plaza standards.

The Coliseum was one of the first houses to temporarily close its doors. The theatre was completely redecorated with new stage curtains, lighting and seats to accommodate an audience of 1,000. The new projection equipment costing £3,000 was made by the British firm BTH. The directorate assured patrons that their new policy would be to show one talkie and one silent film at every performance so that everyone's taste would be served! In addition they announced a programme change twice a week. The future of the Coliseum seemed assured. Do you remember the opening film? Let me refresh your memory. It was 'The Sky Hawk', an all-British epic feature about "a fight between a Zeppelin and a lone aircraft 10,000 feet above London". Shades of the First World War.

The next picture house to receive the treatment was the Super, although on this occasion a new company took over its operation. Again, the auditorium was refurbished and Western Electric equipment installed. Then the Empire made an announcement. The picture house would be redecorated and a similar American sound system installed. On 1 September 1930 the house re-opened with the film 'Charming Sinners', a provocative title with innocent content starring Ruth Chatterton, Clive Brook, William Powell and Mary Nolan; truly an all-star cast. The golden age of the cinema was about to begin. We queued patiently in long lines behind boards which declared our credit worthiness: 6d, 1s, 1s 9d and 2s 6d. We chose the queue we could afford. Our objective was to see the film and relegation to the 6d division made not the slightest difference to our enjoyment from the first few rows of seats.

During that same summer another event took place which was destined to change, once again, the face of Watford. James Cawdell & Co Ltd proudly announced their 'great rebuilding sale' beginning on Saturday 28 June 1930. Cawdells, like Clements, Percy J Wilson and Trewins, was one of Watford's family stores. The old premises had proved inadequate to meet the shopping potential of an ever-increasing population. To provide room for expansion, James Cawdell acquired the Essex Hall and Rooms, which together had become an intrinsic part of the town's social and political heritage. The Essex Hall was subsequently demolished and, in due course, the reconstituted Cawdells became the most modern store in Watford, resplendent in off-white tiles which covered the front elevation; not unlike the treatment given to the Plaza. The proverbial clock was mounted above the second floor to become an integral part of the old Market Place.

The Essex became just a memory, like the 14th century tithe barn of Watford Vicarage which was demolished to make way for the original Woolworth store where nothing cost more than 6d. Another building of much more recent vintage, but equally unique, was put up for sale in 1930: the Watford Labour Church. Few will know where Mr F H Gorle and some of his socialist friends built their church at the turn of the century. Socialism was a virtually unknown political doctrine or force in Watford in those early years. The two party system of Conservatives and Liberals had not been challenged by a third emerging party. As the Labour movement gathered momentum, the church in Durban Road had become the centre of political activities in the municipal elections. It became expedient in later years to transfer their base to the Trade Union Hall and Labour Club. The church became redundant. In the early days, such well-known figures as H M Hyndman, Mrs Despard, George Bernard Shaw and G K Chesterton had spoken to packed audiences, if not congregations, on the theory of socialism. The same little church still exists in its original corrugated iron clad form in what is now Durban Road East.

Watford Labour Church, extreme left, 1908.

During that same summer, a branch of Cakebread Robey was opened opposite the Plaza[33]. In keeping with many buildings in the vicinity, the new building was given a timbered front elevation and its general appearance, at least from the first floor up, has changed little in over half a century. The new shop, which operated both wholesale and retail outlets, sold ironmongery, paints, wallpapers, building materials and farm requisites. Their sale confirms the market town environment which we remember so well. To remind you of the prices, a full-size tiled fireplace with a wood surround complete with back boiler "to give hot water all over the house" cost only £9 2s 6d. A pedestal basin sold for £4 6s 9d and a cast-iron bath on four short legs (side panels had yet to come into fashion) was £7 15s 0d.

Cakebead Robey continued to trade into the '70s. Then the Oliver opened; probably one of Watford's first havens for the younger generation with whom, we are so often reminded, there is an inseparable age gap and lack of communication. By the same token we are also told that this is the age of communication. The latter claim, I would dispute. Who did not own a 'Kelly's Directory' in the '30s, even though it may have been out of date? We had few telephones, but we wrote letters in the sure knowledge they would arrive at their destination the following day. Such was the local postal service that it was possible to post letters at certain boxes in central Watford to catch the 9pm collection. Each week our local papers published the names and addresses of new telephone subscribers, amounting to about a dozen. In addition, we were informed how many patients had been admitted to the Peace, how many were discharged, how many were in hospital and the numbers of accidents and casualties. As I said, local communications were efficient, enlightening and effective. They gave cohesion to our lives. Now the picture houses are closing; shops have changed hands, while some have disappeared altogether. We use the telephone because who knows when a letter will arrive. We are going full circle.

27   The Day of the Ramble

When the Americans introduced jogging as a cure for an overweight automobile-inhibited nation, it was predictable that the pastime would sooner or later be adopted by the conscience-stricken British. Familiar figures frequently pass the garden gate in a state of induced euphoria as they begin their jog, or in a state of some distress on their return.

In the early days we walked for pleasure. I recall the early post-war era when boys from the Junior Masonic School at Bushey[34] filed past the house in their thick dark grey suits, irrespective of the weather, on their regular Sunday walks. They were orderly and well behaved, speaking in hushed voices when the accompanying master was near at hand. Occasionally, hardy walkers passed by with their rucksacks and black leather boots, sometimes stopping to consult their Ordnance Survey maps as they approached the fringe of Watford from Merry Hill Road. The Junior Masonic School closed in the '70s and the ramblers are few and far between. Now we watch the joggers go by and those exercising their dogs, who invariably develop a thirst which they quench at the Haydon Arms[35]

During the inter-war years, rambling was a popular feature of our relatively uneventful lives. Many books were published describing the scenic routes which Watford and district had to offer. One of the recommended walks of some 14 miles was to Park Street and back via Munden Park to Watford Junction, the starting point. I am only concerned with the directions that will take us to Leavesden and Garston before the days of Harebreaks, the North Orbital and even Watford bypass.

St Albans Road, Callowland, 1905.

From Watford Junction Station, directions lead us to the Old Police Station in St Albans Road where we continue into Leavesden Road, or Callowland as it was better known in those days, until we reach the recreation ground. "At the end of this", we are instructed, "We leave the roadway for a path on the right which, after keeping beside the road for a short way, turns to the right. Soon the path, fenced on either side, leads through a wood (east, I suspect, of Gammons Farm). When the left-hand fence bears away and the path forks, keep to the right-hand branch and, on quitting the wood, turn to the right along its outskirts. At the next corner of the wood, we bear left across the open fields (Leggatt's Farm), but soon there is a wire fence on the right and the path ends at Russell Lane where we turn to the right. We shortly enter Leavesden with the Hare Inn on the right and, just past this house at the end of its garden wall, we turn along an enclosed path. Passing through the swing-gate, the path enters a field. We take the left branch through a second swing gate and bear gently to the right across the field to a gate and stile. Over the stile we turn to the right along a cart track and, after half-a-dozen steps, our path strikes off again to the left crossing an open field. In the fourth field, follow the left track and come out at Sheepcote Lane". We have just crossed the fields of the original Kingswood Estate, but we must continue our ramble!

"We turn to the right and, after passing on the left of the carriage gateway to Woodside House, the lane bears to the right and makes a slight dip. As it rises again, we find on the left a field gate and swing gate and we follow a path along the right-hand border of the field. There is a stile at the end of the field, a fence on the right and a narrow copse on the left, until presently the path merges in a rough lane among the cottages of Garston (Horseshoe Lane)".

I suppose we have been walking four or five five miles of the original 14, but that is quite far enough for one day's ramble 60 years ago. The historian William Camden described the county as "rich in cornfields, pastures, meadows, woods, groves and clear rivulets". William Cobbett in his 'Rural Rides in England' records his journey in 1822 with the comment: "Talk of pleasure grounds indeed; what, that man ever invented under the name of pleasure grounds, can equal these fields in Hertfordshire". One hundred years later the local pastoral scene had changed very little. To all intents and purposes we were using tracks and paths in all probability used in medieval times.

Not quite the first major change to affect the town's rural amenities occurred in March 1924 when Hertfordshire County Council accepted a contract for that part of the new 'arterial' road, later to be called the Watford bypass (A41), which came within their jurisdiction as a much needed escape route from London. The reasons for its construction were twofold; to create employment after the First World War and to relieve traffic congestion in Watford. The line of the new road was planned to cut through virgin agricultural land, virtually destroying many ancient farms in Bushey, Watford and Leavesden, before reaching Hunton Bridge. Its arrival heralded the break-up of Watford as a farming community and the fragmentation of the rural landscape. The isolated fields became the source of many new estates which were to finally surround the nucleus of the town centre.

One example springs to mind which we passed across during the course of a short ramble to Garston – Kingswood. In May 1930, the freehold estate was submitted to auction at the London Auction Centre by Stimpson, Lock & Vince, the well-known firm of estate agents. The total area of Kingswood was 105 acres, which included a residence, farm house and cottages with frontages of nearly 7,500 feet to existing roads and the newly proposed North Orbital Road. Bidding started at £12,000 and the estate finally sold at £24,000 to a purchaser intent on its development as a residential estate.

Between 1930 and 1939 the road was completed and the estate almost finished. Despite its position on the borough boundary the houses sold surprisingly well, perhaps because of their modest cost and an efficient bus service to the town. In later years, many employees at Odhams lived at Kingswood because of its convenience to the new printing works. As far as I can remember, a number of plots in Hillingdon Road had not been developed, at least not until after the war in 1948, when the new semi-detached houses sold at government controlled prices of £1,450; roughly twice the price of their pre-war counterparts!

In more recent years the North Orbital Road has become a vital link in the existing road system, far beyond the capacity the planners of the '20s ever envisaged. The Kingswood Estate now gives no clues to its original identity, except at the point where Sheepcote Lane emerges at the east corner on the 'front' as local residents used to call the houses facing the main road. Since those days, the fields of Garston Manor have been developed, the Hare rebuilt and a new road approach to Leavesden has left little evidence of our agricultural heritage. The farms surrounding Watford are now confined to memory.

28   Herkomer's 'Castle'

As a child I frequently walked across Attenborough's fields and through the churchyard of Bushey Parish Church, complete with pond, elm tree and lychgate. Then I turned right and walked beyond the village shops, past the site of the old forge and turned left into Melbourne Road. Just a short distance along the road, which gently dipped to the lower level of Coldharbour Lane, stood Herkomer's 'castle'. The property was derelict. Weeds and grass covered the driveway to the main bronze door. A notice placed there on the instructions of Lady Herkomer threatened trespassers with prosecution; a warning generally heeded in those old-fashioned days of discipline and good behaviour. Weaned on Grimm's fairy tales, we were convinced the 'castle' was haunted. In retrospect, I suspect parents encouraged us to believe the haunting, if only to keep us on the right side of the massive boundary wall. We gazed in fear and dismay at a decaying edifice; an architectural mutation that suggested the crossing of a Bavarian castle with St Pancras Station.

Lululaund, Bushey, with Lady Herkomer's warning notice at entrance, 1920s.

We called it Herkomer's 'castle' and hurried past clutching our towels and swimming costumes, pretending not to be frightened. We almost ran to the safety of King George Avenue and on to Bushey Swimming Baths. How and why did such a strange Victorian structure come to be built in Bushey, a village of Norman origin? The story begins in 1849, with the birth of Hubert von Herkomer in Waal, Bavaria, to gifted but artisan parents, Josephine and Lorenz. Conditions in the country at that time prompted them to emigrate to the United States. After four years, disillusioned, the family decided to come to England and settled at Southampton. Lorenz found occasional work as a jobbing carpenter and Josephine supplemented the family income by giving music lessons. Hubert's grandfather was a master mason, his father a master joiner and his mother a trained musician. From those poor and humble beginnings, the parents managed to find a place for their son at Southampton Art School. Still financed by his parents, Hubert moved to London for further training and later became an illustrator for a London magazine.

He aspired to become a painter of portraits and landscapes and visited his native Bavaria to improve his skills. He sold one of his paintings for £500 and, from that moment, never looked back. He was 29 when 'The Last Muster' was hung at the Royal Academy. Established, and with an assured income, he purchased two cottages by the forge in Bushey and converted them into one residence. Then he brought his parents to Bushey and gave them a new home in surroundings that would remind them of Bavaria. He called the house Dyrham. In the same year, he married Anne Weise. Two children were born, Siegfried and Elsa, before she contracted tuberculosis. He arranged for the services of a full-time nurse to attend to his ailing wife. Hubert inevitably fell in love with the nurse, Lulu Griffiths. His parents disapproved of his conduct and left for Landsberg-am-Lech near Waal.

Herkomer in his garden near the end of his life, photo courtesy of Bushey Museum.

During an extended tour of America in 1881, his wife Anne died and in 1884 he married Lulu. The future promised happiness and stability. He could now concentrate on his paintings and give his new wife the love and attention she deserved. But fate took a hand and, when in York the following year, Lulu saved a boy from the wheels of a passing carriage. She was pregnant and the shock of the incident induced a premature birth. The baby was stillborn and, although very ill, Lulu was brought back to Bushey where she died.

Herkomer's domestic life was wrecked, but his reputation as a portrait painter was now firmly established. His growing international reputation prompted a return visit to America and he left the two children with Lulu's sister, Margaret, in Wales. On tour he met an eminent American architect, H H Richardson, which encounter was to indirectly change the very heart of Bushey. One day a near neighbour, T E Gibb MP, asked Herkomer to give his daughter tuition in painting. Herkomer agreed, but the outcome was the building of a new art school and Mr Gibb met the cost. To reciprocate such generosity, Herkomer became its unpaid principal. The new school was built on the site of the present Rose Garden and opened in 1883; the first rural art school in the country. In 1886 he erected a barn as a joinery shop and picture frame establishment to complement his output and that of his students. Overnight, Bushey became an artists' colony.

Then Herkomer converted an old methodist chapel into a theatre, seating an audience of 150 and accommodating a small orchestra, in which to perform his own musical plays[36]. The invited audiences travelled by special trains from Euston to Bushey Station and were brought to the theatre by carriage. Lulu's sister Margaret Griffiths, who often took the leading roles, married Hubert in 1888. Two children were born – Lorenz and Gwendydd.

As the number of commissions increased it was necessary to build new studios, so Herkomer embarked on designing a Bavarian-inspired structure accommodating a printing workshop in which he had found a new interest, a studio for extra-large canvasses and a residence for a newly-engaged assistant/printer, Mr H T Cox. Houses were erected in Melbourne Road for Herkomer's other employees mainly engaged in the printing shop. With the assistance of H H Richardson, Herkomer designed his "most beautiful house in England". Stone was imported, uncles were induced to design and make the interior décor, tapestries, forgings, furnishings, panelling... almost everything was made by hand. He called the house Lululaund after Lulu Griffiths. The house was completed in 1894 and illuminated by electricity; the bedrooms were supplied with hot water and the kitchen was on the first floor. The appearance of Lululaund belied the detailed and advanced innovations which Herkomer introduced into its design.

Herkomer's fame as a painter was recognised in 1899 when Kaiser Wilhelm II decorated him with the Order of Maximillian. In 1907, Edward VII conferred a knighthood upon him.

Herkomer's Bavarian-style building on Melbourne Road corner, partly occupied by his assistant/printer, Mr H T Cox, 1914.

In 1904 the then famous art school closed because of financial difficulties and Miss Lucy Kemp-Welch, a pupil, acquired the premises for her Bushey School of Painting. Herkomer repossessed the building in 1912, demolished it and converted the area into a rose garden. In 1913 the prospect of making his own films attracted his interest, so he converted the old theatre into a glasshouse film studio. He died at Budleigh Salterton in 1914 and was buried in the shadow of the elm tree featured in his painting of Bushey called 'Our Village'.

The 'castle' was requisitioned by the Crown during the First World War and demolished in 1939 when Bushey Urban District Council declined the deteriorating structure as a free gift. Only a small section of the front elevation remains, behind which the Bushey branch of the Royal British Legion established its headquarters. Semi-detached houses are now built on the old estate. Herkomer's original house, Dyrham, like the art school, was demolished, but paradoxically some of his other buildings remain: the film studios, the barn workshop (part of the original film studio complex), the printing shop and workers' residences. Sir Hubert von Herkomer's presence in Bushey is still very much apparent. He and his family now rest in peace at Bushey.

29   The Mill Stone Grinds to a Halt

Not so long ago I was absent-mindedly thumbing through 'Watford's Official Guide', a veritable mine of information. It was written by Mr George R Bolton, Borough Librarian, and published by Watford Town Council. The booklet is pocket-sized, with at least two maps. It made nostalgic reading, for it was dated 1931. In the reference library it is referred to simply as 'Boltons'. Perhaps you remember the well-illustrated guide. If not, let me remind you of the contents. There was a potted history of Watford, too brief to be anything but a reminder of a past era, but what I found equally interesting were the advertisements which must have helped with the cost of the production. I realised how names with which we were so familiar have vanished. It is not so much that we have forgotten such famous names, for example Rogers & Gowlett, but rather there is no cause to remember them. Rogers & Gowlett were ironmongers extraordinary, as well as heating and electrical engineers of fine reputation. For those who could afford the cost, central heating installations were available. I am sure you will remember their shop in the old Market Place.

The flagpole marks Rogers & Gowlett's shop, Market Place, 1930.

The memory may falter when I mention Timpson's AEC coaches which provided a "service to anywhere" and evening trips to London's theatreland. Their office was to be found at the 'Recreation Stores', 4 St Albans Road. Then there was Trewins of Queens Road. On 1 February 1927 a "no deposit system of home furnishing" had been introduced. The terms were quite simple: 36 equal instalments and "the first monthly payment secures". The new plan was a success. "These very words" decreed Trewins "will conjure up in the imagination a picture of absolute shopping freedom under conditions that inspire a confidence as unshakable as the very foundations of the great pyramids of Egypt (whatever happened to the Rock of Gibraltar?). So far-reaching has been this great new system since it was launched as to become comparable to one of the great social reforms of our land…"

You will surely remember Lea Wiggs and Clarke, whose dairies covered almost the whole of Watford, with branch shops in Queens Road, Whippendell Road, St Albans Road, Leavesden Road, Watford High Street and Oxhey. They were the days when we took our own jugs to be filled with milk, ladled from a spotless churn. Many local farms supplied dairy products to the company: Church Farm, Aldenham; Oxhey Place Farm; Lea Farm; Bushey Hall Farm; Moor Farm, Rickmansworth; Micklefield Farm, Sarratt; as well as farms at Stanmore and Chipperfield. Milk was really fresh in those days; it had to be. Without domestic refrigeration, one of the first precautions was to ensure that all the milk was safely placed on the marble slab in the pantry and covered with a muslin square weighted with beads at each corner.

The average family always endeavoured to keep a little money in a Post Office savings account in case of a 'rainy day'. Very few people maintained bank accounts. Invariably, wages and salaries were almost totally committed on the day of receipt. Today, branch banks are more generously scattered; in 1931 they were generally confined to commercial areas. In those days, Barclays had the greatest number of offices: The Parade; 132 High Street; 128 St Albans Road; 'Hollywood', Garston; and 28 Bushey High Street. Lloyds of 63-65 High Street had just one other branch at 141 St Albans Road, although Midland at 73 High Street boasted two branches: one in St Albans Road and the other at Ye Corner, Oxhey.

Gartlet School, 30 Clarendon Road, 1920.

There was the council school, the Central in Derby Road, and the grammar schools. Many of us were probably educated at one or more of these seats of learning. Some of you, especially the ladies, may have received their education at a private school, of which there were many in Watford. Corran, established in 1892, was perhaps the largest and most sophisticated boarding and day school in the town with its own science laboratory, gymnasium, studio, reference library and playing fields. A more modest school, although not in an academic sense, was Northfield, offering almost the same facilities but, without doubt, the most popular girls' school was surely Gartlet in Clarendon Road[37]. Like Corran and Northfield, it was a boarding and day school with kindergarten facilities. There was a secluded garden rather than playing fields and a single tennis court. Miss M Bellman was principal. Perhaps the most exclusive establishment was The Grove School for Girls at The Grove, the ancient and historic seat of the Heydon family.

Many well-known local names subsequently became residents: the Bucks, Grevilles and Villiers. The Hon Thomas Villiers was later created Earl of Clarendon. As Mr Villiers, he was appointed Envoy Extraordinary to the Court of Madrid and distinguished himself by being instrumental in negotiating a treaty with Spain to abolish the slave trade in their colonies. He died on 27 June 1878. Queen Victoria paid "a visit of condolence" to the Countess. It was on this historic estate of some 200 acres, where its herd of red deer was once famous, that the school aimed to "send out healthy and happy girls capable of taking a useful place in social and professional spheres". Young ladies were accepted until the age of 18.

Like Cassiobury House, The Grove had its own mill. In the late 1870s, the mill and machinery were totally destroyed by fire and later rebuilt. The mill was not used to serve the house and in the 1880s it was let to Mr Weston, miller of Camden Town. I do not know when the mill changed hands, but until the mid-'60s it was operated by a name you will well remember: Arthur East, corn, seed and coal merchants of 34 High Street and 170 Whippendell Road. Their High Street premises, recalled if only for the smell of the animal foodstuffs prepared there, was

The Grove, 1910.

the first to disappear sometime in the late '50s or early '60s as part of a subsequently aborted road widening scheme. Then the familiar shop and yard on the corner of Harwoods Road and Whippendell Road closed, severing yet another connection with Watford's agrarian past.

The passing of a local industry is always to be regretted; the passing of an order is inevitable and irreversible. Grove Mill has changed little externally, but the mill stone turns no more. Now it is a residential complex. The Grove, requisitioned by the Crown during the last war, is now an integral part of British Railways' executive training programme[38] To end on a happy note, the old red brick house has changed little over the years. The ornate stone bridge spanning the Grand Junction Canal, over which the driveway passes to the house from Hempstead Road, may still be admired for its timeless beauty.

30   When the PM Came to Watford

It was cold and the drizzle was fine and penetrating; typical weather for the time of year. The date was 31 January 1931. Small crowds gathered outside the municipal offices at The Elms. Coat collars were turned up and trilby brims pulled down. The overcast sky gave no promise of even a single ray of sunshine, but there was an air of excitement. The local police looked on with patience in the knowledge that their presence was mandatory rather than necessary. The day of the militants had not yet arrived.

The cars arrived from the south and stopped outside the municipal offices. With practised protocol, the accompanying detectives receded into the background as the Prime Minister, the Rt Hon J Ramsay MacDonald was assisted out of the car, followed by his Private Secretary, Mr K Usher. The welcome visitors were met by Alderman H J Bridges, Chairman of the local Labour party. The party entered the building and in the Mayor's Parlour Alderman Bridger introduced Watford's Mayor, Alderman F W Jeffs who then presented the Deputy Mayor, Alderman F J B Hemming; and the Town Clerk, Mr W Hudson. The formalities over, they proceeded to the council chamber where 150 aldermen, councillors and representatives of the courts, public bodies and voluntary organisations waited to greet the PM.

The town clerk first read a letter apologising for the absence of Sir Dennis Herbert MP and then an address of welcome. The address was recorded on vellum, illuminated with the borough's armorial bearings and bore the common seal of the corporation. It was then handed to the Prime Minister. In his reply, Ramsay MacDonald said: "It is a very kind thought on the part of the borough to present me with the address and I can assure you I will value it highly indeed. You have been good enough to refer in it to arduous work and leisure. A Prime Minister has plenty of the former and very little of the latter, especially in these days when there are such tremendous changes going on all over the world. A Prime Minister who presides over the political fortunes not only of this country, but the whole of the empire of dominions and colonies in all stages of evolution has no easy task".

He referred to his endeavours to "straighten out" the cotton industry, having spent the previous day and part of the night negotiating a settlement. He was convinced that "unless we can devise the means of settling industrial disputes other than by warring conflicts, the outlook for this country is not at all bright. On the other hand, if we could settle down and pull our full weight together, doing fair play to each other, being reasonable in relations to each other, looking at the facts and determined to seize our opportunities with all our skill and ability and push that our people possess, there is no reason why anyone should be pessimistic regarding the future of the country". They were prophetic political platitudes of the best tradition.

To many, his next words came as something of a surprise. "Mr Mayor, Watford is not a new place for me. I knew you in your old days; I knew you before your streets were so brilliantly lighted as they are now. I knew you before those magnificent new shops of yours were built, which are so great an attraction to anyone who has a penny in his pocket – so that I am an old friend of Watford or, rather, putting it more accurately, Watford is an old friend of mine".

In due course, the PM was taken to the Sun Engraving Works in Whippendell Road[39] where he was greeted by Mr Edward Hunter, Chairman and Managing Director, and other directors of the company including Messrs Guy Simmonds, David Greenhill, J Hughes, H N Hunter and G M Hunter. The PM was shown the all-British photogravure machines which were capable of simultaneously producing eight colours; a unique feature in the '30s. His visit lasted an hour, during which time he took the opportunity of speaking to the operators.

The highlight of the visit and, indeed its specific purpose, was yet to happen. By nightfall the Trade Union Hall was packed to capacity. The chairs were quickly occupied and members were obliged to stand at the back and round the sides. Although the meeting would foreseeably revert into a good old-fashioned political rally, it was not the prime reason for Ramsay MacDonald's visit to Watford. The hall had been built by voluntary labour between 1921 and 1923 and had become an essential feature in Labour's political activities, including local and parliamentary elections, meetings and demonstrations[40] To aid party funds there were dances, bazaars and other entertainment. Inevitably, a platform and odd dressing rooms no longer proved adequate. Volunteers extended the hall and built a proper stage with acceptable accommodation. The building was completed; a building fit for a Prime Minister.

Watford Trade Union Hall, 1931.

He received a rousing reception. Mr E G Yates chaired the meeting with the support of Mr Frank Summerfield, President of the Trade Unionist and Labour Club; Mr F M Jacques, prospective Labour candidate for Watford; Alderman Bridger; and Mr Usher. Mr Yates said how proud they were that their leader had been given a civic reception by the Town Council. Mr Summerfield spoke of the 13 men who had given their services and who were to be honoured that night. He thanked Messrs Andrews, Wells, Webb, Creed, Cartwright, Barter, Knight, Miles, Hart, Hill, Archie, Hall and Yates, to whom the PM presented specially bound souvenir programmes printed by Sun Engraving in connection with his visit. They contained a full programme of events with illustrations of the Premier, the Mayor, the Town Clerk and the Borough Librarian, who had written a number of paragraphs about Watford, the Sun Engraving Works and Watford Co-operative Movement.

After the presentations, Ramsay MacDonald congratulated everyone on the completion of the building. "You should be proud", he said, "that it was built sometimes in the moods of despair and had taken time, not as a jerry builder did by mere waving of a sort of magic wand, making the walls rise in a night – and fall the next morning!" His speech then assumed a more serious note. The political content of his address may be easily imagined.

The 13 voluntary workers proudly clutched their souvenirs. In their pockets were testimonials to their loyalty and devotion, as well as life membership cards to the Trade Unionist Club. They had been instrumental in creating the necessary pretext to invite a Prime Minister to Watford. Thirteen was a very lucky number for some.

31   Buried Treasure in the High Street

In 1921 the population of Watford was approximately 46,000, but 10 years later the number had increased by 20,000. The town, within the borough limits, has been virtually fully developed in recent years so it is difficult to imagine the ramifications of a population explosion. I have already made reference to the transfer of the street market in Market Place to the Red Lion Yard area because of the ever-increasing volume of traffic and the very real danger to shoppers of passing vehicles. The cost of moving the market was in the region of £25,000.

In recent years we wondered whether the alterations to the High Street would ever be completed. In 1931 shoppers were presented with the same traumatic experience of change. Having cleared Market Place, the next task was to use the area vacated by the market and which served as a car park on non-market days as a road and so create two traffic lanes for the short distance between Cawdells and the Green Man.

The Post Office took the opportunity to lay new telephone cables from Market Street in the direction of Loates Lane. Their first task was to remove the old cobble stones to make way for a 4-foot trench and no particular problems or hazards were anticipated. Indeed, there was no impediment until a workman made a significant discovery. Without warning, his pick revealed brickwork just 12 inches below the cobbles at the southern end of Market Place. There was naturally a good deal of speculation as to the nature of his find and digging proceeded with some caution. As the hole widened, a brick dome was revealed. The dome was removed and, to everyone's surprise, beneath it was a well. It was a find no one had anticipated and the marvel of it was that the fragile dome had supported the weight of cattle, stalls and, in later years, cars and heavy lorries.

The well was found to be brick-lined and in an excellent state of preservation. Just 75 feet below the surface water was found. The water was 10 feet deep and, allowing for the silt which must have accumulated over the centuries, its total depth could quite well have been 90 feet! I can find no record that local archaeologists ever investigated the well or its contents. The depth no doubt made investigation difficult, if not impossible, although today sub-aqua clubs would have volunteered to go down just as they did when a well was found a few years ago at Chenies. Unfortunately the first thought was how to deal with the problem because the well was between 4-5 feet wide. Fears were expressed at the time that just covering the well head with concrete could represent a danger to the public, so it was decided to fill the well. Horses and carts were used to bring in rubble, which was tipped into the cavernous interior. Their modest loads made little impression and eventually lorries were brought in to hasten the process. At last the well was filled and the Post Office went on with the long trench stretching down the High Street. We will never know what treasures were buried in the silt.

The well has, to my knowledge, never been dated although it was then acknowledged to be centuries-old. It was a well of some importance and featured in Watford's historical past. Perhaps it had once been an open well in the tradition of Jack and Jill, but in later years it had been capped with a "large iron box". How the primitive mechanism worked, I have no idea; but to draw water it was necessary to turn a handle on a large wheel. Local residents were dependent on its supply and, because of the quantity needed, at least in the 17th and 18th centuries, the carriers used a wooden yoke across their shoulders with a bucket suspended at each end. Shades of the proverbial milkmaid!

No doubt for very good reasons the town pump, the stocks and the old Market House were grouped together in current terms. The building has been described as 100 feet long and 24 feet wide, built primarily of wood. It had "lofts and corn stores standing on numerous strong wooden columns; it was open at the bottom and round the columns were shambles and stones on which goods were exposed for sale at the annual fairs and on market days".

High St Watford, 1853

Watford Market House, 1830.

The story is told that two or three days after one of the fairs, a spark from a flare "settled in some crevice" and, fanned by the wind, eventually set fire to the building. The year was 1853. Grain which had not been sold at the last market was stored in the loft and, once it had caught alight, all attempts to put out the fire were in vain. The old pump was cranked by many willing hands until it ran dry. Then they resorted to the nearest pond, which would have been in the vicinity of Dudley's Corner, as well as the pump at the Essex Arms. All hope of saving it was abandoned. "The Market House, left a prey to the fire, soon became a vast body of flame and great was the excitement of the thousands of persons present when the bell turret, with its tinkling bell that had been rung at the opening of the corn market each week for years previously, fell with a loud crash onto the road together with the machinery that had denoted the changes of the wind. Shortly after the roof fell in and forced out one of the ends of the building which, burning fiercely, fell in a piece against the house then occupied by Mr Taylor, a boot maker". That is how Henry Williams in his 'History of Watford' described the end of the Market House.

I mentioned earlier Watford's population explosion. Another consequence of the town's expansion proved to be an inadequate sewerage system and, as a result, new sewers of greater capacity were required to direct effluent to the farm beyond West Watford. Among the many roads affected was Market Street. In the same year, 1931, the road was closed to all traffic and new pipes laid to take advantage of the Market Place reconstruction scheme. It was chaos for the shoppers and traffic in the High Street.

The ever-vigilant management of the Plaza cinema, realising the growing problem of parking a car in or near the High Street, responded by opening their car park between 9am and 5pm for a nominal charge of 6d. If you had time to spare, they also opened a very attractive miniature 18-hole golf course at the rear of the premises. Perhaps you had a go putting the golf ball round and over all sorts of obstacles for 6d a time. I wonder how such leisure activities would go down with shoppers today. Shades of the future: it was open from 10.30am on Sundays!

32   Watford's Oldest Inhabited Building

We now call them the Bedford Almshouses, that little row of quaint antique cottages that border George Street and face the churchyard of St Mary's. In the '30s they were known as the Essex Almshouses. Traditionally, they have always been regarded as the oldest inhabited buildings in the town. For many years no one doubted or disputed the claim. Watford historian W R Saunders in his 'History of Watford' published in 1931 perpetuated that belief. Perhaps one of the reasons was the fact that their origin and history were so well documented.

To put you in the picture I quote Henry Williams, whose earlier 'History of Watford' was published in 1884. "Francis, second Earl of Bedford and Bridget, Countess of Bedford, his wife, by deed dated 21 of February AD 1580, granted a piece of land containing by estimation three roods and two perches, lying in the town of Watford between the Parsonage Barn Yard and a certain lane called New Street; and also eight tenements with their appurtenances, there lately built

Bedford Almshouses, 1910.

upon a parcel of land with eight crofts thereto adjoining, to hold them the said feoffees, their heirs and assigns forever; to the intent that they and succeeding feoffees should permit from time to time, forever, eight poor women, such as should be appointed by the Earl and Countess aforesaid, to dwell and be maintained therein, during the rest of their lives". Another deed of the same date clarified the above deed by further declaring "that eight poor women who from time to time might inhabit and be maintained in the said eight almshouses should be appointed and chosen by them only". The deed further provided that the women should be the "poorest and most needy who should be found within the parishes of Watford, Kings Langley and Chenies". Due provisions were then made to ensure the wellbeing of tenants for all time.

The almshouses were founded in the days of Queen Elizabeth I. With few exceptions, the construction date of an old building is a matter for the experts. In this instance, there was no doubt and it is easy to imagine the irresistible temptation to credit the almshouses with the distinguished label of being the oldest inhabited building in Watford in the absence of any information to the contrary.

By 1930, due to neglect because no funds were available for repairs, the almshouses looked even older than they really were. The front elevation had deteriorated to the extent that plaster was falling away from the walls and some of the woodwork was rotting. Inside conditions were little better. The Charity Commissioners indicated that the income provided by the endowments could not be expended on repairs and the suggestion was made that the building could be sold.

The Highways Committee immediately jumped on the bandwagon and recommended the purchase of the almshouses, not for philanthropic reasons but something much more down to earth. They proposed to pull them down and convert the site into a car park! As soon as their recommendation became known, even HM Office of Works became involved. While the row was still simmering, our usually reticent citizens made their feelings known. In such circumstances, the council declined to take any action, no doubt for the reasons that if they made the purchase they would, under public pressure, be forced to renovate the ancient building. In other words, they washed their hands of the whole affair and the position was back to square one. The consensus was that the almshouses should be saved, but by whom? Inevitably the cost of the renovations became a matter of public concern and, in due course, sufficient money was raised by public subscription, primarily through the efforts of Alderman Bickerton.

By 1934 the almshouses had been restored, much to the delight of the elderly lady residents and the citizens at large. The generosity of the townspeople of the early '30s was directly responsible for saving Watford's "oldest inhabited building". Some 40 years later, that claim was invalidated. The Bedford Almshouses were not the oldest, not by any means. The discovery of even older properties may never have happened had it not been for the Phase 5 road scheme in which Exchange Road and Beechen

Rearward wing 177-179 High Street from northeast, 1976.

Grove were to be joined by a new link road crossing Watford High Street just north of Watford High Street station. The enormity of the junction, slip roads and bus lanes demanded the sacrifice of many properties of mature years in one of the oldest parts of Watford.

Stephen Castle (left) and Ian Mackay surveying first floor of 177-179 High Street, 1977.

Of his own volition, Mr Stephen Castle had voluntarily surveyed and recorded those buildings still surviving in the borough between 1970 and 1971. In 1974 he was first granted access by the Town Hall to survey the first floor and roofs of 177-179 High Street; a rambling timber-framed building almost opposite Watford High Street station, the side of which overlooked the deep cutting carrying the railway line below street level[41]. The last tenants of the shops, which faced the White Hart, were DER Television and David Leslie, Estate Agents. After an extensive and detailed examination of the first floor and roof area, Mr Castle ascertained that the rearward wing dated from the 15th century and the frontage and middle range from the 16th century. He had discovered a building that had been occupied until its compulsory purchase and predated the Bedford Almshouses by a century! With the construction of the Watford – Rickmansworth railway in 1862, the cutting is believed to have severed the original building, of which 177-179 was the surviving part.

When Stapleton's (195) was dismantled, it was also found to be of timber-framed construction. It was a town house, with crown post roofs dating from c1500[42]. The building was inhabited until 1977 and, before its removal, was the oldest inhabited house in the town. The front and middle sections of 177-179 were removed to St Albans and reconstructed at considerable expense. The 15th century rearward wing was transferred to the Chiltern Open Air Museum, together with timbers from No 195, where they are stacked under polythene, awaiting the time when sufficient funds are available to restore the buildings as they would have appeared 500 years ago. There was a public outcry to keep the buildings in

195 High Street on left, 1906 (later Stapleton's).

Watford and the 'Evening Post-Echo' published a composite photograph illustrating one of the buildings re-erected near the site of the old Cassiobury Park Gates, but to no avail.

193-195 High Street, Swann's (Watford's first Police Station) and Stapletons, 1977.

With the removal of these ancient buildings, you will be tempted to surmise that the Bedford Almshouses must now surely be Watford's oldest building. On good authority, I am told that The One Crown public house, the earliest parts of which date from c1500, carries that rare distinction[43].

33   The Oldest Film Studios in the World

I have already written at some length about Sir Hubert von Herkomer. Now he crops up again, but for a very different reason. One of his last interests before he died in 1914 was the creation of new film studios at the junction of Melbourne Road and Bushey High Street. In 1913 Herkomer dismantled his neglected theatre and on top of the building he erected a glasshouse. On the intermediate floors he provided a viewing theatre, cutting and dark rooms, as well as dressing rooms. With his son Siegfried, he formed a film company and started a new industry in Bushey. The father wrote shooting scripts and the son, after taking a course with Pathe Frères, became responsible for the technical side of the unit. A generator was installed to provide electricity for arc lamps to supplement natural lighting during inclement weather.

With experience gained during trial short films, they moved on to more ambitious full-length features. For their first film, 'A Highwayman's Honour', Bushey actor A E Matthews was engaged to take the leading role. The story was influenced by the infamous Dick Turpin who, it is said, once operated in the Watford area. The heroine in the spectacular finale was trapped in a burning house. Herkomer didn't bother with film sets; he set fire to a real house! When the film was completed, the structure was restored and renamed Burnt Cottage.

Hubert von Herkomer (seated) in 'A Highwayman's Honour', his last screen appearance, 1914.
Photo courtesy of Bushey Museum.

Among the invited audience at the preview were two Americans who conned him into parting with the negative from which the prints would be made for release in the United States. Without so much as a deposit to regularise the deal, they departed with 'A Highwayman's Honour'. That was the last Herkomer ever saw of the Americans and his beloved film. Undeterred by the loss, production continued until his death in 1914. For many years the search has gone on to locate his old films, but without success. Ironically, some still pictures of Herkomer filming have survived.

Then A E Matthews bought the studios and all the equipment for £3,500 and once more the cameras turned. His first production was a skit on 'Macbeth', which was written and directed by Sir James Barrie. On the strength of its success, Matthews formed the British Actors Film Company. The shareholders were either connected with the industry or stage actors. Siegfried was taken on as a scriptwriter and he gave the company the run of Lululaund and the estate to use as ready-made film sets. There were financial difficulties, but these were overcome by an amalgamation which provided the necessary working capital. Between 1916 and 1921 some 20 films were produced. By this time, Herkomer's old workshop opposite had also been converted into another, larger studio.

At about the time production stopped, Minerva Films rented studio space and made a number of short comedies. The directors of the new company included such well-known names as A A Milne, C Aubrey Smith and Leslie Howard. After little more than a year, Minerva ceased production. Leslie Howard was the first to leave for Hollywood, closely followed by C Aubrey Smith. There they both enjoyed successful careers in the balmy pre-Second World War days.

Adrian Brunel, originally a scriptwriter with the British Actors Film Company, returned from North Africa where he had been making films with another organisation and made a number of humorous shorts between 1923 and 1924. By 1927 the studios, now known as Bushey Film Studios, were purchased by George Humphries and Randall Terraneau, ostensibly for the purpose of renting out studio space. One of the first productions to emerge in 1928 was the 'Dr Sin Fang' series produced by Fred Paul. The first film, 'Living Death', was shown at the Empire almost exactly one year later.

Since the '30s the studios have operated on a rental basis, which arrangement has always attracted the small producer, although ownership has changed hands many times over the years. As late as 1932 the viewing theatre was still embellished with Herkomer's wood carvings, but they have since disappeared as a result of the many interior changes during the last half-century. In that year, Delta Pictures leased the studios and the company was busily engaged making a series of shorts called 'Pets', directed by Widgley Newman. For the series, almost every pet imaginable was gathered at Bushey. The collection included flying foxes, snakes and lizards. Everything went well until a kangaroo, frightened by the lights, decided to escape by bounding up Clay Hill. It was later captured where Elstree Road crosses the A41.

Delta's success prompted another series called 'Tailwaggers', followed by 'Derby Secrets' and the sports series 'According to Widgley'. In 1935 Milheath produced 'Our Royal Heritage' with Widgley Newman, and 'Faust' in 1936 with Anne Ziegler and Webster Booth. By 1937 the Bushey Film Corporation had taken over the studios and produced films until 1940. In 1948 Gilbert Church acquired the property in the name of Bushey Film Studios Ltd, producing 'The Mysterious Mr Nicholson' with Anthony Hulme and Lesley Osmond and, in the same year, 'Black Memory' with Michael Medwin, Winifred Melville and Sid James. Films continued to be produced by the company until Mr Church decided to adopt the concept of renting or leasing. In later years, a number of television commercials were made there with jingles played in some cases by a local band. Then Cygnet took over the studios and soon made a name for themselves in educational, medical, scientific and commercial documentaries. As Cygnet Ltd, a new title acquired in the last few months, production still continues (1982)[44].

Although Borehamwood and Elstree jointly represented the very heart of the British film industry, there was a time when Watford could well have eclipsed Denham and Pinewood. In March 1932, plans for studios on the Russell Estate, Hempstead Road, were submitted to Watford Rural District Council, as well as a suggested layout of land at Hunters Lane, Leavesden, for the same purpose. Whether they were separate or alternative proposals, I cannot say. The area in Hempstead Road was close to Russells House, while 50 acres were earmarked at Leavesden where both houses and shops were allocated, as well as stages, workshops and offices.

Imagine how the face and character of Watford would have changed had either or perhaps both projects come to fruition. But it was not to be, and the old studios at Bushey continue to be the only studios in the area. However, that is not their only distinction. They are undoubtedly the oldest film studios in Europe and no one disputes that they could be the oldest studios still in use in the world[45].

In recent weeks (1982) Oxhey Grange and the estate upon which it stands came onto the property market for only the third time in well over a century. To refresh your memory, the Ely family acquired the virgin estate and built a hunting lodge, which they later developed into a home. Mr Ely died in 1881 and a drinking fountain was erected on Watford Heath in his memory by his sisters.

Oxhey Grange, 1977.

The next owner of Oxhey Grange was Mr James Doyle Penrose who moved there in 1908 and commemorated his arrival by setting a stone block near the main entrance in the red brickwork bearing the date and the initials of his wife and himself. Although a contemporary of Sir Hubert von Herkomer, I do not recall that their names have ever been connected either as near neighbours or fellow artists. All the same, I cannot believe that they were unknown to one another. If they were not friends, they were surely acquaintances. Whether they were tolerant of each other is quite another matter, since Mr Doyle was Quaker by religious persuasion. He is unlikely to have approved of Herkomer's domestic entanglements.

Like Herkomer, he painted in both watercolour and oils and received his artistic training at South Kensington, probably around the same time. He also trained at St John's Wood and the Royal Academy Schools. It is practically certain he would have met Herkomer in the early days, if not in later years. Penrose gained his first silver medal and thereafter specialised in landscapes, subject pictures so dear to the hearts of the Victorians, as well as portraits. Here there is a distinct parallel with Herkomer's initial interests. On other levels, the similarity must surely end.

Penrose was born at Mitchelstown, Co Dublin and was educated at the Friends' School at Kendal. As a Quaker, perhaps it is not surprising that his pictures reflected his religious convictions. They were quite numerous, although I cannot believe he was as prolific as Herkomer. To his paintings he gave such titles as 'The Presence in the Midst', depicting the congregation at the Jordan's Meeting House. There were others, for example 'The Last Chapter' depicting the death of the Venerable Bede, 'The First Easter Morning' and 'None Shall Make Them Afraid'. His portraits included those of Lord Russell as Lord Chief Justice of England; Lord Jessell as Mayor of Westminster; and his father-in-law, the well-known Quaker banker, Lord Peckover of Wisbech, of whom he also executed a bust in bronze. I do not think he achieved the popularity, or notoriety for that matter, enjoyed by the self-made Herkomer, perhaps for the reason that he had never known or experienced abject poverty. Certainly his interests were different, unobscured by artisan crafts.

Penrose was a collector with a fascination for antiques, but not in the generally accepted sense of the word. He acquired the wrought iron gates of Drayton Manor when they were being dismantled. They were no ordinary gates; in fact they were very special gates and quite unique, for they had originally been made for and presented to none other than Oliver Cromwell. After restoration work, they were re-erected at the entrance to Oxhey Grange. On another occasion he attended the sale of Cassiobury House in the '20s and successfully bid for the yew hedge and what has been described as a "remarkable" bay tree. These he had transplanted in the estate and no doubt they are still there, although their origin may now have been forgotten. At the same sale he acquired a chiming clock, for which he carved two ivory figures representing war and peace and, presumably with some modification, each figure appeared as the clock chimed hourly. He was also credited with a copy of a 'Breeches' bible, which was said to be one of his most treasured possessions.

What brought James Doyle Penrose to Oxhey we may never know, but we do know what attracted him to Oxhey Grange, quite apart from its other splendours. He loved its mature and beautiful gardens, the beauty of which was further enhanced during his lifetime by his dedicated gardeners. Before coming to Oxhey he was Deputy Lieutenant for Cambridgeshire and Justice of the Peace for Wisbech. Despite bad health in later years, he continued with his public duties in Watford. Mr Penrose joined the Commission of the Peace for Hertfordshire and sat on the Bench. As a keen and active Liberal, he declined a number of invitations to stand for Parliament. In addition, he was Treasurer of the Watford Temperance Council of Christian Churches (Herkomer was a teetotaller), Vice-President of the Watford branch of the League of Nations Union and a hard-working elder of the Watford Quaker Meeting, as well as a keen supporter of the Adult School in Derby Road to which he leased, rent-free, one of his fields for their cricket club.

He was a fervent believer in the League of Nations and practised what he preached. Each year, Oxhey Grange prepared for his International Garden Party. As the title suggests, it was truly international and he made a special point of inviting the Chinese ambassador as well as many Indian friends and visitors.

In 1893 he married the Hon Elizabeth Josephine, daughter of Lord Peckover. They had four sons. She died in 1930 and he died on 2 January 1932 at the age of 68 at Bognor Regis, following a long illness. And so ended the era of the Victorian Irishman who had spent 24 years of his life in Oxhey. He had guided Oxhey Grange and his vast estate from the near-feudal Edwardian era safely into the '30s and was ever-thoughtful of the welfare of those who served him. He improved their housing, which was so primitive in the early years. In fact, he largely created Watford Heath as we know it today. Now it is one of Watford's few residential beauty spots which, in their infinite but doubtful wisdom, the borough refuses to make a conservation area[46].

James Doyle Penrose's death, although anticipated, brought sorrow to the family and his many employees who were accommodated on Watford Heath. His dynamic presence, his love for people, as well as the things he created were an essential feature of life at Oxhey Grange. By 1934 it had changed hands once again and now (1982), it is for sale for the third time. We are at the end of yet another era.

35   Peaceful Arts and Crafts

Today we take time for granted. I do not mean its passing, for surely it passes all too quickly. What I really mean is that we know or have access to the time to the nearest minute, if not second. What with mains electric clocks which are automatically regulated, quartz clocks and watches accurate to a few seconds a month and time checks with the radio and television, we always know the right time.

As children, one of our most treasured possessions was surely the 5s Ingersoll watch, which generally found its way into the top pocket of our flannel jackets when we wore our 'Sunday best'. At other times, especially during the summer holidays, we simply waylaid the first adult and uttered the once very familiar request: "Please, mister, can you tell us the time?" If the response was accurate to the nearest hour, we were quite satisfied.

Queens Road looking to Wesleyan Church, 1917.

So how did we cope before mains and battery clocks? All families had at least one good and solid clock, usually ticking away on the mantelpiece, upon which everyone was dependent. From the mid-'20s it was possible to take time checks from the wireless, but what happened before radio, or telegraph for that matter? There is a simple answer. We were largely dependent on our local clockmakers and none was more famous in Watford than Mr B S Morse who originally set up business in Queens Road and later moved to the High Street. In those early days, Mr Morse was the only local clockmaker to have his own observatory, from which he took the time from the sun! His services to the local Post Office became indispensable. For many years he regulated all their clocks. I am in little doubt they were the most accurate in the town.

He made many clocks, but the last public clock made at his premises was in 1924 and, believe it or not, that clock is well-known to most citizens. It is the clock gracing the Peace Memorial Hospital, which may be seen from Rickmansworth Road. I do not know whether the original mechanism is still in place or even working, but if the day ever comes that the hospital is demolished, I sincerely hope that this historic Watford-made clock will be saved[47].

In March 1932 Mr H J Sturman of Chalk Hill, Oxhey, died. His name is more likely to be remembered as an organist who for many years, until about 1924, was associated with the Bushey Baptist Church. He later served as organist at St James' and St Matthew's Churches. Now you may well wonder what connection Mr Sturman had with the Peace Memorial Hospital. Let me explain. When Mary Bromet of Heath Road, Oxhey, created her 'Peace Memorial' statuary, Mr Sturman was the model for the figure depicting 'grief'; the figure on the left

Mary Bromet's Peace Memorial statuary in its original location, 1930.

of the group. The Earl of Clarendon unveiled the memorial.

I have had occasion to refer to Mrs Bromet in the past always, it seems, in the context of her famous 'Peace Memorial'. I now realise that such parochial references may imply this gifted lady was a local, rather than an international celebrity. To put the record straight, let me tell you something about her. Ironically, in the same year that Mr Sturman died, Mary Bromet was elected an Associate of the Royal Society of Sculptors. Her election has been attributed to the tremendous success of the 'Peace Memorial' statuary, but such a claim would ignore the reputation she had carved herself since the end of the 19th century. She received an 'honourable mention' at the Paris Salon as early as 1899. With the deserving recognition for her work, Mary Bromet began a distinguished career as an exhibitor and such was the respect shown for her that she was invited to participate in almost all the colonial and international exhibitions that were such a popular feature between the reigns of Queen Victoria and George V. She exhibited at the Franco-British Exhibition at White City in 1908, of which only the stadium is left as evidence of one of the biggest exhibitions since the Great Exhibition of 1851.

In 1911 Mary Bromet was selected to represent British sculpture at the International Exhibition in Rome. One of her last exhibitions of that particular era was at Wembley in 1924 where examples of her work were displayed at the Palace of Arts. Other examples of her work were frequently exhibited at the Royal Academy and Salon.

She was, as I have tried to illustrate, far more than a local celebrity and we are privileged to have an example of her skill on permanent display in Watford, although the group has lost much of its impact following its relegation to the backwater of the Town Hall on a site for which it was never designed or intended. Despite its ill-chosen location, I do recommend that you take another look at the 'Peace Memorial' by a Watford resident who deservedly achieved international fame and whose major work is available to us all. Her name is perpetuated in Oxhey Road, where Bromet School has been named after her. I hope the pupils are told something of her background, her genius and about the 'Peace Memorial', and why the school bears her name.

The house in which she lived has long since disappeared; a large symmetrical house of uninspired design with sash windows and a slate roof that some would claim as being a typical 19th century residence. Its rather quaint exterior was compensated by the beauty of the garden in which it stood; a large garden extending almost from Pinner Road to Oxhey Avenue containing her glasshouse studio.

I remember a garden of numerous winding paths, isolated lawns and rose arches; a garden full of colour and surprises. In retrospect, I suppose it could be described as an Italian garden full of marble columns, on top of which were busts of unnamed people.Perhaps they were examples of her earlier works, or they could have been specially sculpted for display in a garden setting. The static marble heads in an ever-moving floral setting left a lasting impression on the eyes of a child unfamiliar with cold eyeless heads with features unimpaired by scars and skin blemishes; unseeing heads and yet seeing all. These are my memories of Mrs Bromet's garden. I have even fewer recollections of the garden party on that Saturday afternoon. There were happy sounds of parents' voices, forgetting for a few minutes the activities of their off-spring who, as likely as not, were munching sandwiches, helped down by glasses of real lemonade served from large glass jugs and ice cream that, in all probability, was home-made. They were carefree days for children; precious days which one now wishes could be recalled in absolute detail. That, I suppose, is what nostalgia is all about.

Council houses and privately-owned dwellings now occupy the site of Lime Lodge, Mary Bromet's house. The road is still unadopted and the same wooden barrier separates one end of the gravel road from the other. The wooden fence surrounding the garden has gone. There is nothing to remind us of her presence; it is as if she never existed.

36   The Mystery of the Fig Tree Tomb

The legend of the fig tree tomb in St Mary's Churchyard was known throughout the country. It brought the curious, if not the pilgrims to Watford to see for themselves the fig tree that had lifted the lid of a tomb and, by so doing, proved the existence of God.

I have often quoted Henry Williams' 'History of Watford', published in 1884. With your indulgence, I will quote him once again. "… I fear I must upset an old legend, the fame of which has pervaded the whole country and brought hundreds of strangers to St Mary's Parish Churchyard. Under the south wall of St Catherine's Chapel stands a tomb through which is growing a fig tree that each year exhibits considerable luxury of growth and sometimes produces figs. This fig tree has probably grown there for close on a hundred years, as some fifteen or sixteen years ago I inquired of one of the oldest inhabitants what knowledge he had of its age and he told me he remembered that when he was quite a child it was growing there and apparently as large as now. The little legend alluded to above is that the lady buried in the vault from which the tree is growing was an atheist and that on her death she adhered to that tenet and expressed a wish that a fig tree might grow out of her heart if there was a God. Of course the thing is absurd, but it was not thought so by the credulous of the 18th century who handed the tale down from one to the other, giving it such an air of truth that it came to be looked upon as a fact by a great number of persons, not only at Watford but throughout the country and hundreds visited the churchyard, many making long excursions for the purpose of seeing the notorious tree".

Fig tree tomb, 1910.

In 1871 St Mary's was restored at a cost of nearly £7,000. The work, which included the facing of its crumbling walls with flint, also necessitated lowering the level of the churchyard which had become so high as to require three or four steps down to enter the church. Mr Williams no doubt seized the opportunity to examine the tomb and his impressions were recorded in the following words: "The root of the tree was not in the vault but in the crown of the arch, 4-5 feet above where the lady's heart must have been". Notwithstanding Williams' revelation, the legend persisted. He then described the coffin which he could now see. "The peculiar shape of the coffin in which the lady was buried attracted attention also; it had a projection at the top which led to the conclusion that the person must have died with her knees up and that after death her legs could not be straightened".

Williams tells us he had spoken to the "oldest inhabitant" 15 or 16 years before writing his book, so it would have been in about 1868. Let us suppose the "oldest inhabitant" was about 80-years-old. As a child of five, that person would have remembered the fig tree around the year 1793 as being "as large as now". It would not be unreasonable to suppose the interment occurred earlier that same century. Since the name of the person buried there was never disclosed, we must also conclude the stonemason's inscriptions had weathered away by 1884.

Williams' disclosures did not go unchallenged and in September 1898 the parish magazine offered an entirely different version. The author of the article appeared to give a definitive account which, as far as I am aware, has never been questioned. "Ben Wangford, as he was generally called, lived about the middle of the last century (c1750). I can't say if he was a native of Watford or if married. But he was buried in St Mary's Churchyard and had a handsome tomb for that period. He was a man of enormous size; it is said that his boots could contain a bushel of corn. He did not believe in a hereafter state and wished, when buried, to have something placed with his remains that would germinate and then his relations would know that his soul was alive. If nothing appeared they might know his opinion was correct. I have not heard what was placed in the coffin, but a fig tree appeared and for years passed unnoticed by strangers. Now it is very much talked of and people travel for miles to see the tomb".

It seems that Williams got his dates right, but the gender of the occupant of the tomb wrong and, in consequence, has caused confusion over the years. On the other hand, the parish magazine account leaves a lot to be desired. There is even doubt about his name. If he was "generally called" Ben Wangford, by what other names was he known? The writer did not disclose the date of his death or appear to know whether he was married or single, or even if he was a native of Watford. What we can conclude is that he was a man of means to be able to afford an elaborate tomb and, by all accounts, a man of remarkable proportion. To give you some idea of his size we can draw a parallel with the landlord of the Rose & Crown, James Rogers, who died in 1829. One of his boots, we are told, could hold a bushel of corn, so he was presumably of greater girth than Ben Wangford. James Rogers was "a great eater" writes Williams "and when invited out to dine he would eat the greater part of a shoulder of mutton with a corresponding quantity of vegetables and bread before he left home, so that a moderate meal might suffice and prevent his host looking upon him as a gourmand".

When James Rogers died he was placed in a specially-built coffin and the weight was so great "that it required a larger number of men to carry the coffin than could get under it". As a last resort, it seems, a window of the Rose & Crown was removed together with some of the brickwork! I mention this incident by way of verifying Williams' comment about the coffin having "a projection at the top". Not for the reason he stated, but in all probability to accommodate the rotund Mr Rogers whose stomach, it was said, was so large that to enable him to take food at the table with his family "a piece, half-circular in shape, was cut out of the table and then, by placing dishes on either side of him, he was enabled to take his food with tolerable comfort". While we know a lot about James Rogers, we know little or nothing about Ben Wangford. He will remain a mystery, although there seems little doubt that he was the occupant of that once famous tomb.

James Rogers, founder of Rogers & Gowlett.

What of the legend of the fig tree? I remember reading that a rector of the Parish Church of that period was partial to figs and had a habit of spitting out the seeds. On second thoughts, I prefer to think of the legend which we always associated with the tomb as we walked past those tall iron railings which once protected the churchyard and looked at the lid, precariously balanced as the boughs of the fig tree reached for the sky from the depths of the tomb.

37   The Post Office

When we recall the Watford scene 50 years ago, we invariably relate the changes which have taken place and the shops and buildings that have disappeared. The irresistible temptation is to forget, if not ignore, the service industries we have enjoyed over the years. The reason is simple; we have taken them for granted. The Post Office is, perhaps, the best example.

We are told that in the early 19th century our local Post Office was to be found at a house opposite the Green Man; "the second door above Butcher's Yard". In those far-off days the cost of sending a letter to London was 11d, a small fortune by any standard. With the tremendous growth of the town, attributed by all local historians to the arrival of the railway in 1837, the Post Office was transferred to a house in the High Street, almost opposite Water Lane. Here an old but agile lady used to wait for the London-bound coach which stopped outside her house each weekday morning at five o'clock. A series of thumps on the front door roused her from her sleep and she lowered the mail bag on a piece of string from the bedroom window. The driver untied the string which the old lady hauled back; she then closed the window and went back to sleep as the whip and shouting of the driver encouraged the horses into a gallop. The first delivery of letters did not arrive until 10 o'clock.

During the next few years the Post Office moved to 87 High Street and then to the bottom of Carey Place. At that time there was just one delivery a day by one postman who handled some 30 or 40 letters. For this task he received 7s a week. The Post Office moved yet again, this time into the High Street opposite Carey Place. From there it passed to a stationer's shop opposite King Street, where Mr Graves became the first Post Master. He was succeeded by Mr Morley and, under his guidance, the business was transferred to a house in Queens Road dealing solely with postal matters. This was thought by many to be permanent premises, but the continued growth of Watford forced the authorities to look for an alternative property. Mr Humbert was given the task of finding suitable accommodation.

Watford's less than philanthropic property owners offered their premises at inflated prices; they had no qualms about overcharging the government! But Mr Humbert finally solved the problem by purchasing a site from Waterman Brothers at the junction of Queens Road and Derby Road where "a very unsightly office" was erected around 1880 as a temporary measure. The story is told that the postal authorities wished to ascertain "before commencing a permanent building" the amount of space required for the parcel post side of the business. Some statistics are available from that period which may come as something of a surprise. In one week 30,000 letters were posted in Watford and, for the corresponding period, 47,000 were received for delivery. Our residents were thoroughly spoilt. There were four letter deliveries a day, except Sundays and Bank Holidays when there was just one delivery. There were three 'receiving houses' and nine pillar or wall boxes, one of which was on No 1 platform at Watford Junction Station. In those days Mr Morley had 10 employees at Queens Road. There were, of course, other employees engaged in the sorting and delivery of letters and parcels, as well as maintaining the telegraph system.

Watford Post Office sorting room at 6am, 1907.

Queens Road. Large three-chimneyed building was Watford's Post Office for 50 years, later Theodore Greville's Studios, 1910.

The old Victorian building in Queens Road was cold, uninviting and dreary on the inside and very ornate on the outside. It was constructed of red brick and trimmed with Portland stone. The design was fussy rather than functional. The counter accommodation may have been adequate in 1880, but the 'temporary' building continued to serve an increasingly irate public until the '30s. Watford's population had increased fivefold and so had the tempers of people queuing, especially on Saturdays when everyone worked – if only in the morning.

Considerable pressure was applied by the council on the Post Office through Sir Dennis Herbert to provide a building worthy of Watford, then a mature town, reflecting our architectural past from medieval times through the centuries to the latest the '30s had to offer. After 20 or more years of protests, the Post Office finally demurred and acquired a site in Market Street backing onto the old cattle market. There, another red brick building was erected in what has been called a "traditional Hertfordshire style". The handsome front elevation was graced with an imposing portico in stone, from the top of which Mercury looked down on the shoppers in Market Street[48].

On Monday 28 November 1932 the new Post Office was completed. Present at the opening were the Postmaster General, Sir Kingsley Wood; Sir Dennis Herbert MP; and the Mayor, Councillor J Evans. In his opening speech the Mayor, who had a reputation for saying what he thought, took the opportunity of reminding Sir Kingsley Wood of the strong representation made by local telephone subscribers against the proposed merger of Watford's directory with London's telephone directory. He voiced good reasons for Watford retaining its own identity, at least in the context of telephone subscribers who, he added "should be given a rebate for every three minutes they lost searching for numbers in the two large directories which were like family bibles". The Mayor was adamant that we should retain the facility of a local directory and made his point in no uncertain manner.

The occasion was treated light-heartedly and Sir Dennis Herbert spoke of "the flattery and cajolery and even threats" with which he had pressed the Postmaster General to acquaint him with the existence of Watford. Responding in a similar vein, Sir Kingsley Wood complimented the two speakers for not "badgering" him to restore the penny post. He referred to the new building and stressed that provision had been made in its design to accommodate Watford's expansion and growth over the next 25 years – and that was 50 years ago!

After the opening ceremony, Sir Kingsley Wood purchased the first stamp to be sold over the counter. The interior was bright, spacious and unencumbered. There was a long mahogany counter surrounded by head-height bronze grilles with ornate serving hatches. The area was warm and inviting; in complete contrast to Queens Road. Alas, in more recent years the old grilles have been removed and in their place security screens in glass and wire mesh rise to almost ceiling height, while illuminated signs indicate the hatches giving service. Now we have the choice of entering the Post Office by one of two insignificant doors. The massive portico has disappeared, although its outline may still be seen where new bricks have been used to seal the original entrance. To all intents and purposes, its removal has neutered a once attractive building.

The old Queens Road premises survived until the late '70s and you may remember that Greville Studios, one of Watford's oldest photographers, were established there for many years; in fact, until the time of its demolition when they acquired alternative accommodation a few doors away. The old Post Office became one of the best examples of Victorian architecture, notwithstanding the criticism voiced at the time. It was sad to see it go the way of so many of our buildings worthy of retaining – for the sake of a new road system.

Theodore Greville's sons, Richard (left) & Ivor, at Greville's Studios, 64 Queens Road, 1980.

38   Watford's Grammar Schools

The prime seat of learning in the Middle Ages was St Alban's Abbey and if there is a person to be named as being responsible, the honour must surely go to a monastic chronicler named Matthew Paris. In Watford, those seeking tuition were dependent upon the priests of the Parish Church. We do not know when the first school was established here, but records indicate that George Redhead was a schoolmaster in 1595. In 1601 there is a reference to one Nicholas Hall who had graduated at university and was licenced to "assist our pastor in the ministry and to keep a grammar school".

In 1640 a name with which you will be familiar, Francis Coombe, donated £10 a year to a free school in the town for teaching poor and underprivileged children to read and write and cast accounts. Their schooling was conducted in a room above two houses, the property of the church near St Mary's Churchyard. It is a matter of conjecture whether the teacher was Nicholas Hall. In 1821 the houses were demolished and the school moved to other premises.

Mrs Elizabeth Fuller lived at Watford Place at the end of the 17th century. Of her own volition she acquired land said to be part of the orchard of the vicarage and in 1704 built at her own expense a new Free School, large enough to accommodate 40 boys and 20 girls. Her generosity knew no bounds. She endowed the school with £52 a year to pay the salaries of the school master and mistress, the fuel and other necessities. All the children were to be taught to read and write, but the boys were also required to cast accounts and the girls such useful domestic duties as sewing and knitting.

They were all required to wear regulation dress: the boys, grey bonnets and cloth coats with brass buttons, and the girls, linsey-woolsey gowns and blue aprons. How proud the poor parents of Watford must have been when they sent their children off to school early in the morning. And it was early. Between Candlemas (2 February) and All Hallows (1 November), school started at 6am and, for the subsequent three months, at 7am. School finished at 4pm, so it was a long day. In fact it was a long week as Saturday was also a school day, with the afternoon devoted to religious instruction.

The Free School was popular with benefactors. Between 1760 and 1768 donations totalled over £4,000 and for many years the school thrived. Dame Elizabeth Fuller died in 1709 at the age of 65, having survived three husbands. She was buried in the graveyard of Bushey Parish Church in the shadow of the tower. The tomb is in surprisingly good order and if you happen to be passing, do take the trouble to find it. The inscription is still legible. But her endowment and the donations were sadly insufficient to maintain the Free School in perpetuity. The story is told that Thomas Deacon, which one I do not know, provided for the school in his will. The problem was that he died in a debtors' prison and was penniless. Impressed with his brother's intended benevolence, Charles Deacon assumed moral responsibility and paid up.

Inevitably, expenses exceeded income; a situation with which we are only too familiar today and the school closed in 1882. One of the trustees, Dr Brett, successfully applied to the Platt's Charity at Aldenham and Consuls to the value of £13,333 were assigned to Watford, conditional that "a scheme for the management of Watford Charities shall be framed". No time was lost in preparing the necessary scheme, which was presented to the Charity Commission in 1881. It was accepted and the funds were made available. A new Board of Governors was appointed and they decided to acquire a site in Derby Road to accommodate boys and girls under one roof, but effectively segregated. A design was submitted by Sedgwick, Son & Weall which was chosen, and a tender by Thomas Turner was accepted. In 1884 the school was completed and on 21 April the Earl of Clarendon duly opened the Watford Endowed School for Boys. On 22 April he opened the girls' section and apologised for not mentioning on the previous day the part played by Dr Brett in making it all possible. In 1903 the schools were renamed the Watford Grammar Schools, thus ending the era of Endowed Schools.

All went well until the Education Act of 1902 which specified that each pupil should enjoy a space of not less than 18 square feet. To meet these mandatory demands, a second storey was proposed and rejected. There was only one solution to the problem; one section should move out, leaving the other with sufficient space to meet the requirements of the Act. The decision was made to rehouse the girls and leave the boys behind. Unfortunately, insufficient funds were available and the county authorities became involved by helping to fund the costs involved. That really put the cat amongst the pigeons. Why, the public asked, were public funds being utilised to uphold the historically sectarian nature of the schools' activities? They were placated by the reconstitution of the Board of Governors with county representation and the introduction of denominational safeguards.

Watford Grammar School for Girls, assembly, 1907.

Watford Grammar School for Girls moved to a new site bounded by Wiggenhall Road in September 1907 without so much as an official ceremony to celebrate the occasion. It really was a hot potato and, for once, our local politicians were forced to play it cool. C Brightman of Watford built the new premises. Miss A Coles, who succeeded Miss Kennaby in 1895, became the school's third headmistress.

Watford Grammar School for Boys, late 1930s.

Within three years, Watford Grammar School for Boys became overcrowded and the Board of Governors searched for a site on which to build a new school. Twelve acres of the diminishing Cassiobury Estate were acquired and the new school was completed in 1912. Lord Clarendon presided at the opening ceremony. Nearly 300 boys had marched from Derby Road to their new school, an event that was to become known as the 'Derby Road Trek'. Each year at the Old Fullerians' annual dinner, held in the school hall for as many years as I can remember, the Chairman has traditionally toasted those present who took part in that trek. The numbers of old boys who responded to the toast and raised their glasses amidst thunderous applause have sadly diminished during that time. In January this year (1982) there was no toast because the weather and the distance proved too much for Gp Capt Leslie Bonnet who left Watford some years ago.

39   Watford Swimming Baths

By 1933 the days of the Five Arches bathing place were numbered. For almost 30 years pressure had been applied by various groups and individuals on the old Rural District Council and, in later years, the Borough Council to provide the town with new swimming baths. For 30 years the councillors had procrastinated. Their first excuse was the advent of the First World War. After the war and until 1931 the scheme was shelved and all further appeals were seemingly ignored. The accusation that the council was adamant was not without foundation. In the meantime, the Five Arches were maintained as the official municipal baths. At least we know that the water of the River Colne was still pure and free from pollution.

Five Arches, 1919.

Five Arches bathing place, 1913.

Then the borough acquired The Elms for the express purpose of building a Town Hall and Municipal Offices. New swimming baths featured in their forward planning and there was adequate space at the rear of the site. At last this much-needed amenity became a reality. Application was made to the old Ministry of Health and sanction was given for a loan of £36,900. It was argued that site clearance and preparation, as well as the building, would provide employment and that the project qualified for an 'unemployment grant'. That, too, was granted in the form of an interest period of eight years which, even in the days of low interest rates, was estimated as being equivalent to £20,000.

As soon as the funding of the new baths was assured, work commenced. After considerable soul searching and debate whether the baths should be open-air or closed, the views of the local swimming community and local teachers were respected and the decision was made to provide closed baths. Mr Newman, Borough Engineer and Surveyor, was directly responsible for the design and no doubt the decision to go "all electric". Watford, at least in that respect, pioneered the new concept. Electricity would be used for heating, lighting and the power necessary to operate the filtration plant.

A few weeks before the baths were due to be opened, Prince George paid Watford one of his rare visits. His first question was: "What are you going to do with the baths in the winter?" It was explained that they were hoping to open during the winter months, to which the Prince replied: "What a glorious place for a dance hall". This was no idle comment, since it was then common practice to cover baths with flooring for recreational purposes during the closed season. In fact, it was the intention to remain open as long as the public attended. Already local schools had applied to use the baths and the elementary schools were planning to teach 1,000 children a week to swim.

The new Watford Public Baths were officially opened by the Mayor, Councillor J Evans on the afternoon of Wednesday 10 May 1933. He had good reason to be proud of the completion of the latest municipal project. Architecturally and technically, the bath building was believed to be among the best in the country. The ceremony began on the steps outside. On one side were gathered members and officials of the corporation and representatives of Hertfordshire County Council, St Albans, Bushey and

Rickmansworth. Guests included Lord Knutsford, Lady Herbert and representatives of the Electricity Board. On the other side were children and parents, overawed by the pomp and circumstances of the occasion.

Watford's aldermen in their scarlet gowns duly followed the mace bearer and Mayor and Mayoress through the swing doors, to be received by the chairman of the Baths Committee, Councillor W J Clarke, who handed the Mayor a ceremonial key. With deliberation, but with excitement in his voice, he addressed the Mayor: "We are asking you to perform the opening ceremony of these baths on 10 May 1933. May they still be going strong in 2033". We know they are still going strong in 1982, so there is no reason to doubt these prophetic words[49]. The Mayor formally declared them open, unlocked the door with his new key and entered. The guests and the public followed, taking up three sides of the baths.

In his speech the Mayor made special mention of Mr Newman who, he said: "In my opinion has with the help of his very efficient staff produced a piece of architecture pleasing in design and admirably adapted for the purpose which it is to serve and a monument of which this borough may well be proud." Councillor Evans replied that the ceremony would be a "red letter day" (no political connotation) in the history of the town and he expressed his pleasure at seeing so many young people present. The Mayor responded: "We have an up-to-date Public Library, the people of Watford have built a wonderful hospital and now we have the baths. But on the corner we have a derelict hotel (The Elms). I shall not be satisfied until we have a worthy building there with a town hall worthy of Watford". In 1938 his wishes came true. Then seven-year-old Terry Woodcock of Sussex Road, the youngest member of Watford Swimming Club, climbed 14 feet to the top diving board, executed a neat dive and received a tremendous ovation. A swimming display followed by Miss Valerie Davies, Welsh champion and a distinguished member of the Olympic team, and a diving display by the Amateur Diving Association.

That same evening a long queue patiently waited at the entrance in the hope of seeing a swimming gala arranged by Watford Swimming Club. As most of the seats were already booked, very few in the queue were allowed in. Two young but nonetheless enthusiastic lads decided they would find another way in and climbed through one of the top windows. We will never know whether they gained illicit entrance or were apprehended.

The local support given to the baths during the first week exceeded all expectations and there were times when queues formed. On three consecutive days the total for the period was 2,500 and on Sunday when the baths opened at 7am there was already a queue. I have not overlooked the installation of 24 slipper baths, the inclusion of which were criticised by some councillors. Practically every house has a bathroom they claimed, so what is the use of providing something which so many people already have. But they were proved quite wrong, as the slipper baths were equally popular.

The diehards who preferred the open air kept faith with Five Arches, but inevitably the original baths went into decline and finally the old superstructure was demolished and, to some extent, the river banks were restored. There is still sufficient evidence of the old swimming baths left today to see where they were located in the shadow of the viaduct. No longer can we hear the shouting or buy a penny biscuit as the steam trains roar above and belch smoke and cinders into the air. Those halcyon days are gone for ever and the sounds from the Five Arches are echoes of the past.

40   The End of an Era

To many mature residents of Watford the name Ashwell will be synonymous with gentlemen's outfitting. No doubt you will remember the shop in the High Street by the name of Ashwell & Sons with its windows cluttered with sombre ties, caps, bowlers and, by present standards, heavyweight worsted clothing, gloves and all the accoutrements that made the well-dressed man of the '20s and '30s. Everything, or nearly everything, was made of natural materials: wool, cotton and leather. They were the days when man-made fibres and plastics were virtually unknown; when boots were losing favour as a fashion item, but braces were still holding their own, and garters were supporting thick long woollen socks.

Ashwell & Sons on right, 73 High Street. Demolished in the 1920s.

Mr Albert Ashwell was thought by many to be a native of Watford, but he was born at St Albans and learned the fundamentals of his trade in London before coming to Watford in 1881. Here he became manager of a business and eventually the proprietor. At first he traded in his own name, but in later years he changed the title to Ashwell and Sons. He retired in 1922, although the shop continued in business. When he first arrived the population was about 15,000 and during his lifetime he saw the number quadruple. Mr Ashwell was proud of Watford and took every opportunity to express his sincere and profound feelings for the town of his adoption. As a successful businessman he did not isolate himself from the rest of the trading community. He became one of the first members of the Tradesmen's Association and enthusiastically supported the movement for an early closing day in order to give hard-pressed staff an extra half-day in addition to Sunday, which was their only day of rest.

He lived at Ashlyns in Marlborough Road and remained active even during retirement, but he never recovered from a stroke. After contracting bronchitis he died in a nursing home in February 1933. About the same time, another member of one of Watford's old established family businesses died: Mr Alfred White. For nearly a century the family had traded in china and glassware at 83 High Street, but in the late '20s moved to The Parade. Like Mr Ashwell, Mr White involved himself in the welfare of the town and became a very active member of Watford Rotary Club and one of the organisers of the club's annual garden parties to which foreign students were invited.

Clutterbuck is another name with which many will be familiar, but in quite a different context. The name was known to many generations of local residents for reasons as diverse as landowner, the church, brewer, historian and philanthropist. Capt T R C Clutterbuck became the soldier of the family. His father was Thomas Meadows Clutterbuck. On his death, Capt Clutterbuck, the eldest son, inherited the centuries-old brewery of T Clutterbuck & Co at Stanmore, which had been in the family for a number of generations. It was the period when many local breweries surrendered to larger progressive breweries and in 1923 the old brewery on Stanmore Hill was sold to the Cannon Brewery Co Ltd of Clerkenwell, London (no connection with Cannon Brewery of Watford). In 1930 Taylor Walker & Co Ltd acquired Cannon and in 1959 Taylor Walker was taken over by Ind Coope. Two years previously, Ind Coope had acquired Benskins Brewery.

Thomas Clutterbuck joined the Army and was gazetted to the Coldstream Guards, with which regiment he served in France during the First World War. He returned to England and was posted to Bushey Hall which had been requisitioned by the Crown as an officers' training school. With an unimpeachable war record and being of independent means, he became interested in politics and was elected Chairman of the Watford Divisional Conservative Association. He was a good friend of Sir Dennis Herbert MP and actively supported him during his election campaign over a period of 12 years. He became a member of the Management Committee of the Peace Memorial Hospital and joined the Board of Management of the London Orphan School in 1925. In 1931 he was elected to the Hertfordshire County Council as representative of Watford Rural District and succeeded the Earl of Clarendon who had been appointed Governor General of South Africa. A keen sportsman, his favourite game was cricket and he served on the committee of the Hertfordshire County Cricket Club.

Well known to Capt Clutterbuck was Mr W S Langford who lived in Durban Road. Mr Langford was born at Malvern Wells in 1862 and came to work in Watford in 1905 as secretary to André & Sleigh, a printing firm which later amalgamated with the Sun Engraving. He became secretary of the old Watford Cottage Hospital in 1916 until the opening of the Peace Memorial Hospital in 1925, when the administration was transferred to the new hospital.

Mr Langford was a dedicated and industrious secretary whose efforts to maintain the Cottage Hospital and later the Peace were better known to the administrative and nursing staff than either patients or the public. Virtually single-handedly he guided the hospital into the '30s, in the knowledge that as Watford's population increased so the accommodation and medical facilities, thought to be adequate at the time, had to keep pace. The burden of that responsibility was great, but Mr Langford never failed or faltered in his task and always maintained his sense of humour.

In his earlier years he belonged to the now forgotten Linden Entertainers, a concert party comprising personalities from Watford which, in its time, was popular and successful. Mr Langford's forte was the writing of witty and topical lyrics which he composed for the concert party and, on occasions, performed them himself as a salon singer. His interest in entertainment never waned and he still found time and energy to become a member of another very elite concert party organised by the nursing staff at the hospital each Christmas. Sadly we do not have on record any of his pieces but he was still writing and singing his own songs, one with 36 verses, at the age of 70.

He died four weeks before Capt Clutterbuck and at more or less the same time as Anthony Ashwell and Alfred Wright. Watford's last four personalities of Victorian birth who had successfully survived the traumatic transition into a new century, were all dedicated in their own particular manner to the welfare of the town. Their loss was mourned by the community at large, for Watford was still a town with an indigenous population whose lives had been temporarily disturbed by the calamity of the war years of 1914 -1918. Men of this calibre helped build the foundations upon which the town was founded; men whose interests were so closely related to the community. In this day of multi-nationals, we miss the personal touch which was then a way of life we took for granted.

41   Watford Rules OK

I have heard it said that brewing put Watford on the map but football kept it there. I accept that there is more than a grain of truth in the old saying. In retrospect, I realise I have already written about Watford's brewing industry, but nothing concerning football. I shall, therefore, make good that inexcusable deficiency.

We all think of Vicarage Road as the home of Watford FC and not without good reason, but it was not its birthplace. To trace its origin we must go back to the time of the Hertfordshire Rangers and the Watford Rovers, the town's best teams. In 1890 they amalgamated for the express purpose of giving Watford one first class team with individual loyalty. For the next season the new Rovers changed their name to West Hertfordshire, prompted by the availability of eight acres of land which had been part of Harwoods Farm. The team still enjoyed amateur status, but it now had a ground of its own. We know the old football ground as the West Hertfordshire Sports Ground, bounded on the east by Cassio Road.

Thoughts naturally turned to the prospect of going professional and, by 1894, the proposal was put to a meeting but, surprisingly, was rejected. However, the seed was sown and in 1897 the club changed its mind and gave up its amateur tag. The transition took some time, due largely to lack of funds, but despite the problem two players were signed up. Now it was 'pay for play'. The proportion of professionals to semi-professionals increased over the years and, in 1898, West Hertfordshire and another top local team, Watford St Mary's, amalgamated. On that day Watford Football Club, already conceived, was born.

Watford's 4-0 victory over Reading, 19 October 1907.

At the end of their first season, Watford FC was placed third in Division Two of the Southern League and in 1890 became champions. Those of the old West Hertfordshire who had pressed for the team to go professional knew their militant views had been vindicated. But victory did not bring its just monetary rewards and by 1907 the club headed for financial disaster. To stave off the evil day, their centre-forward, Foster, was sold to Sunderland for £800. The team was now fully professional and the club was incorporated as a limited company.

The new broom swept clean. The colours were changed from red, yellow and green (the Wasps) to white shirts and black shorts (the Magpies). In later years there were more changes, from black-and-white striped shirts and black shorts to blue shirts and white shorts. Their hour of glory came in the 1914-15 season when, under the management of Harry Kent, they became the Southern League champions. Competitive football was barred during the years of the First World War and Watford FC did not resume league matches until 1919 when they were beaten on goal average by Portsmouth. Then in 1920 Watford joined the brand new Third Division and in 1922 moved to their new home at Vicarage Road.

All connections with the West Hertfordshire were severed. Watford had gained independence, but fame and fortune were still a long way off. It is true they made the last 16 in the battle for the Cup in 1924 and the match with Newcastle was lost by an only goal. In 1931 Watford got through to the fifth round, but went down to Birmingham. The next year they did even better, but were again defeated by Newcastle. It was a long time before Watford reached such heights again. It happened in the 1949-50 season. A replay with Preston was won by an only goal and the next clash came in the fourth round with Manchester United. Cup fever gripped the town and on that memorable occasion 32,419 people attended the match, breaking earlier attendance records. Pulling out all the stops, Watford played as they had seldom played before and all but stopped United in their tracks. The match was lost with honour, again by that one goal.

In 1936-37 Neil McBain had raised the club to fourth place in the division and Billy Findlay who succeeded him equalled the achievement. In 1953-54 Len Goulden did the same but their finest year, in a historical context, was without doubt 1959-60 under Ron Burgess, so ably assisted by Len Goulden. Under their guidance, you will recall the fifth round Cup battle with Sheffield United when nine fit men finally acknowledged defeat. There have been few occasions in competitive football when supporters and opposition have praised the losing side on or off the field. Those moments of greatness are surely what soccer is all about.

I have referred to the team as a corporate body, but what of the players, player-managers and managers of the past? Did they not build the foundations on which future successes were based? In the very distant past there was John Goodall, a member of the Preston team of 1889 which won the League championship and the FA Cup in the same year, who became player-manager. During the inter-war years you will surely remember Tommy Barrett, an inside forward who established an incredible record by appearing in 445 games. Whether that record has since been bettered I cannot say, but mention of his name brings to mind W Chapman, with whom he formed a triumphant partnership. Then there was Frank McPherson, an ex-Manchester United player who gained a reputation as centre-forward and treated the football like a cannonball. He moved on to Reading and in 1934 returned to the club. As his career came to an end, Len Dunderdale was signed on and in no time became the idol of the terraces before his transfer to Leeds during the 1938-39 season for the local record fee of £3,750.

Then there was Fred 'Paggie' Pagnam way back in 1921. He was recruited as centre-forward, having played for Huddersfield, Arsenal and Cardiff, at a cost of £1,000. He became manager in 1926 by succeeding Harry Kent. Remember Taffy Davies, a contemporary of Chapman, McPherson and Barnett? He played for 21 years and gained a wartime international cap playing for Wales. Barson may be remembered for a very different reason. He was sent off in a September game with Fulham in 1928. His next game at Shepherds Bush was the last for the season. That was the term of suspension inflicted on him by the FA.

The supporters were naturally incensed by what they considered to be such an unjust suspension period and 5,000 of them signed a petition deploring the decision and pleading for reconsideration of the harsh verdict. At that time the suspension period was the longest on record and it was no ordinary petition. The Mayor, Alderman Thomas Rushton, presented the documentation directly to the FA Secretary, Mr F A Wall. The occasion was unique in another respect. It was the first time that supporters had rallied to the defence of a player who had been sent off by an irate referee. But the protestations were, unhappily, of no avail and Barson was duly suspended.

Any reference to Watford FC cannot pass without mention of one of the Club's best-loved figures of all time – Arthur Grimsdell. He joined Watford in 1910 and left to play for Tottenham after only two years, where his success was legendary. Fortunately he was not lost to Watford and later returned in the capacity of director. Arthur was always regarded as one of the 'greats'.

Now (1982) Watford has achieved the success that eluded the Club for so many years, as it competes in the FA First Division. Past boards, managements and players have always worked to that end, but it has taken 60 years at Vicarage Road to make the dream come true.

42   The Slums of Watford

The word 'slum' is defined in my 1930 dictionary as a "low, dirty street of a city or town inhabited by very poor or criminal classes". The inclusion of the word "criminal" was no doubt a left-over from Dickensian times. It is a word that has gone out of fashion, due largely to the national rehousing programmes of the two World Wars. The expression is certainly alien to Watford in this day and age, but memories can be notoriously short when recalling some of the town's less than desirable areas and dwellings.

Woodman's Yard and medieval wagonway from rear (195 High Street) prior to dismantling, 1977.

In the early 19th century, before the arrival of the railways, Watford was without any public authority to care either for the welfare of its people or the immediate environment. There was then a large proportion of poor to the few aristocratic land owners, men of independent means and prosperous tradesmen who lived in or near the town. The drainage system was almost non-existent, in consequence of which killer diseases thrived and the mortality rate was high. There was no running water and the communal pump in the Market Place was the only source of supply. The overcrowded residents then lived in 'courts', which have now all but disappeared. They were squalid, dirty and damp cobbled cul-de-sacs where lines of washing hung out to dry across open 'courts' as children splashed in stagnant pools of water. Some of their names may be familiar: Old Yard, Woodman's Yard, Chapman's Yard and Chequer's Yard, to name a few. The yards were generally accessible by medieval wagonways giving access to the High Street. Other areas containing dilapidated properties included Crown Passage, Meeting Alley, Church Street and New Street.

One of the most notorious areas which undoubtedly subscribed to the criminal element in the definition of 'slum' was surely Ballard's Buildings. Ballard was a railway contractor who built the embankment between Bushey Station and Watford Junction. He imported hundreds of labourers whose sweat, blood and even lives came cheaply before the era of mechanical aids. The prospect of the railway coming to Watford was resisted by both the poor and rich elements of the indigenous population. The former featured the fusion of fire and water as the manifestation of the devil himself, while the latter counted their losses in land and property values. The arrival of Ballard's work force did nothing to allay those fears.

Ballard had to find accommodation for the men, but they were unwelcome as lodgers in the town. Their negative reception forced him to the yard off New Street where the first John Dyson had brewed in the early 18th century. There the 'navvies' were housed in the already old properties and the yard soon became known as Ballard's Buildings. After the embankment was completed the 'navvies' moved on, but the buildings remained. They were perhaps Watford's only slum area of more recent times. In 1926 the tenants were found alternative accommodation when the buildings were finally condemned and demolished. The process of demolition started as late as the 19th century, but in 1933 Watford Corporation made one of their biggest efforts to rid the town of many of the remaining slum properties. They were not slums in the old-fashioned sense, but the houses lacked certain amenities which landlords had neglected rather than provided. In the period 1924-1928 as many as 152 houses had been condemned and the tenants rehoused in council houses. At the beginning of 1932, Watford's Medical Officer reported 200 more dwellings as unfit for habitation.

In anticipation of the displacement of many more families the Leavesden Green housing estate was started, with completion planned for June 1934. It was estimated that 600 people would be immediately affected, followed by another 400 when the estate was completed. The Ministry of Health approved the greater part of Watford's recommendations which involved 120 dwellings, subject to the findings of a Public Enquiry. The enquiry was held in May 1933 and many tenants were present at the meeting, frequently interrupting the proceedings with shouts and applause.

Application was made by the Town Hall for clearance orders for 11 areas and compulsory purchase orders for three. These included houses in Beechen Grove and Red Lion Yard, Upper Paddock Road, Meeting Alley, New Road, Chapman's Yard, Wells Yard, Chater's Yard and Albert Street. Purchase orders were requested for Grove Circus, Beechen Grove and Riverside Road. In Upper Paddock Road, Oxhey, terraced cottages of wooden construction had been built in 1883 by, it was said, a Dutchman called Van Yean. It was claimed that the structure was past redemption, being riddled with rot and damp and it failed to comply with building standards. In Red Lion Yard eight houses were said to be in a state of disrepair, with rotting floors, stairs and woodwork. Of the dwellings in Beechen Grove/Loates Lane area, it was explained that the small cottages had once been a 17th century manor house and had been divided up in a most "extraordinary manner". The corporation asked for their demolition due to dampness and lack of sanitary accommodation. Loates Lane was once the main road to Aldenham and Radlett.

Cottages in New Road and Chapman's Yard were criticised because the toilets faced the front doors! In addition there was no running water, although it was noted that sinks had been provided. Eleven houses in Chater's Yard and four in Albert Street were also reported as being in need of repair, with no water supply and only two toilets to four houses. The cottages in Meeting Alley were in good order, but they were condemned for having no rear access. The cottages at the Rookery were said to be from the 18th century and once accommodated families working at the old Silk Mill, but little was wrong with them that could not be rectified. The displaced residents did not take kindly to being sent to an estate over 2½ miles away. It was not the distance involved, as much as the additional cost of getting to work in Watford. They complained too at the rent of 7s a week and the lack of educational facilities for children. However, this omission was rectified with a new school scheduled for 1934 at Leggatt's Way, in addition to another school in the planning stages. For the time being, children were accommodated at Parkgate Road School.

Virtually none of the dwellings could correctly be called 'slums'. It is true they did not meet existing health regulations, but little evidence could be found that they were unfit for habitation. Ultimately, many of the houses were demolished and the residents moved to council properties. Even in 1933, old Watford was fast disappearing.

43　　The Day of the Semi

By 1933 the land acquired during the sale of Cassiobury House and its estate was already being developed. A skeleton road system had been built and detached residences now bordered the new roads in what was then regarded as Watford's most exclusive estate. In those days, the prospect of a new house convenient to the town and Cassiobury Park was the sole prerogative of the middle classes who employed at least one maid or housekeeper. The concurrent working class development was confined to the more remote parts that had once been farmland.

Kingswood estate was the subject of an earlier article, but development was not confined to this once fringe area. One of the most popular in the early '30s was the Tudor estate built by one of the town's most respected developers by the name of Rice Brothers Builders. Here the houses, known as 'Rice's Remarkable Residences', were sold at prices between £700 and £1,000 and achieved special distinction when some international delegates attending the Building Societies Conference chose to inspect the estate as an example of modern English houses selling at moderate prices.

Nearby Bushey Mill Lane was another area ripe for development. It was known as the Bradshaw estate and, unlike the Tudor Estate, many different builders were involved. Wm King and Sons, established in 1885, offered their semis at a freehold price of £700. The customary deposit was then £50 and the balance of the loan was repayable at 19s 11d weekly. The design and layout of the '30s semi was fairly traditional and often differed only in finish. The specification was virtually identical; bay widows with gabled roof over, three bedrooms, two reception rooms, small kitchen (sometimes conveniently called a kitchenette), a coke stove supplying hot water, and two toilets. The price was inclusive of legal fees and road charges. The purchaser invariably acquired a property soundly built with seasoned timber, clay roof tiles, cast-iron gutters and down pipes, lead cold water pipes and steel hot water pipes with galvanised steel tanks, one electric socket per room, and a white vitreous enamelled bath with earthenware bowls and basins. The toilet system had a chain pull and the kitchen would have been equipped with a dresser.

Other builders at Bradshaw included F J Allen responsible for some, if not all the houses in Knutsford Avenue, and there were the Howard Houses, claimed to be decorated with "the finest materials and equipped with the most up-to-date fittings". They were, the builders claimed, "second to none". A Howard semi was yours for £675 freehold, or rather £50 deposit and 17s 8d a week.

Hillingdon Estates claimed to offer the prospective customer seeking a house the "biggest bargain". The bargain was a "seven-roomed house for £695 freehold with no road or legal charges; the keenest bargain in property since the war. Wonderfully well built, excellently appointed, large rooms, spacious gardens, room for a garage. Two reception rooms, three bedrooms, tiled kitchen and bathroom with panelled bath, chromium fittings and two WCs. £5 secures, all-in deposit £39, weekly repayments 21s". Quite a deal, by any standards.

With such specifications, although the provision of hot water is not always quoted but may be assumed, we can visualise the '30s semi. The inclusion of garage space was an indicator of changing times. Some builders required an additional £25, but none ever quoted the cost of a garage as a separate item. We had progressed from terraced houses to semis in less than 50 years or, put another way, we had gone from the primitive outdoor 'privy' to the cosy 'loo' in half a century.

Unemployment in the early '30s was still a problem, but things were getting better rather than worse. Watford's unemployed were well below the national average, which seems to have always been the case. Competition in the building industry was fierce and cut-throat. Each developer fully equipped a show house which was not just open to the public by appointment, but every day of the week. Families wondering what to do on a Sunday afternoon would often visit a show house and were content to regard the visitation as offering adequate but harmless entertainment, although the feeling persisted that it was not the right thing to do on a Sunday. We have come a long way since those days and those guilty thoughts. We marvelled at the latest gadgets and work-saving devices, although we could never quite understand why kitchens were getting smaller and smaller, until they became no wider than the entrance hall. Perhaps it was just fashion or a ploy to make the dining room a little bigger, but whatever the reason the situation was accepted in the name of progress.

At about the same time another slightly up-market estate appeared on the south side of Cassiobury Park, then called the Cassiobury Station estate. The developer was Chas Brightman and Son. The frontages were advertised as 30 feet, rather generous by any standard, and garage space was included. Houses with either three or four bedrooms were offered from £816 freehold; £50 deposit and 24s 9d a week.

Another well-known Watford builder, Clifford and Gough, was building at Munden Grove. Weekly repayments ranged from 21s 10d. to 22s 7d, but the specification was sufficiently attractive to warrant the higher costs. Wireless sockets were fitted in the sitting room, the front garden was finished in crazy paving and the roof tiles were "best handmade". At the same time, Kempster and Williams were selling their houses on North Western Avenue at £430, with repayments of 13s 8d a week.

I have told you of the estates which were in an advanced state of development in 1933, but there were more and more houses still to come. Russells estate was earmarked for development and plots were offered along the existing road frontage of 6,000 feet. The same was happening at Croxley Green where Durrants estate was sold. A more modest road frontage of 2,500 feet on Baldwins Lane became ripe for development. Building was also taking place at Stanborough estate and Bushey Lodge farm.

In retrospect, 1933 was the year when Watford finally severed its connections with its agrarian past. The sale of farms and estates was accelerated by the arterial road or the by-pass, as the A41 became known. It was foreseeable that the affected land in North Watford sandwiched between the new road and the limit of the old turn-of-the-century developments would ultimately suffer the same fate. It was in that year that the face of Watford could be said to have changed more than at any other time. It is the Watford we know today; a town largely built in the '30s, the day of the semi.

CLIFFORD & GOUGH,

Clifford & Gough advertisement, 1915.

44　The Carlton and the Palace

The recent (1982) demise of the old Carlton cinema was for many of us a timely reminder of the ever-changing face of Watford. It was a structure of little architectural merit and yet part of our young lives was inextricably involved with this house of entertainment. Its physical presence, despite the peeling paint and neglected mahogany entrance doors, somehow bridged the gap between childhood and maturity. Although the stripped auditorium had been relegated to a furniture emporium, it was still a nostalgic reminder of those far-off days. A stay of execution for a year or so could not change its ultimate fate and now another memory of old Watford has gone forever.

It is common knowledge that this oddly-shaped building, both inside and out, started life as a roller-skating rink. The temporary rink that opened on the corner of Beechen Grove in 1909 was soon replaced by a permanent structure in March 1910, when indoor roller-skating suddenly caught the public's imagination like the skate boards of a few years ago. But the popularity of the rink was short-lived due, no doubt, to the First World War. It remained closed during the immediate post-war years and reopened as the Super in 1921 under the managership of Fred Farleigh.

Roller skating at what became the Super (later the Carlton), 1909.

The extent of the conversion of the rink to a picture theatre was minimal. The viewing area, where spectators once watched the antics of the skaters, was left largely intact except, of course, the area occupied by the screen. The new owners merely replaced the floor and seats and erected a projection room on the edge of the roof. The unfortunate patrons who sat on the perimeter of the near-round auditorium suffered a partial loss of vision in the days of silent movies and, when sound arrived, a noticeable distortion of voice and music. Although commercial talkies came to Watford in 1929, the Super could well have been the first picture house in Watford to show a sound film, that is a film with the soundtrack on the film rather than on an accompanying record. On 15 December 1928 the audience was treated to a fully synchronised British Talking Picture demonstration film in which the Celeste Octet played the 'Bacarolle' from the 'Tales of Hoffman'! Brought up on wind-up gramophones with steel needles that played 78 rpm records, the quality of the sound must have enraptured the audience who little imagined their technological experience that night would soon revolutionise the industry.

On conversion to talkies, the theatre changed hands and became the Carlton. Little was done to the interior until the early '60s when, at a cost of £70,000, it was given a long-overdue facelift. The old viewing galleries disappeared behind acoustic walls and the shape became almost, but not quite identifiable with the traditional auditorium. The central dome was made a feature with dozens of tiny light bulbs. A great deal of careful planning was applied to the old carcase. The film which hailed its reopening was 'Tom Jones', that rumbustious bawdy 18th century English comedy starring Albert Finney and Susannah York.

The scene outside the Carlton was rather like the old days – queues in all directions, but television was already making inroads on our lives, our habits and, where it hurt most, the box office. Within a decade rumour had it that the Carlton would close, which was perhaps not surprising when films were playing to audiences of two or three dozen on some evenings. Few people were prepared to believe that it could possibly happen but in 1980 the curtain came down, the doors closed for the last time and the staff looked elsewhere for a livelihood.

The same picture theatre had entertained the young and old of Watford for nearly 60 years. The period had spanned almost the birth of the popular movies to their near eclipse; from Charlie Chaplin to Woody Allen, from Mary Pickford to Jane Fonda, and from childhood to the present. The memories linger on as bulldozers clear the site of tangled metal, wood and bricks which was once the Carlton. The Palace Theatre next door, offering live entertainment, nearly suffered the same fate when audiences changed their allegiance from the stage to the silver screen in the mid-'30s, before the days of Baird.

The Palace Theatre, which was originally built for the Watford Hippodrome Co Ltd, opened its doors on 14 December 1908 under the proprietorship of the Watford Palace of Varieties Co. It put on two performances nightly at prices ranging from 4d to 1s 6d. The management promised to secure the top London names and musical shows and, of course, present a Christmas show. 'Aladdin' was the first pantomime which opened the following Boxing Day and was performed by a London company of players. True to its word, the management presented Little Titch, George Robey and Harry Tate with his legendary sketch, 'Motoring'. Also direct from the London stage came such greats as Nellie Wallace, Marie Lloyd and Vesta Tilley. It was the day of fulfilled promises. The Palace of Varieties thrived and Watford's public was given the opportunity of seeing for themselves London's most famous theatrical personalities.

Palace Theatre. *The Pearl Girl* is advertised. Oct 1914.

Clarendon Hall advertisement for two January 1904 performances of J M Barrie's 'Quality Street'.

Even before the new theatre was built, in fact before any of the old familiar picture houses were built, Watford's residents had already been thrilled by moving images projected on a silver screen. The Kinetic at the Corn Exchange, which once stood on the site of Cawdells store, attracted visiting film projectionists, who also showed 'animated pictures' at the Clarendon Hall. The other day I was talking to 'Buck' Buckingham, who served Watford in the capacity of councillor and alderman for many years. We chatted about the old days and, without hesitation, he recalled a visiting circus at the Clarendon Hall at which he saw his first film. "I can't remember its title" he admitted "but I remember the story well". It appears that a young maid servant was treated badly by her master and to get her own back slipped a piece of ripe cheese into the tail of his coat, with foreseeable results!

By the mid-'30s the Palace was forced to abandon regular variety shows and introduced repertory companies which, in direct competition with cinemas, succeeded in attracting large audiences. Having survived the pre-war years, the war and the difficult post-war years, in 1956 a dynamic husband and wife team, Mr and Mrs Jimmy Perry, arrived on the scene to restore the ailing fortunes of the Palace Theatre at a time when even the cinemas were feeling the pinch. Against all odds, they succeeded in keeping the theatre alive and it is largely due to this indefatigable couple that the Palace was still there to be saved in later years when there was no alternative but to seek financial support from other quarters.

Ironically, the Carlton had no benefactors. Tied to commerce, it had to pay its way or go to the wall. With dwindling audiences, it could not compete against the challenge of television and the inevitable happened. Now an office block will be erected in its place. If all goes well, additional space will be acquired in the new building by the recently-restored theatre which is now listed by the Department of the Environment. "It's an ill wind" I can hear you say.

The Carlton's last show, days before it closed on 12 July 1980.

45   Throwing More Light on Watford

It is on record that in August 1883 a shop by the name of Roger Bros in Watford High Street abandoned its gas lighting of bat jets and glass shades in favour of electricity. The proprietors decided they could no longer tolerate Watford Gas Company's ill-smelling gas and made the momentous decision to go "all electric". Roger Bros became the first shop in Watford to convert to electricity for lighting purposes. A pair of three light 'electroliers' (ornamental metal pendants for supporting electric lamps) were fitted, one inside the shop and one outside.

At that early date there was no municipal supply and it is doubtful if a private company would have provided electricity within the central area. I think it is more likely the brothers purchased a gas engine and generator to light the primitive bulbs. The new lighting system caused a minor sensation and the shop attracted many people who came to see the new luminant. They were not disappointed. Local shopkeepers were envious of the entrepreneurs who first introduced electric lighting to the shopping centre.

Fourteen years passed before a municipal supply became available to the public. Our enterprising council had successfully applied for an 'Electric Light Order', which presumably gave public utility status to their new enterprise. The experiment was less than successful in the early days and disappointed ratepayers found themselves with an additional rate burden. The prospect of ever getting into the 'black' looked so remote that the council seriously debated whether to offer the ailing enterprise to a private company. It appears that good reason or an element of stubbornness prevailed and the council retained ownership hoping, no doubt, for better days to come. They came, but some years later.

In the '20s modest profits were made; for example in 1923 an annual profit of £14,618 was declared. In 1925 and 1927, however, losses of £603 and £3,605 respectively were recorded. After 1927 the position improved considerably, especially in the early '30s. You may recall my recent article about the new estates and developments which were a feature of pre-war Watford. It could be called a population explosion, but it had little to do with the birth rate. Demand for electricity increased as people moved into the town to take up permanent residence. By 1931 profits exceeded £330,000!

Electricity meter card, 1940-1941.

Since the council effectively controlled the utility, which included the massive generating station in Cardiff Road, it was argued in the '30s that the ratepayers could look upon themselves as shareholders and thus enjoy the fruits of their investments! In fact it did not quite work out that way. There was a formula which determined the proportion of profits that could be transferred to the rate fund. As a municipal undertaking, an Electricity Committee made up of councillors and aldermen controlled the purse strings and policy which included the administration of profits.

The operation was efficient and Watford became the first local authority in England to convert all their street lamps to electricity. The reason for doing so was no doubt prompted by the fact that the gas company was in private hands and did not therefore contribute to the increasing wealth of the borough, except as a nominal commercial ratepayer. On the other side of the coin, however, the Electricity Committee did not enjoy particular popularity and came in for a lot of criticism because of its miserly attitude. In 1933, for example, the committee grudgingly voted a sum of £4,500 to the rate fund when the amount it could have legitimately transferred was in the region of £7,800.

The reason for such meanness became apparent that year when the request was made to the council for land adjacent to the old Council Offices on which to build a showroom. The request was refused so, undaunted and to wave the flag of independence, if not defiance, the committee agreed to the acquisition of a site opposite the Pond almost next door to their competitors, the Watford and St Albans Gas Company! When it became known that the price paid for the land was £80 a foot, the committee was subjected to even greater criticism for depriving the ratepayers of the full allocation of profits. The accusation was made that only the money available to the utility justified the high cost paid for the land. Perhaps you may have forgotten, unless you had a penny-in-the-slot meter, that electricity bills used to be payable at their offices in Cardiff Road. Very few families had bank accounts in those days and, in consequence, it was necessary to go with cash to the generating station, of which the offices were part. A visit to that area needed courage. The huge chimneys belched out black smoke which was carried away by the prevailing wind. The smell of burning fuel was not altogether alien to our environment as coal was our staple fuel. We took little notice of the pollution and accepted the frequent fogs as a natural hazard. After all, we used coal for heating and contributed in our own small way to the problem.

The new site at the Pond was large enough to accommodate not only a showroom, but also the offices and perhaps, after all, it was not a coincidence that the electricity offices were so close to the gas company. The rivalry between them was now physically apparent. In due course a very pleasant red brick building was erected and by the mid-'30s both structures brought a semblance of harmony and continuity to the Pond area by countering the alien architecture of the Plaza cinema. In those pre-war and more recent post-war days, that end of Watford was a feast of colour, making us not a little proud of a town which seemed conscious of its appearance. Unfortunately times have changed; our priorities are confused and our sense of pride relies on memories of the past rather than the present. Our local gas and electricity services were nationalised and the old manufacturing undertakings have virtually disappeared. Now we are dependent on supplies, the origin of which remain a closed book to the layman. There is little doubt that even the showrooms would still have been occupied today had the town planners had a greater regard for the consequences of their actions. Their biggest mistake was to create the psychological barrier of the flyover, effectively sealing off The Parade. Both the electricity and gas authorities chose to relocate to the busy shopping area and the Pond end of The Parade is now (1982) but a ghost of its former affluence and beauty.

46   Lady Capel's Wharf

If you have driven along the northern section of Hempstead Road at regulation speed, you will have observed a small signpost pointing away from the road towards the canal. The hand-painted letters read 'Lady Capel's Wharf'. The spot is well known to local fishermen, walkers and those travelling at an even more leisurely pace on pleasure cruisers. However, of the many familiar with the name, few will know the origin of the wharf or why it should have been named after Lady Capel.

The story begins at the end of the 18th century when the Duke of Bridgewater engaged the services of engineer James Brindley and built the Bridgewater Canal to convey coal from the Duke's mines at Worsley to Manchester. Within the next 70 years, 3,000 miles of canals straddled the country. Inevitably, plans were made to connect London with the Midlands to avoid the circuitous route via the Oxford arm to the Thames. Two companies contributed to the creation of that connection from Braunton over the Chilterns to Berkhamsted, Watford, Rickmansworth and Brentford.

The new canal was originally planned to enter a tunnel at Langleybury to avoid more locks over rising ground and work may have actually started. A counter-proposal was made to approach the Earls of Clarendon and Essex, the major landowners, for permission to utilise the course of the River Gade which ran through both estates. They would jointly be offered the sum of £1,200, which represented the difference between the cost of the tunnel and the new route.

The Earl of Essex rejected the proposed compensation out of hand, but after long drawn out negotiations, he settled for £15,000 and a seat on the company board. The Earl of Clarendon accepted £5,000 plus the cost of the land. There was one other condition upon which both insisted. Each stipulated that the canal was to be landscaped and made compatible with the local environment. These conditions are said to account for the presence of the attractive bridge carrying the drive to The Grove and the carefully planned setting as the canal passes through Cassiobury Park. In 1797 work was completed on both estates and the 'navvies' moved to the north beyond Langleybury along the Gade Valley. By 1890 the new canal was complete.

You may wonder what the Great Fire of London in 1666 has to do with Lady Capel's Wharf. Let me explain. With the major part of the City destroyed, the corporation decided to impose a toll on 'sea coal', which had traditionally been shipped by coasters to the Port of London to help finance the rebuilding of St Paul's. As soon as the Grand Junction Canal was completed, coal was brought down from the north by longboat and by-passed the London docks and, in theory at least, the coal tax. At this time coal tax revenue was being utilised to improve London's embankments. Restrictions were immediately placed on the movement of coal on the canal and, at one stage, it was not allowed to be transported beyond Watford.

In due course the prohibition was eased and a collector was permanently stationed at The Grove to record the coal tonnage in transit for London. Then a flat rate of 1s 1d a ton was imposed on all coal cargoes taken beyond Watford. To avoid payment of tax, a wharf was constructed where coal could be off-loaded without contravening the Coal Duties Act. A thriving business developed as haulage contractors and coal merchants loaded their carts and wagons to supply Watford and the surrounding area with duty-free coal! The wharf became known as Lady Capel's Wharf. There are conflicting versions concerning its ownership. We know it was vacated by the Grand Junction in 1847 when the lease expired. It is reasonable to suppose the government collector stayed on for some years at least. The wharf is said to have belonged to the Earl of Clarendon but, having regard for its name, I am inclined to subscribe to the version that attributes ownership of Russells, one of the dower houses of Cassiobury House, to the Essex family.

William Capel, third Earl of Essex who died in 1743, had two sons and four daughters, two of whom died in infancy. The surviving daughters, Lady Diane and Lady Anne, remained single. They both died in their 70s at Russells, Diane the eldest in 1800 and Anne in 1804. The wharf would have been built during their lifetime on the Russells estate and who would dispute that the Lady Capel after whom it was named was the eldest daughter Diane?

Eventually, the railways took over coal transportation and the coal duty was abolished by the turn of the century. Lady Capel's Wharf became a memory as nature took over the abandoned site. Silt, trees and undergrowth obliterated what was once Watford's coal supply depot. It was all but forgotten when the Grand Junction became the Grand Union Canal in 1929. The new company made many improvements to the canal. By August 1933 a new diesel-engined dredger arrived at the wharf. In three months the width at that point was doubled and the depth increased to 5 feet. In the process, a strip of land 18 yards by 55 yards, a shallow bay consisting largely of silt and reeds and a small backwater, disappeared. It was estimated that between 7,000 and 8,000 tons of earth was moved to complete the task.

The presence of the old wharf was confirmed on the removal of huge oak and elm piles, all in perfect condition, together with bricks and gravel. The debris was transferred to floating hoppers for unloading at the ballast pits at Kings Langley. The work was watched by hundreds of curious onlookers who were fascinated by a dredger that could remove mud and earth at the rate of 1 cubic yard a minute. Lady Capel's Wharf disappeared without trace and the little signpost, to some extent, is slightly misleading. Besides carrying coal, the old working boats also brought to Watford and London grain, flour and, of all things, ashes. The bricks used for building Leavesden Hospital are said to have been off-loaded at the old wharf.

Why were the canals built at all? At the time of the industrial revolution, our roads were totally inadequate and no mechanical means existed to carry heavy or bulky loads from one place to another. A long boat could be pulled along by a man or a horse with relatively little effort. If time was not of the essence, transportation on the waterways was cheap and efficient. But within 50 years our railways did the job much better and more quickly, and gradually the canal system deteriorated – although some working boats survived locally until the '70s.

The legacy of the rustic canal is at last being appreciated. We may count ourselves fortunate that the final route chosen to London passed through Watford's largest estates which have been preserved over the years. We can walk along the towpath and envy the drive, vision and passion of the pioneers whose engineering skills and surveying abilities changed the face of the country in general and South West Hertfordshire in particular.

Long boats approaching the Navigation Bridge, 1938.

47   Industrial Watford

Watford's earliest major industries were milling, malting and farming, which together provided the option of not living on bread alone. There were four mills in the area recorded during the Domesday survey: Cassio, Oxhey, The Grove and Watford, all located on our two rivers, the Colne and the Gade. The mills were controlled by the Lord of the Manor, effectively the Abbot of St Albans, in the best tradition of a feudal system. It was then mandatory that all farmers brought their corn to the mill for grinding as they were not permitted to own or operate a mill for themselves. Driven by water power, the mills operated for centuries.

Grove Mill, 1910.*

The once famous mill in Cassiobury Park, acquired by our council, was allowed to deteriorate to the extent that application for its demolition could not be reasonably withheld. The mill at Oxhey was at the Rookery. Grove Mill is presently residential accommodation, as is Hamper Mill. Watford Mill was gutted by fire in 1924 and never rebuilt.

Apart from crops, sheep farming was relatively important and the earliest record of a wool industry occurred when John, Abbot of St Albans granted a fulling mill at Cassiobury to Petronilla d'Amneville. In the 14th century, six merchants and two salesmen were employed there. The merchants purchased the wool from local farmers, which was then bleached and, we must assume, the salesmen took to the road on horseback. Inevitably some yarn was woven locally, but whether in another mill or as a cottage industry we will never know. The last record of a local weaver was in the 17th century. His name was Jeremiah Smith. The demise of his occupation may well have been caused by the popularity of imported linen.

Parliament was concerned about the loss of foreign exchange and the adverse effect on the old established woollen industry. In 1667 an enactment made it illegal to be buried in a covering made of a mixture of flax, silk or hemp, or lining a coffin with a similar material. The alternative was, of course, wool and perhaps that is why Mr Smith managed to stay in business.

In the 17th century some would claim that water was put to its best use. Although maltings had been operated on a small commercial basis, the brewing of ale and the like had been all but another cottage

99

industry. I will not dwell on the history of brewing, about which I have already written at some length. Suffice it to say that the brewers had no difficulty marketing their products.

At the beginning of the 18th century came a new era of papermaking. The early industry had almost disappeared due to the importation of continental paper. For some reason that escapes us now, the movement started in 1660 but it was over a century later after Mill End, Batchworth and others, that Hamper Mill converted to the manufacture of paper. The new venture was a success and handmade paper continued to be produced into the 20th century.

Another industry, already established in the 18th century, was the 'throwing' or weaving of silk. At that time, silk was one of Watford's principal industries. Why the town should have adopted this industry in the first place is not clear, but the presence of the Houses of Essex and Clarendon suggest they were good customers, if not dedicated patrons. The biggest and most prosperous silk mill was sited at the Rookery and used the Colne for its power. The Rookery Mill at the height of its fame was said to employ 400 to 500 people. The mill owner lived in a large house by the side of the mill and many mill hands lived in small cottages, which together formed a thriving local industrial enclave.

But the mill became a victim of either changing fashion or cheap imports and closed in 1881. The mill and the residences were sold and soon the mill was converted into Watford's biggest and most progressive laundry. There were two other silk mills operating in the town, both powered by horses; one in Red Lion Yard and the other at North End House by the Pond. Small local industries such as tanning and candle making declined early in the 19th century. Concurrently, a saw mill on the bank of the Colne in Lower High Street and a small iron foundry prospered. Straw plaiting, a cottage industry, also declined. So bad was the unemployment situation that between 1800 and 1818 Watford's population diminished for the first time from 3,500 to 2,500.

The arrival of the railway reversed the trend and by 1880 the population had increased to 10,000. Watford rapidly changed into a residential town and commuting became a new experience. Even in those days, 100 trains a day stopped at Watford Junction. The railway helped to change the sense and nature of local industry. The convenience of the railway offered an attractive method of distribution, especially to the London markets. Industries previously alien to an agrarian environment discovered the land was relatively cheap on which to establish new factories. By the '30s, engineering, electrical goods, printing and picture reproduction, magnetos, heavy lorries, boot and floor polish, electric batteries, ice, military clothing, pianos and confectionery were some of the diversified products that were made in Watford. Since the '30s, two piano factories closed, one in Bushey Grove Road and the other at the Rookery. Then there was Fowlers of Sydney Road, whose jam of the day was an open secret to most of West Watford; also Rembrandts, Delectaland, Ever Ready and Norths, to name a few. Change was accelerated by the First and Second World Wars and, in more recent years, the multi-nationals, the M1 and finally the recession.

There is one other name which cannot go unmentioned: the Watford Engineering Works. The company was established in 1827 by George Tidcombe who, with Bryan Donkin, produced an early Fourdrinier-style papermaking machine. Until its closure in the '70s, Watford Engineering Works was one of the oldest in the town. After George Tidcombe's death, Henry J Rogers carried on the same type of business and a new company was formed in 1911. Since that date the company thrived in parallel with the paper milling industry in this country. Not so many years ago their machines, allied to the manufacture of paper, were exported to 35 countries. Their empty factory premises in Lower High Street[50], together with Ever Ready, are a grim reminder of the effects of the recession. The accent now seems to be on service industries, brought about largely by our change of shopping habits and no longer buying British. But history has a way of repeating itself and Watford is resilient enough to weather the change in economic patterns as it has done for the last 1,000 years.

48   Watford Schools in the '30s

In a recent article I wrote, albeit briefly, about the origin of the Watford Grammar Schools at Derby Road. The building, which dates from 1884, was still relatively new and ideally suited for educational purposes. The Education Act of 1870 had changed the face of our educational system, which had previously been supported by local churches on sectarian lands, or by benefactors such as the Earl of Essex who established an independent non-sectarian school for children of the working class in Rickmansworth Road. Schools became a direct charge on the rates and the newly constituted Local School Board became responsible for the education of children. During those early years at the turn of the century the first elementary schools were built. Their names will be familiar: Watford Field, Callowland, Alexandra, Parkgate, Victoria and, just across the Watford/Bushey border, London Road.

Victoria Senior Boys class, 1907.   Alexandra Senior Mixed School, 1903.

The council schools provided an elementary education and the leaving age was then 14. Discipline was strict and the cane was frequently used to instil the need to conform to regulations and behave in a proper manner. Those responsible for locating and planning the new schools were well informed, as events proved. No new school was built in Watford until over 30 years later and that was at Garston where residential expansion forced the educational authorities to think in terms of providing adequate schooling facilities.

The empty buildings in Derby Road were put to good use as a means of bridging the educational gap created by the grammar schools, which offered only a small proportion of free places. Here the Central School was established, ostensibly to increase the number of free places available to elementary school children of ability. Each year children between the ages of 11 and 12 had the opportunity of taking a set examination for a free place at either the grammar schools or the Central School. The most promising entrants were creamed off by the grammar schools and the Central had second choice. Each year, the chosen 40 boys and 40 girls were subjected to yet another exam set by the Central School staff before their final acceptance. The course lasted for five years and, on completion, the leaving age was 15 or 16.

The total number of children being taught at any one time was about 400. The course required that the pupils studied for the standard academic subjects which would allow them to take the matriculation examination, although additional courses such as art, handicrafts and commerce for boys and domestic science and needlework for girls were mandatory. In the third year boys were required to specialise in commercial subjects or maths, science and handicrafts with a view to entering engineering or allied trades.

The most promising pupils were offered an additional two years' training as pupil-teachers. The intensive educational curriculum proved highly successful and, as an example, on one occasion only 6% of the entrants failed their Cambridge School Certificate. Such enthusiasm was not necessarily confined to the classrooms. The sports field of 5½ acres was the scene of much healthy rivalry and keen competition for the many trophies to be won. As we all know, there is far more to school life than study and sports, however important they are in the life of a successful school. The dedicated Central

School staff encouraged the involvement of pupils in activities as diverse as summer camps, the school magazine and drama. The success of any scholastic establishment may be judged by the strength of the relationship which exists after pupils leave school. There was no doubt about the support given by the Old Centralians' Association, which flourished during the years the school was an intrinsic part of Watford's educational system. As far as I know the association predeceased the Old Centralian Players which continued to flourish as one of the town's leading amateur theatrical companies until the 1970s.

London Orphan Asylum, 1905.

Royal Caledonian School, Bushey, 1912.

It would be misleading to omit some of the other schools in Watford and District for the reason that they were not an integral part of the local educational system. In the early years the St Pancras Schools at Leavesden and the London Orphan Asylum near Watford Junction cared for children who qualified as waifs or strays. The Royal Masonic School in The Avenue, Bushey, was an orphanage and in 1926 yet another school was built, no doubt to accommodate the orphaned children of the First World War. Although the buildings remain, these once familiar names and landmarks can no longer be associated with our area. There is one important exception: the Royal Caledonian School, once in complete isolation at the eastern end of Aldenham Road[51]. The school was originally established in 1815 to provide homes and schooling for boys and girls of Scottish parentage whose fathers had been killed in the Napoleonic wars. The London establishment could no longer accommodate all the orphans and in 1903 new premises were built on the borders of Bushey Hall.

The Royal Masonic School, Bushey, 1907. On reverse 'Tom' wrote: "This is a view of our school. Very imposing, is it not. I am going down again Saturday week 15 June 1907 to the Old Boys' reunion and cricket match. We have fine sport there."

Our elementary schools, which had existed for so many years undisturbed by any radical changes within the borough, could no longer cope with a rapidly expanding Watford. The slum clearance of 1933 had precipitated the problem and, in that year, the Borough Council were obliged to consider a massive capital expenditure budget by pre-war standards. The sum of £15,000 was allocated for a new school in Bushey Mill Lane to accommodate the children of Bradshaw estate; £5,000 for an extension to Victoria School; £1,500 for a site in the Eastbury Road area for the children of Oxhey Hall Estate; £800 to the Central School for an extension of their workshop; and, lastly, £1,000 to the Technical School which had its eye on properties in Chater's Yard adjacent to the school annexe and separated by a narrow passage, which were scheduled for demolition.

In those days, the cost of acquiring land and building council schools was mostly met by the local authority. Not surprisingly some of the councillors, shocked by the sudden demands on the municipal finances, made accusations of lack of forward planning. However, the proposal to offer £200 from the Mayor's Special Fund to meet the labour costs of constructing a 12 feet by a ¼ mile-long cinder track at Garston School was well received. The fund was administered by the work committee for any project that would help the local unemployment problem and the track was regarded as such a cause.

49   Christmas Day 1929

As children we were not aware of the existence of the workhouse at Christmas, or any other time for that matter. It is true we were familiar with the occasional visit by tramps who invariably proffered a tin can with a wire handle with the request: "Can you spare some tea?" and with a "God bless you" when their wishes were granted. We had seen disabled ex-servicemen proudly wearing their medals and selling matches, asking: "Can you spare a copper?" We could, but never took the matches. The true meaning of unemployment and deprivation escaped us. Christmas, however, did have a special meaning and this was reaffirmed at Sunday school. We knew there was yet another side to Christmas, when the family would be together again. There would be fun and laughter and endless cups of tea.

Christmas greetings postcard, Aldenham Road, 1911.

We further understood that Father Christmas would pay us a visit and, if we were good, perhaps leave us a present which we badly wanted but did not necessarily deserve. Structurally there were no features which could impede the progress of our nocturnal visitor. He had a full range of chimneys by which to make his inconspicuous entrance.

The first signs of Christmas were not evident until December, when Trewins, Cawdells and Clements each invited a substitute Father Christmas who would generally arrive by horse and carriage. As far as I can recall there was no municipal tree, but there was one outside St Mary's Church. It was illuminated by electric bulbs and beautifully decorated. Artificial snow was applied to the branches and on the ground under the tree. Our own Christmas tree had been purchased at the market and, as soon as we got it home on the bus, it was placed in a galvanised bucket filled with earth. Little tin candle holders complete with coloured candles were clipped to the branches, tinsel and baubles were added for good measure as well as small presents. To keep me out of mischief, I was given strips of coloured paper and a bowl of flour paste. It was with satisfaction if not pride that when the paper chains were pinned to the picture rail and stretched from corner to corner the theory of the weakest link was disproved. Mistletoe was strategically placed above doorways and holly lodged on the oak picture frames. Coloured balloons were added to complete the transformation of the dining room and sitting room into magic grottoes.

As children, we did not appreciate the preparatory work involved. The pudding and the cake had been made months earlier. Only the icing had been added later. The turkey had been plucked and drawn; the grocer had made his last delivery, adding to the order tea and biscuits as gifts demonstrating his appreciation of our custom. Aunts and uncles began to arrive, some just visiting, others staying. The coal bucket was filled to the brim and the curtains were pulled together in a vain attempt to stop the draughts. We were allowed to stay up beyond our usual bedtime. Yawns were stifled and eyelids forced open. Nuts, fruit jellies and chocolates were handed round. Someone sat at the piano and played a selection of well-known tunes and one by one we joined in; 'All by Yourself in the Moonlight' and 'The Road to Mandalay' were the favourites. We happily consumed ginger beer, while our elders daintily sipped port and lemon. The fight against sleep was a losing battle. "Time for bed", a gentle voice whispered.

Prayers said, but too excited to sleep, I snuggled down and put my cold feet on the 'stone' hot water bottle that my thoughtful mother had not overlooked, despite the demands of the festive occasion. I hardly heard the fond "Goodnight, God bless". It was still dark; perhaps I did not sleep after all. There was no sound. Had Father Christmas paid his annual visit? My small hands found the bed rail and groped for the pillow case tied to the end of the wooden bedstead.

The same thoughts occurred to the children in the Peace Memorial Hospital who were not well enough to spend Christmas at home. They too were not disappointed. The ward had been decorated by the ward sister and the nurses with pictures of the ever-popular Mickey Mouse. A Christmas tree in one corner was festooned with coloured lights and decorated with tinsel, glass baubles and parcels. In the centre of the ward miniature elephants were enjoying a tea party sitting on tiny chairs around an equally small table. The children's first intimation of Christmas began with nurses carrying lanterns and singing carols. Christmas stockings had been directly placed beside each of their beds. After breakfast Dr Maycock, dressed as Father Christmas, took down and distributed presents from the tree to the delight of the young patients. Their day began with all the excitement they would have experienced at home.

The poor and needy families of Watford were not forgotten either. In the '30s there were two organisations dedicated to their relief at Christmas. Traditionally, the Mayor's Christmas Fund appealed for donations and then distributed vouchers that could be encashed at various grocers. They were issued to some 700 families whose names had been supplied by the Labour Exchange and local welfare organisations. Paradoxically, Oxhey was not included in the municipal scheme. Oxhey was once called New Bushey and that same but nebulous link still exists today. Established in the '20s, the Bushey & Oxhey Welfare Committee took care of its own impoverished residents. In 1933 as many as 253 hampers were distributed, of which 73 were delivered to Oxhey and 51 to the Rookery.

But what of the unfortunates who walked from town to town seeking work? The workhouse, renamed Shrodells, operated under new administration but its function remained unchanged[52]. In the late '20s accommodation was so inadequate that inmates slept on the floor between the beds. In the early '30s, when the economy was visibly improving, numbers had decreased to 200.

On Christmas Day they were roused at the crack of dawn by the staff singing carols. For breakfast they were given sausages and bacon and presents of fruit and tobacco. In the morning they went to a service at St Barnabas' Chapel in the workhouse. For dinner the inmates enjoyed roast pork, beef and turkey, followed by the proverbial Christmas pudding and custard. Once a year the poignant scene was camouflaged by a thin veneer of gaiety. Their entertainment was more frugal as they listened to the wireless and a number of short speeches by members of the Guardian Committee who no doubt stressed that the food that day had been provided through the generosity of some of Watford's citizens. We should be grateful that social changes wrought during the 20th century have eliminated the need for the workhouse.

50   New Year's Day 1934

The New Year revellers who celebrated the arrival of 1934 too well did not have the benefit of a bank holiday during which to reconsider the advantages of sobriety. New Year's Day was just another day as far as the employer was concerned and little or no allowance was made for over-indulgence or intemperate habits, not to mention lack of sleep. For the majority of Watford's commuters working in London, a good night's sleep was their dearest wish.

The weather pattern on the morning of 1 January 1934, aggravated by industrial and domestic coal fires, gave notice if not warning of what was to happen. By mid-afternoon fog was widespread and thickening; by late afternoon in Watford visibility was down to five yards. The Automobile Association's patrolmen on their motor cycle combinations were instructed to take the usual precautions and they headed for designated junctions and crossroads which were hazardous in normal conditions. There, flares were ignited as a warning and guide to road users. Later that evening visibility was declared to be nil in the usual notorious areas. The truism "I couldn't see my hand in front of me" was fact. The sulphurous fog was a lethal green and yellow mixture; its acidity attacking the sinus, throat and lungs. Londoners had a name for it – a pea-souper – and that was no exaggeration.

The newly-constituted London Transport had its first initiation in trying to keep the bus service operational, if not on schedule. All available inspectors were deployed at key points where telephone communication could be maintained with base and they could report from time to time on the density of the fog. Between times they advised drivers where they were! In the best tradition, the service was maintained – although over an hour late. Long distance coaches suffered delays of four to five hours and the Green Line's Watford to Golders Green service was eventually withdrawn.

The LMS railway fared even worse. At 6pm two electric trains collided in the fog at Camden Town junction, one running into the back of the other. The ramifications of that accident upset the whole system. The electric train services were suspended for the night and only one line remained clear for steam trains to leave or arrive at Euston. There were many anxious wives waiting at home, wondering what had happened to their husbands, sons and daughters. When the weary travellers finally arrived back at the Junction, they faced further delays finding their way home. The weather conditions that day were exceptional. In normal circumstances Watford enjoyed the fastest suburban railway service in the world. The claim was well founded and, as far as I know, never challenged. Some credit must be accorded to Robert Stephenson who originally created the railroad for the London and Birmingham Railway. The track maintenance gangs also contributed but the record was ostensibly made possible by Stanier's new tank locomotives, with which the Watford sheds were now equipped.

All the many steam trains leaving Watford Junction were fast, frequent and reliable, but there was just one commuter train, the 8.25 which, for some reason, earned the passengers' affection and became known as the 'Watford Flyer'. Having earned that reputation, the engine crews were conscious of the responsibility to uphold the fame of their train six days a week. You will recall that on Saturday mornings everyone went to work.

The fully-laden 'Flyer' was boarded promptly by the passengers who were secretly as proud of the train as any of the LMS employees. The carriage doors were closed and checked in seconds. The guard waved his flag and blew his whistle. The driver needed no second bidding before it was on its way, hardly visible in a mixture of steam and smoke which smothered the station. It roared through Bushey, accelerating hard and by the time it reached Harrow the speed was 70 mph. For the rest of the journey, as far as South Hampstead at least, the speed was maintained – if not bettered. Beyond this point, permanent speed restrictions applied. Only the joint expertise of driver and fireman made such remarkable times possible, which were only a little short of their electric counterparts a half-century later.

London & North Western Express overtaking a slow train, Oxhey Road bridge in distance. Early 1900s.

In normal circumstances if the going was not sufficiently exciting, the return journey certainly was. When the humble 5.53 pulled out of Euston on the slow line, the engine attached to the Merseyside Express was already breathing fire and smoke like an impatient dragon. It was timed to leave at 5.55pm. Its crew had one objective and that was to catch up and pass the local train with its two minute start. By the same token, the crew of the tank engine were equally determined they would not, at least not before they reached Wembley, their first stop. The co-operative passengers alighted with all possible haste and the train accelerated as fast as the available head of steam would permit. A little beyond Wembley, the Merseyside Express would pass the steaming tank engine with a victorious blast on its whistle. Then the race resumed as the trains raced neck-and-neck to reach Harrow first. It is little wonder that young train spotters littered the boundary fences and walls to witness the daily duel. The gallant local train generally overtook the express between Harrow and Bushey with a blast on its whistle, before losing speed on its approach to Watford Junction.

That is how it should have been on New Year's Day 1934. Hours later the 5.53 finally arrived. The weary passengers alighted, thankful that their nightmare journey had come to an end. The station forecourt was deserted; the street lamps offered little light in the swirling vapour. Some valiantly, if not optimistically, waited for buses; others started to walk and almost instantly disappeared into the fog. Even the puffing of the locomotive hardly disturbed the silence. The occasional policeman in cloak and helmet passed by with a "Goodnight" or "It's a real pea-souper tonight". Strange footsteps were a welcome sound and not to be feared that night. An occasional vehicle would pass by in the opposite direction at walking pace, some with a guide walking in front and a number of cars tagging along in its wake. The front door was a welcome sight, as was a coal fire, a hot drink, then a meal that had been kept in the oven for three or four hours. Just 24 hours ago the party was getting underway. "Another two hours", someone had said "and it'll be 1934". It seemed like an eternity. We had grasped hands at the magic hour and sang 'Auld Lang Syne', wondering what 1934 had in store for us.

51   Watford's Buses of the '30s

On 1 January 1934 the last train trundled between Watford Metropolitan Station and Rickmansworth. Since the '20s a shuttle service operated to give local passengers direct access to the London North Eastern Railway or a quick, if not convenient means of travelling to Rickmansworth. It operated in direct competition with the LMS line from Watford Junction via the High Street station and was never a popular route. By 1933 the train carried an average of five passengers per journey and, inevitably, the service was discontinued. The line connecting Watford and Rickmansworth was a ½ mile in length and ran along the north side of the canal at Croxley Moor. The embankment is still visible above the canal towpath.

By this time Watford's many independent bus companies had disappeared with the arrival of the all-embracing London Transport. One of its many tasks was to re-organise the bus routes to take into account a rapidly expanding community. The old private bus services were not co-ordinated in any way and remained independent in operation and attitude. In acquiring all the old routes, it was necessary to restructure the whole Watford operation. On 31 January 1934, with the new plans completed, Watford's revised public transport system was introduced to an unsuspecting travelling public. The immediate effect of the numerous route changes was most apparent in the central area. Fourteen services would use the High Street, nine Leavesden Road, seven St Albans Road and eight Clarendon Road, as a means of reaching Watford Junction. Only a small number of routes were left unchanged and these included London's 142 and 158, and the 301 and 302 service to Aylesbury from Watford and Watford Heath respectively.

The circular route that was once operated by Lewis buses between St Mary's Church and the Metropolitan station was abandoned, no doubt in empathy with the withdrawal of the Watford – Rickmansworth shuttle service mentioned above. The 395 was also withdrawn. The former was the old Watford West – Abbots Langley service which was routed via Hagden Lane and Station Approach to the station. The latter was the old 'Elite' service which had plied between Bushey Mill Lane and Cassio Bridge. Now it would terminate at the station by turning off Rickmansworth Road at Station Approach instead of proceeding on to Cassio Bridge. The other end of the route was extended over the railway crossing of the Watford – St Albans railway to the junction of Radlett Road. This extension was intended to accommodate the new residents of the ever-expanding Bradshaw development.

Other services that had traditionally terminated at Watford Junction were extended to Gammons Lane. These included the 306 to Enfield, the 311 to Boreham Wood, the 312 to Little Bushey, the 336 to Berkhamsted via Rickmansworth and Chesham and, lastly, the 335 to Windsor, the old route worked by the Lewis buses. Four services were extended to Leavesden, including the former Biggerstaff route between the Market Place and Sarratt. Arriving in Watford, the route was Rickmansworth Road, the High Street to Clarendon Road, then Gammons Lane and across the by-pass to Leavesden.

In those days there were no bus shelters and for a very good reason. Buses were invariably so frequent that a shelter was not really necessary. The fact that shelters are now provided surely indicates the present-day service is quite inadequate! One service operating between Abbots Langley and Watford was every 10 minutes at busy periods, otherwise every 20 minutes. That was one of the poorest services of them all. The service between Garston and Watford was every five minutes and there was no bus garage at Garston in those days. Do you remember the time buses came down Harwoods Road and then turned into Rickmansworth Road? London Transport considered the turning too dangerous and all Rickmansworth buses were directed along Whippendell Road following the old Lewis route.

No buses served the newly-built Brookdene Avenue and Eastbury Road areas until 1934, when the new 346 route operated between Leggatt's Rise and Hamper Mill via the Harebreaks, Bushey Arches and Eastbury Road offering a 15-minute service.

The fare structure had remained the same for many years and, even after London Transport's takeover, bus fares generally remained unchanged. However, much capital was made out of the few reductions which were well publicised. The fare from Ganders Ash to the Market Place was reduced from 4d to 3d; from Clarendon Road to the by-pass the reduction was 1d, making the new fare 2d; and to Sarratt a single fare was reduced from 8d to 7d and on a return from 1s to 11d. Critics were quick to point out that the fare from Rudolph Road to Bushey Station was doubled because of a change in fare stages, while a quarterly season ticket to London was increased by £2 1s 6d to £6 9s 0d. Fares were, of course, based on the numbers of passengers utilising public transport facilities but in those days few people owned cars and almost everyone travelled by bus in terms of local journeys. The frequency of the service made travelling a pleasure, in contrast to today's frustrations of waiting for a bus that may never come. At points such as Watford Junction or Bushey Station where many routes converged, the service was almost too good to be true. Few people ran for a bus. "There'll be another one along in a minute" was the favourite expression and, of course, there was.

Looking back nearly 50 years, I cannot be without nostalgia for the public transport system which we were inclined to take for granted. They were the days of service from which the so-called service industries today could learn so much: politeness, efficiency, punctuality, care, attention and, above all, a smile. The attribute we miss most of all is the smile, and there was precious little to smile about in those days of depression.

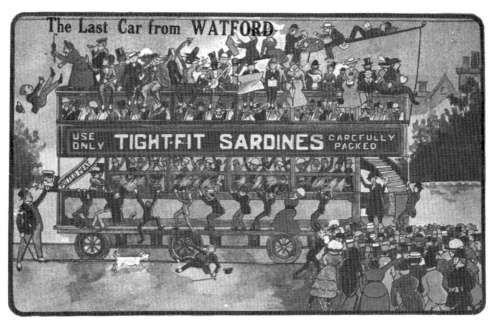

Cartoon postcard, 1918.

52   Carnival Time

Apart from the wireless and the new all-electric radiograms introduced by HMV at 25 guineas, there was no electronic gadgetry to keep children indoors at any time of the year. Families involved themselves in a variety of activities in the '30s which demanded both their time and attention outside the home.

A sign that winter was all but over came with the official announcement by the Watford and District Peace Memorial Saturday Fund of the forthcoming Whitsun carnival programme. Although our present carnival raises money for old people's welfare, in those days it was organised by and for the Peace Memorial Hospital[52]. Since its opening, 23,000 patients had received medical care and the annual maintenance costs in 1934 were £15,000. Watford's residents were proud of the hospital, for which they had personally contributed. Public support for the carnival was a foregone conclusion.

Whitsun Carnival procession in Market Place, 1910.

You may remember that fundraising activities continued throughout the week and not just Saturday and Monday. Let me remind you of the ambitious programme arranged for the period 13 to 21 May 1934. Officially it was the 10th carnival, but in the early days there was no Carnival Queen. In 1932, Watford had introduced the first competition and the honour of becoming the first Carnival Queen went to Miss Joyce Rolls. Two years later, Miss Joyce Baldwin of Victoria Road was chosen and her Maids of Honour were Miss B Mead of Mill Lane, Kings Langley and Miss Yvonne Oake of Brookdene Avenue, with two supporting pages: Masters Kenneth Bray of Harebreaks and Alan Soper of the High Street.

Celebrations began on the Sunday in brilliant sunshine with an open-air interdenominational church service at the bandstand in Cassiobury Park. A procession formed at the Park Gates headed by the Mayor and Mayoress, Councillor Charles and Mrs Griffin, and members of the corporation together with representatives of the local churches and members of the Watford British Legion including the Women's Section. They all marched to the music of the South West Hertfordshire Boy Scouts' Band from the Park Gates to the bandstand. The bandstand enclosure with its hard green wooden seats was already full. The service, which started at 3pm, was conducted by the Vicar of Watford, the Rev H Earnshaw Smith, assisted by the Rev G H Ruffell Laslett, Pastor G Walker, the Rev F J Gould, the Rev E D P Kelsey and Viscount Knutsford. The local Salvation Army band accompanied the service in their inimitable manner and the congregation responded in an equally hearty voice.

Two events commenced on the Monday and lasted throughout the week. One was called the Motorists' and Sportsmen's Appeal, which was an ingenious method of raising money. The object of the exercise was to sell combined draw tickets and 'immunity' badges. You may well ask immunity from what? They were stickers that could be attached to car windscreens and the windows of shops and private houses. Their display promised immunity from enthusiastic carnival collectors. Mr F H Gurney of Beechen Grove accepted responsibility for 'painting the town red'. The lucky badge holder won a new Ford 8 worth £120.

The second event was equally original and caused a great deal of fun, while appealing to the competitive spirit of young people. You may remember the Hercules bicycles which sold for less than £5. The firm also produced home training machines and they were made available to the public at a number of cycle dealers including Norwood of Whippendell Road, Emery in the High Street, and Tissier and Bishop of Vicarage Road. Here the early heats for sustained speed were held. The quarter, semi-finals and finals of the contest were judged by Mr W Bailey, son of ex-world champion Bill Bailey, at the Plaza cinema. The winner of the Watford and District Hercules Cycling Championship was presented with a cup by the Mayor and the runners-up received medals the following Saturday on the stage of the cinema.

On the Monday a Grand Swimming Gala was arranged at the corporation baths by the Watford Swimming Club, with the assistance of the Sun Engraving Swimming Club. Displays of diving and swimming in both light and serious vein warmed up an enthusiastic audience to a local derby water polo match and team races – Watford versus Luton! I have to tell you that Watford won at water polo, but lost the team races. On Wednesday evening in the grounds of The Elms, the Christ Church Girls' Gymnasium Club gave a sparkling display lasting about half-an-hour, followed by a whist drive and dancing to the music of one of Watford's oldest and best-known bands, the Blue Rhythm Boys. The cost for the evening's entertainment was a modest 1s 6d. On Thursday a well-known local sportsman, Lt Col R de Sarigny, arranged a boxing tournament at the Crown Hall, venue of the Watford Sports Club. As a special attraction, Don McCorkindale, contender for the British title, and Jack Grant made an appearance. The cost of entrance ranged from 1s 6d to 5s.

The hard-working organisers wisely made no special arrangements for Friday, although the semi-final cycling competition took place that night at the cinema. Cassiobury Park, the now traditional venue of the celebrations, was officially opened by the Mayor and Mayoress. Tickets were 6d for adults and 3d for children. No special events were planned, except the fun fair with a steam tractor generating electricity and steam-driven roundabouts with pipe organ music. To the delight of the youngsters, a firework display concluded a highly successful day.

The big day was Whit Monday, which was fine and dry. Thousands lined the route of the carnival procession which started from Rickmansworth Road, over the Cross Roads to St Albans Road, Station Road, Woodford Road, Queens Road and into the High Street, then to Market Street, Cassio Road, Whippendell Road and Harwoods Road and back into Rickmansworth Road. The spectators enjoyed the colourful parade of children and adults in fancy dress, the large banner carried by members of the Chamber of Trade with the simple message 'Shop in Watford', the decorated cycles, motor cycles and cars and, lastly, horse-drawn vehicles and motor vehicles. The formula has changed little over the years, although the number of entries is now on the decline.

Equestrian group at Caldecote Towers, Bushey Heath, formerly Rosary Priory, now Immanuel College, early 1900s*

In the afternoon, the customary Mounted Gymkhana arranged by Capt Younghusband of Stanmore Riding School thrilled children and parents alike with open jumps, musical chairs, trotting races and competitions which proves, at least, that some things never change. That is certainly not true of the Quaint Dog Show. To end the evening a children's play was presented, followed by a cabaret, dancing and fireworks. In detail there have been many changes, but the carnival and the procession are a legacy from the past and one of the few remaining links with the '20s and '30s[53].

53   Bushey House

The 'White House', as it is so often called, still dominates Bushey village. In the '30s it was better known as the family seat of the Bethells, a respected family whose presence in Bushey gave the village the status it so richly deserved. The estate was vast, stretching from the High Street in a westerly direction as far as the eye could see with oaks and elms obscuring the true horizon. The gardens surrounding the house were immaculate and the outbuildings, including the stables, were neat and tidy. Here Lord and Lady Bethell lived for many years, witnessing the dissolution of many local farms and comparable estates as suburban development made inroads into traditional farming areas. Bushey was an artists' colony and Ivy House had only recently opened as a private school. In 1934 it was still very much a village community, with the Parish Church and the mature elm almost overhanging the pond. There was little to disturb the peace, except the 142 and 158 buses which trundled through the High Street.

On Saturday 16 June 1934 all that changed, at least for one day, when over 6,000 people arrived in the village and made their way to Bushey House. The occasion was a very special one, as Lord and Lady Bethell had opened their house and gardens for the National Society for the Prevention of Cruelty to Children, which was celebrating its Golden Jubilee. Many local people had spent months planning the biggest fête ever held in Bushey. The Chairman of the Fête Committee was Mrs Eleanor Wilson and the Vice-Chairman was Mrs Amy Wheelwright. The Executive Committee included many local celebrities, such as Armand Blackley, Lady Caulcutt and Arthur Kingham. Supporting them was a large band of voluntary workers who came from Bushey and beyond.

Her Royal Highness Princess Alice, Countess of Athlone, accepted the invitation to open the fête. She arrived by car from Kensington Palace and was received at Bushey House by Lord and Lady Bethell, members of the NSPCC and fête officials. To the relief of all present, the weather was on its best behaviour. Princess Alice was conducted through a guard of honour made up entirely of Girl

Young Jennifer Bethell with her grandfather, Lord Bethell, and Princess Alice at NSPCC Golden Jubilee, Bushey House, 1934. Photo courtesy of the Hon Mrs Jennifer Brown (née Bethell).

Guides, representing every group in Watford and Bushey, to a platform where Lord Knutsford and Lord Ullswater, President of the Society, greeted her. Lord Knutsford, in good form, welcomed the Princess. "Surrounded as you are by black coats" he jested, "I can assure you we are more peaceful than black shirts". Little did he realise in those innocent days that his words would be so prophetic.

Princess Alice was cheered by the thousands of spectators when she rose to respond to the speech of welcome. "I am sure everyone present is an enthusiastic believer of the NSPCC, of which I have been a member for many years", she said. The applause left her in no doubt that the audience was in total empathy with her speech. In reply Sir Dennis Herbert thanked the Princess for her gracious presence and in a lighter vein warned everyone to beware of a large gang of pick-pockets headed by none other than Lord Knutsford. The opening ceremony successfully completed, the ever-increasing crowds spread themselves over the estate. Beyond the main lawn behind the house and protected by a number of trees, temporary signposts pointed to the 'shopping centre' where a number of stalls offered useful and luxury items, a good choice of homemade jams and chutneys and the season's vegetables, as well as cakes of all sizes. Other stalls were scattered around the lawn, where a pretty girl in crinolines and a hooped skirt sold flowers from a large straw basket.

Parents were dragged by permanently hungry and thirsty children to the ice cream and lemonade stalls, the ingredients of which were as genuine as the names implied. The ice cream was made of cream and the drink was made of lemons. No synthetic additives were needed to enhance their appearance and flavour. Duly refilled and refreshed at their parents' expense, the child still craved excitement. He was not disappointed: clock golf, crazy golf, swings, roundabout, coconut shy, hoop-la, darts, smashing crockery, hunting for treasure, all games that were once the prerogative of the English garden fête. For the sport enthusiasts, a full-blooded tennis tournament was being waged on the court between local tennis club members from Northwood to Edgware. Meanwhile teas were served by a team of voluntary waitresses under the guidance of Mrs Poro, who also supervised suppers served in the late evening by another band of voluntary helpers.

Later in the day the ballroom was opened for the presentation of entertainment by local children. St Hilda's School presented a play with the unlikely title 'Six Who Pass While the Lentils Boil' and St Andrew's School presented A A Milne's play 'The Princess and the Woodcutter', based on Tennyson's immortal line "Kind hearts are more than coronets". The Bushey branch of the League of Pity under the direction of Mrs E Vaughan Williams offered a short two-act comedy called 'Wanted, A Governess', which was well received and produced much laughter. Then the Studio School of Dancing of Nascot Road directed by Miss Winifred Sharp and Miss Marie Breukelman presented a captivating display of dancing by their gifted and well-rehearsed pupils. This was followed by another display by pupils of Miss Elsie Christmas of the West Hertfordshire School of Dancing of Clarendon Road. An enraptured audience showed their appreciation with thunderous applause.

The day was hot and sunny and the evening was almost welcome, giving relief to the 200 volunteers and the 6,000 visitors. In the late evening another concert was arranged with adults in mind. The formula was very much in the nature of the old 'musical evening'. There were songs by soprano Hilda Freestone and baritone Donovan Cross, and violin selections played by Alice Harford, accompanied on piano by Winifred Clotworthy. The star attraction was a name you will surely remember, if only because of his frequent BBC broadcasts: Ronald Gourlay, the blind pianist who not only played with his back to the keyboard, but also played selections of tunes requested by the audience.

The event was a complete success. Bushey village had not experienced a day like it and the fête was the subject of conversation for many months to follow. Perhaps you were there on that auspicious day. I certainly was. In retrospect, we were lucky that such events, made possible by our local philanthropic aristocracy, have enriched our lives and left on our minds an indelible impression of a past era. Lord Bethell died in 1945.

54   The New Educational Era

In my more recent articles I have mentioned, perhaps even laboured the point, that the many early '30s housing estate developments determined, irrevocably, the residential and social character of Watford. The non-indigenous population that settled in the fringe areas brought their children with them and the planning of new schools became an inextricable part of the town's expansion problems.

The first school to be completed as part of the long-term plan to accommodate children between the ages of 11 and 14 was Leggatt's Way School for boys and girls. In those days it was designated as a senior school. The choice of the site was determined by the availability of land on which to build. A suitable plot was located at the highest point in the borough, but it was found to be too small – until the authorities acquired a number of allotments to increase the area of the land. Building started in 1933. The front elevation and the materials used were, in every sense, traditional but there any similarity with the old elementary ended. In fact Leggatt's Way School, in both structural and educational terms, would reflect the wind of change blowing through the enlightened Board of Education.

The boys and girls were to be segregated and some parents, I am sure, would argue that there was merit in retaining such a precept. The building was designed around an open courtyard, across which two main halls would cross the open space in the centre. This arrangement, it was argued, would allow additional light into the classrooms and provide good air circulation. The classrooms would not open directly into the halls and, as a consequence, there would be no distractions. Corridors around three sides would provide the necessary connections with other classrooms and the main halls. On the north side were special classrooms, to which I will make reference later. In the open quadrangles formed by the division of the two halls it was intended that children were to receive their physical training and, weather permitting, open air tuition. The school could be accessed by three entrances. The main entrance was from Leggatt's Way, with subsidiary entrances from the by-pass and Harebreaks Recreational Ground.

The customary use of a classroom for such activities as handicrafts and art was abandoned. Special rooms were set aside for both subjects and classes would report to special teachers for tuition. The principle, for a council school, was revolutionary in its day. The handicraft section was provided with chairs and tables, and the children were to be taught the art of bookbinding and lino cutting. It was intended that one day the school, as well as pupils' homes, would be decorated with the pictures they produced. Since Watford was a 'print town', the introduction of basic techniques suggested a possible future in print which was then very much a growth industry.

Other rooms were devoted to art, geography and science. The science room was equipped with mobile benches and flexible gas connections with water troughs on one side and balances on the other. The concept of the new educational system was without parallel, but that was not all. Leggatt's Way was to become a 'Hadow' school. The new educational system was relatively unknown in the south so Leggatt's Way was unique, inasmuch as it was yet another first for Watford. The principal of 'Hadow' seems to have been a negation of the concept that the child is moulded to the prescribed cast of the school curriculum. Instead, education would evolve around the child. The ultimate goal of 'Hadow' was to prepare him or her to a given standard of education, but also to nurture existing talent and discover latent abilities! So you see it was a revolutionary principle in its day.

Although children were admitted to the school at the beginning of the new term, the official opening was not arranged until Saturday 30 September 1934. Mr W J Tovey was appointed headmaster. He was no stranger to Watford as he had been headmaster of Callowland School for some years. On the other hand the new headmistress, Miss Clifford, was not recruited locally and came from Clacton to take up the new appointment. She controlled a staff of 11 assistants, while Mr Tovey was allocated only 10. However, headmaster and headmistress were in accord on many matters, including one of the most important factors concerning the inception of the joint schools: the school colours and the names of the school 'houses'. The children had settled into their new and relatively luxurious surroundings before the official day of opening. Sir Henry Richard, ex-senior chief inspector of the Board of Education, performed the opening ceremony. Sir Dennis and Lady Herbert; the Mayor, Councillor C E Griffin; the Mayoress, Mrs Lovell; Alderman W Graveson, Chairman of the Hertfordshire Education Committee; and members of Hertfordshire County Council and Watford Borough Council were present. The hall was filled to capacity. The ceremony began with a short service jointly conducted by the Rev E D P Kelsey, Vicar of Christ Church, and the Rev W G Baldwin of North Watford Methodist Church. Alderman Graveson presided and congratulated the school for being the best equipped senior school in the county. He reminded his receptive audience that at that time Watford was responsible for educating 6,750 school children, of which half were resident in the south and central areas, while the other half lived in North Watford. After time-consuming speeches, parents were given the opportunity of inspecting the school and speaking to the headmaster and headmistress, as well as supporting staff.

The macadam-surfaced playgrounds were immaculate, but the playing fields were so rough as to require ploughing before hockey and football pitches could be laid down. The cost of the school was £33,000, furnishings £1,000 and the site was another £1,000. The costs sound so modest by current standards as to be suspect.

Only one incident marred the otherwise cordial relationship with the local school Management Committee. Miss Clifford and Mr Tovey had approached the committee for a piano. A reasonable request, you may think, when Elliott's were selling pianos from £35. But their request was rejected on the grounds that the committee's position would become intolerable if all the schools made a similar request. The heads jointly replied that they regretted the decision, since music was an integral part of the school curriculum. However, I am pleased to tell you that the story ends on a happy note as grants of £20 were made towards the pianos. But another request for a typewriter was flatly refused! Economy in education in those far-off days reflects the cutbacks being applied in these more austere times (1983).

55   Women's Lib in 1934

I have been told that in 1931 only 25% of the houses in this country were supplied with electricity. If you doubt this revelation, may I remind you that electricity was not brought to Sarratt until 1932. Watford's residents were more fortunate, although many householders still depended on gas for their lighting until the First World War and some did not convert to electricity until the late '40s.

Tenants of terraced and cottage properties with gas lighting downstairs generally depended on oil lamps or candles with which to go to bed. Candles were cheap enough and paraffin was about 9d a gallon. Semi-detached houses on the new estates were, of course, supplied with gas and electricity; gas for cooking and electricity for fires and lighting. The range of electrical appliances available at that time included vacuum cleaners, cookers, fires and, for the well-defined middle class, imported refrigerators and washing machines. All-electric radios and radiograms were making an appearance, but many listeners remained faithful to their primitive wireless sets powered by batteries and accumulators.

The housewife had been brought up with a kitchen range or cast-iron gas cooker, a coal-fired washing boiler and the proverbial flat iron. She was less than familiar with the mysteries of electricity and the complexity of appliances. The man of the house, who may well have built his own wireless, knew the rudiments of wiring circuits and fuse boxes. In those days only two wires were involved: one black, the other red. There was no earth wire to worry about. Paradoxically he would, in all probability, engage the services of a contractor to erect his wireless aerial to the recommended height of 30 feet and not more than 100 feet in length, which was the mandatory limit set by the Postmaster General. The installation usually included a copper wire connecting the set to a long copper tube buried outside the window, which required frequent watering!

The introduction into the home of electrical appliances generally bemused the housewife and because of the lethal nature of electricity a group of women, on a rational level, decided to combat the unnecessary risk to which women in the home were exposed. In 1925 the Electrical Association for Women was founded by a small group of enlightened women who could foresee revolutionary developments once electricity was made available to domestic users. They felt the housewife should be instructed as to the best use of this new source of power. In the years between 1925 and 1933, 40 branches had been formed in the provinces and in 1934 plans were made to set up a Watford and district branch. Its activities would include lectures and demonstrations to illustrate the many uses of electricity in the home and the factory. Additionally, the officers and committee members would be drawn from those women already involved in the public life of the town and sufficiently responsible to impart their newly acquired knowledge as invited speakers at the many women's organisations throughout Watford.

In July 1934 an inaugural meeting was held in the old council chamber at which Lady Herbert accepted the residency. The Mayor, Councillor G E Griffin, presided with the support of Councillor Mrs Armitage and Miss Margaret Partridge representing the association. The committee, conveniently pre-arranged, was formally appointed. Three lady councillors were included: Mrs Armitage, Mrs Ward and Mrs Bridger. Other committee members included Mrs Manuel, Mrs Gifford, Mrs Mosley and Mrs Ginger.

Miss Partridge spoke of the aims of the association, its scope and aspirations to an already converted audience, after which Councillor Mrs Armitage proposed the formation of a Watford and district branch. Councillor Mrs Ward seconded the motion which was duly carried and the town found itself with an amazon ensemble ready to do battle. In fact, the first sign of militancy showed itself sooner than anyone expected.

An onlooker, Mrs Jones, rose from her seat and asked whether it was within the scope of the new committee to negotiate a reduction in tariff charges under the 'Norwich' system as well as the cost of

ELECTRIC COOKER

Complete with a **4 PINT ELECTRIC KETTLE** CAN BE HIRED FOR

PER **7'6** QTR.

INCLUDING FREE MAINTENANCE

Particulars sent on application.

Electric cooker advertisement, 1930s.

electrical appliances. This question caused a great deal of mirth at the time, but I cannot think why. Wisely, Miss Partridge chose to reply. She confirmed that the association had indeed entered into discussions with other electrical authorities but, as far as Watford was concerned, she thought there was no need because of the favourable tariff enjoyed by the town's consumers. The Mayor suggested that the matter could be referred to the Electricity Committee, but the Watford tariffs "were practically as low as any in the country". However, he did agree that the charges for appliances were too high.

Their first public meeting was held at Watford Central Library the following November with the Mayoress, Councillor Mrs Bridger, presiding. Addressing a large audience, she announced she was a member of the Electricity Committee and could appreciate the difficulty experienced by women without technical knowledge dealing with electrical matters. "It is our job as women", she continued "to get into the houses of ordinary people. It would be so useful (for them) to know how to mend a fuse so they would not find themselves without electricity". Soon, she explained, there would be a new showroom with a small theatre where demonstrations would take place and appliances would be on display. The women's liberation movement in Watford started a lot earlier than some young people suppose and the arrival of the Electrical Association for Women cannot be ignored as one of the first incursions into an otherwise male-oriented subject.

Do you remember the old 'Norwich' tariff system? If a house was rated over £37 per annum, the consumer was charged 12½% of the rateable value plus the cost of electricity at ¼d a unit during the summer and 3s 8d during the winter. Unfortunately many houses in North Watford were rated under £37 and could not enjoy the financial benefits of the 'Norwich' tariff. One critic pointed out that the minimum charge under the system was £4 12s 6d, which represented 20% of the rateable value of his house. He certainly had a case.

In January 1935 the town mourned the death of one of its favourite personalities, the Hon Arthur Holland-Hibbert, Lord Knutsford of Munden. He died while speaking at a luncheon following Labrador retriever trials at Idsworth Park in Horndean, Hampshire, the residence of Lorna, Countess Howe. A few years earlier he had suffered a severe heart attack from which he never fully recovered, but it was in character that he remained fully active until the end.

Munden Park, Watford.

Coles Watford

Munden Park, 1905.

He was born on 19 March 1855 and was a twin brother of the second Lord Knutsford and son of the first Viscount Knutsford and Elizabeth, youngest daughter of Nathaniel Hibbert and Emily, who was the daughter of the renowned Rev Sidney Smith, Canon of St Pauls. In 1874 he succeeded to the Munden estate and took the surname of Hibbert. He married the eldest daughter of Sir Wilfred Lawson, second baronet of Brayton in 1884.

Lord Knutsford's early life was colourful and adventurous to say the least, but, as he admitted in later life, total success did not always follow in his footsteps. He spent seven years in the Navy and served in the last of the old wooden ships commissioned by the Naval authorities, two years at Trinity Hall and a similar period at Cirencester Agricultural College. There is little doubt that these impressionable years, if nothing else, moulded the character that was to become so beloved by his contemporaries. He was proud of his ancestry and claimed his family had resided at Munden since 1707.

In 1880 he was appointed director of the old London and North Western Railway and later, following its amalgamation, was appointed director of the London Midland and Scottish Railway. He retired from the board in 1923. During those years he became one of Hertfordshire's leading public figures. In 1889 he was a founder member of Hertfordshire County Council and one of its most respected aldermen. Such was his reputation that in 1890 he was appointed High Sheriff. He had been appointed to the Commission of Peace in 1879 and became one of the senior magistrates in the county. He sat on the Watford bench.

Between 1924 and 1933 he was a keen member of the Avon Vale Foxhounds, although his participation in the hunting scene diminished with the passing years. Despite the fact that he was involved in the public scene at county level, he never deserted Watford. In his life he had many passions, acquired in his youth and practised in maturity. Temperance was one of them and, in common with so many other local personalities, he always associated himself with those who upheld the need for temperance in an increasingly alcoholic society. Given even the smallest opportunity, he expressed his condemnation of alcohol as an evil within society. In fact he was a born after-dinner speaker – the best, it was said, in the county. He had an infectious sense of humour not always associated with the role of a country squire. His observations were meticulous, his criticisms forceful and to the point, especially with regard to any apparent wastage of public funds. Whatever his chosen subject, he could still have his audiences rolling with laughter and, with that sort of reputation, he was in constant demand. The stories and anecdotes he told were endless, moving from pathos to puns with the ease of a professional entertainer.

His unswerving passion in Watford was, without doubt, the assistance of the poor and the treatment of the sick. He worked as hard as anyone to establish the Peace Memorial Hospital and, having done so, retained an active interest in its welfare. His last appeal was for the erection of a home for nurses and it was duly completed after his death. He was instrumental in creating a highly successful hospital contributory scheme, presided over the Finance Committee and, with the Earl of Clarendon and Mr E Henry Lloyd (about whom I will be writing), was one of the trustees.

His involvement at the Peace was not necessarily at administrative level. He was a frequent visitor to the wards and seldom missed a Sunday afternoon when he visited the patients, always greeting them with a sympathetic smile and words of encouragement. In 1934, on behalf of the Peace, he appealed on the wireless for funds – with rewarding results. His interests extended into the realms of childbirth and during the last year of his life he became interested in the use of anaesthetics, then in an experimental stage. Not surprisingly, his love of humanity and hatred of cruelty prompted him to work for the NSPCC and, you may recall from my recent article, he was present at the Golden Jubilee fête held at the invitation of Lord and Lady Bethell at Bushey House.

His twin brother Sydney, second Viscount Knutsford, had the same driving force and dedication to the alleviation of suffering. He became chairman of a London hospital and in a short time earned for himself the title 'The Prince of Beggars'.

On 5 November 1933 Lord and Lady Knutsford celebrated their golden wedding. In his 80th year he looked tired and drawn but still he did not heed the warnings. He attended the Beggars Ball held in Watford in deference to his health because it was in aid of his beloved Peace Memorial Hospital. Then he departed for Hampshire, which he no doubt regarded as something of a holiday. There he died making a speech. Those who knew him were shocked at his sudden death, but in their heart of hearts were aware that he died as he would have wished – in action. Such attributes as vitality, energy and enthusiasm never deserted him and his presence as a driving force within the town, and of course beyond, was sadly missed.

Lord Knutsford was succeeded by his elder son, born in 1888, the Hon Thurstan Holland-Hibbert who received his education at Eton and Cambridge. He married Viola, daughter of Mr P M Clutterbuck, and they had two children. Lord Knutsford left a younger son, Wilfred Holland-Hibbert, and a daughter, the Hon Mrs R C Faulconer. But the day of the traditional country squire was drawing to a close. If a finger may be pointed at any one man as a prime example of an enlightened squire, then it must surely point in the direction of Lord Knutsford, yet another man whose influence in Watford is still apparent today.

57   The House That Never Was

If, in the mid-'30s, a stranger had walked along Bushey Mill Lane, he would have noticed two or three houses being conscientiously erected on the corner leading to Southwold Road. He would not have been surprised, since house building was a normal activity in that area of North Watford and houses were springing up everywhere. Just suppose he made a return journey three or four weeks later, he would not have believed his eyes. The new houses had completely disappeared! Local residents were getting used to the phenomena of disappearing houses. There was nothing paranormal about these strange events. As soon as the houses were completed in a frenzy of activity, another gang would arrive and dismantle them brick by brick! Within days, the Herculean task would start all over again. With regular monotony, the houses went up and down for years on end. There was a relatively simple explanation for this strange sequence of events.

The early '30s were a time of depression and unemployment, not unlike the situation we are experiencing today (1983). Watford was affected by the prevailing economic conditions, but not to the extent experienced by the iron, steel and cotton industries and, by the same token, coal. Scotland, Wales, Yorkshire and North East Lancashire, as well as the cotton manufacturing areas, were badly hit.
Hertfordshire adopted the Durham area and a passionate appeal by the High Sheriff raised many thousands of pounds for the relief of distressed families. By the end of 1934, £10,000 had been collected within the county for this purpose. Meanwhile the Ministry of Labour, acquired a site that was once part of Delectaland where it established a Government Training Centre as a practical scheme to aid young men expressly from the distressed areas.

Each prospective trainee was carefully selected by his local Labour Exchange. In many cases the individual was required to have served his full apprenticeship in the building or allied trades, followed by a long period of unemployment. He was given a ticket to Watford with instructions to report to the Centre. At any one time, 400 trainees were receiving instruction. The maximum training period allowed was 26 weeks. If anyone proved unsatisfactory they were sent back home, but the proportion of failures was very small. In essence, the training was a refresher course which included such trades as bricklaying, plastering, wood machining, house painting, carpentry and joinery. In the allied trade section cabinet makers and French polishers were given instruction.

However, the Training Centre was not confined solely to housing. Another emerging industry was the manufacture of motor cars and a department was created to cater for all aspects of the trade, from panel beating to engine repairs. There was yet another industry still in its infancy, which was quickly gathering momentum: neon signs. Here, inexperienced men were taught the fundamentals of glass tube bending. In a few months they were capable of creating individual letters and finally whole words in glass tubing. Perhaps they were the most fortunate ones, as the demands of industry for such tradesmen exceeded supply. Invariably they left the Centre and immediately found work. The Watford Training Centre was unique in providing this highly specialised form of instruction.

In 1935 the centre was administered by Mr R C Douglas, a Scot from Glasgow, with the support of an assistant manager and a chief instructor who came from Watford. The complex nature of the centre dictated that it was run on factory lines with factory discipline. The trainee received 17s a week for his lodgings and 4s pocket money. His mid-day meal was provided free of charge. Having checked in, he was told that the centre had a good reputation nationally and locally and that his behaviour was of paramount importance, not only at the centre but also in the town. He was expected to attend a course of lectures on the theory of his craft, as well as taking a practical course which would be thorough and productive.

Leaving the administration offices he would be shown the workshop, which was a hive of industry. First to catch his attention would have been 'Placingwell Lodge', the front elevation of a house which had been erected by bricklayers and carpenters for instruction purposes. Beyond the house were some 20 men painting and glazing and, in the same area, cabinet making and joinery shops were humming with the noises of various saws, of which few were mechanised. The engineering section was concentrated on the other side of the building. There was a noisy machine shop with humming lathes, squeaking files and screaming drills. In another bay, panel beating was in progress and the metal from which cars were then made could be slowly worked back into shape. Motor car engines in varying degrees of dismantling or rebuilding littered the wooden benches. The instructors' voices were raised to counter the noise that was a permanent feature of the centre.

The new incumbent was no doubt overawed by the activity, noise and general efficiency of the whole operation. For six months he would be back at school, regaining his confidence and practising his craft. At first it seemed strange; away from home in a strange town that was spilling into green fields. The contrast of his own impoverished village or city with relatively prosperous Watford would have come as something of a shock. His lodgings were sparse but comfortable. His 4s pocket money, while frugal, was almost adequate. In the canteen, where he ate his mid-day meal, he could play billiards, darts or table tennis one evening a week. On another night a dance was held where he could bring his new girlfriend.

The six months passed quickly. Some of the trainees elected to return home. Others turned their backs on the mountains of Wales and Scotland or the dales of Yorkshire and found work in the south. Historically it was possibly the last involuntary migration, bringing into Watford many regional accents that were unfamiliar to a largely indigenous but generous population. It is significant that in 1934 the British Legion distributed over £500 in relief to the distressed folk who had been brought to Watford for training. I would not be surprised if some remained in Watford.

The Watford Mfg Co Ltd advertisement, 1915. Delectaland was at the junction of Sandown Road and Bushey Mill Lane.

58   Watford – the Premier Print Town

The crisis that has overtaken Watford's printing industry during the last few months, culminating in the projected closure of Odhams, begs the question why Watford ever became a print town in the first place[54]. I will endeavour to explain how this came about and why the town achieved international status in the print field.

From 1476, when Caxton set up his printing workshop at Westminster Abbey until the beginning of the 19th century, London dominated the printing and publishing scene. Paradoxically, the paper used in London was in all probability made in Hertfordshire, at least from the beginning of the 19th century. A total of 24 mills were built on the banks of the Colne, Gade, Chess and Ver to produce handmade paper. A name synonymous with those far-off days is still familiar to us all: John Dickinson. He founded his business in Watford during the reign of George III and applied the techniques manifested by the Industrial Revolution. By 1809 he had patented a process for the manufacture of machine-made paper. Until then its manufacture had been dominated by the French. He acquired the water-driven mill at Apsley, then Nash Mill and Home Park Mill and, lastly, Croxley Mill. In an age when transport was still in its infancy, the availability of locally-manufactured paper must have attracted the printers.

Printing may be said to have arrived in Watford when, in 1823, John Peacock published the town's first newspaper, the 'Watford Weekly Advertiser'. By the 1850s, other printers chose Watford as their operating base and, by the dawn of the 20th century, hand presses had changed to power presses. The first evidence that Watford was to become a print town occurred in 1903 when David Greenhill was approached by Harvey Dalziel of the Dalziel Foundry with a view to acquiring a four-colour French press to begin a new printing venture. The Derby-based firm of Bemrose & Sons with premises in the town joined the team. A new company was formed with the title Bemrose-Dalziel Ltd and the first multi-coloured printing on a large-scale in Britain was carried out at the old Bemrose works. David Greenhill was appointed manager.

In 1908 Waterlow Brothers and Layton, the security printers, acquired the firm, which was already printing Weldon's fashion journals. At the turn of the century, two other printers – André & Sleigh and Acme Tone Engraving Company – were already well established in Watford and, under the guidance of David Greenhill who founded the Bushey Colour Press for André & Sleigh, the firms took over the colour printing of the Weldon journals. In 1914 the Anglo Engraving Company, André & Sleigh, and Bushey Colour Press merged to become André Sleigh & Partners. After the First World War they acquired Menpes Printing and Engraving Company in Whippendell Road and, after extensive alterations to the building, adopted the new title Sun Engraving Co Ltd.

During the halcyon days of the '30s, the Sun employed more than 2,000 staff and produced over 25 magazines. In one year a total of 380 million copies were printed, consuming the almost unbelievable figure of one million tons of printer ink. The Sun weathered the loss of Odhams' publications after the announcement that Odhams intended to build their own printing works in Watford by attracting new contracts, of which the most outstanding must have been 'Picture Post' in 1938. When 'Picture Post' was a household name, its weekly circulation was 1½ million.

From humble beginnings in 1847, when William Odhams published 'The Guardian' and after a merger with John Bull, Mr W H Parrack investigated the means by which the company could produce 1¼ million copies in their own printing works by the gravure process. Mr J S Elias, later to become Lord Southwood, acquired a prime site in North Watford with convenient road and rail connections and formed a new company in 1935 – Odhams (Watford) Ltd. By 1936 a building of 140,000-square feet designed by Sir Owen Williams and with a Goss machine installed was ready for action. The transfer of 'John Bull' to Watford created more problems than it solved. To fully utilise the machinery already printing 'Film Weekly', a new magazine was devised called 'Woman', which became a success story in its own right. In 1938 the accommodation was doubled and new presses installed.

With the coming of the First World War and the rationing of paper for domestic consumption, the production of Odhams' magazines was curtailed. However, the presses were not idle as they churned out millions of propaganda leaflets and later printed the US Army publication 'Yanks'. However, there was floor space to spare, which Lord Southwood offered to Lord Beaverbrook as Minister of Aircraft Production. During the war years aircraft were repaired and component parts manufactured. After the war, demand once again increased and in 1954 work started on the massive front elevation with its 180-foot spire, the building with which we are so familiar today. Here, many of the Companion Book Club volumes were printed for Odhams Press Ltd, which venture was another of their success stories, until television took command of our leisure hours. In the '60s over 2,700 people were employed and seven million magazines were printed weekly including 'Woman', which claimed the largest circulation in the world. Such was the confidence expressed by management that, even in more recent years, an additional 8½ acres were acquired for expansion.

During the war years, the Sun continued limited production and several ministries used their services. Perhaps it is not generally known that the invasion maps of the First World War were printed there under the strictest secrecy. Unlike Odhams, the available floor space was given over to war-time engineering projects and components of the atom bomb were developed there but, as you will appreciate, little information is forthcoming about this country's contribution to the bomb that halted the war in the Far East.

In the mid-'50s and again in 1960 the works were increased in area by another 185,000 square feet. A Goss press was installed to print 'The Sunday Times' supplement and, in more recent years, an Albert Frankenthal press was added to produce mail order catalogues. In the mid-'60s, in excess of 10,000 people were employed in the paper printing and publishing industries. Nearly 40 firms of printers were listed locally. Printer ink was made by the Sun, Fishburn and Ault & Wiborg. In retrospect, they were the halcyon days when our printing industries were working to full capacity. Perhaps a straw was blowing in the wind, even then, to advise caution in the future. Now we are counting the cost of retrenchment.

The Sun Engraving Co Ltd, Whippendell Road, 1931.

59   Fun and Games at Bricket Wood

If mention of Bricket Wood conjures up childhood memories of steam trains and fairgrounds rather than woods carpeted with wild flowers, you will have been born in the early '20s or before. The chances are that your first introduction to the pleasures of Bricket Wood was on a Sunday school treat. I would go so far as to say it was an experience you could never forget.

We were not well travelled youngsters in those days. No continental package holidays; more likely a quick visit to Southend. The prospect of travelling by steam train from Watford Junction generated excitement and the spirit of adventure because the legend of Bricket Wood had spread far and wide. I will explain why this little village surrounded by farms and dense woodland once became a mecca for children and parents, even before the arrival of the pleasure grounds.

It all happened when the rail link connecting St Albans with Watford was completed in 1858. At that date there were no intermediate stations. In 1861 a new Bricket Wood Station was built primarily to serve the farming community. However, the beautiful countryside suddenly became accessible to railway travellers and the Victorian passion for seeking out-of-the-way places at which to spend the day soon singled out this new venue. The Sunday school leaders and teachers, desperate for somewhere to take their young people, also adopted this little known area. In fact, the honour for discovering Bricket Wood surely goes to Watford's Ragged School, which held its first Sunday school excursion by rail from Watford in 1865.

In 1887 two brothers, Henry and Frederick Gray from North London decided to include the area in their cycle tour. They were impressed and quick to appreciate the potential of Bricket Wood as a desirable rural area favoured by teetotal and innocent pleasure-seeking Victorians. The brothers acquired a cottage on Smug Oak Green and opened a teashop. They were duly rewarded for their imagination and hard work. Soon after they purchased a new house called Woodside where they found space to expand their enterprise. Over the years a roundabout, a miniature railway, swings and a joy wheel provided the necessary thrills for children of all ages. Towering above all the other amusements was a helter-skelter which became a landmark, if not a trade mark, of Gray's Fair.

The fairground reached the peak of its popularity just before the First World War by which time, it has been said, 5,000 teas

" Woodside " Retreat,
BRICKET WOOD.

The most Popular resort North of the Thames for
SCHOOL EXCURSIONS AND SUMMER OUTINGS.

WOODS, COMMON, RIVER, MEADOW.
Trips to St. Albans with its Ancient Abbey and Roman Walls.

Sports Ground. "Woodside," Bricket Wood.

" Woodside " comprises 50 acres of Playing Fields and Woods.
UP-TO-DATE AMUSEMENT PARK.

Large Permanent Tea Pavilions with accommodation for 4,000. Established 1889 by Mr. H Gray, and still under his personal supervision. Nearly two million have visited and enjoyed a happy day here, and it is more popular than ever.

Write for Illustrated Prospectus with Tariff,
Railway Fares, and full particulars.

H. GRAY, *Refreshment Contractor,*
" WOODSIDE," Bricket Wood, near St. Albans.
Phone: Garston, Watford 13.

Advertisement for Woodside, 1930s.

were

served in the tea rooms daily. During the war it closed to the public and became a wartime camp. In 1919 the fair was restored and once more the trains were packed with young visitors, whose memories of the deprivations of war were all too vivid.

My first visit to Bricket Wood, together with my Sunday school contemporaries, bristled with expectation. I was not disappointed. The eye-catching helter-skelter with its wooden slats tapering into the sky, surmounted by a flimsy wooden balcony topped by an equally flimsy circular roof over which was mounted a flagpole, captivated the mind of a small child. Here we could emulate the exploits of Douglas Fairbanks Snr. Not the re-enactment of a fantasy, but the real thing.

Mat in hand, we mounted the entrance stairs leading to the cavernous interior of the wooden cone. Once inside, the security of the outside world vanished. The stout timber frames and cross beams failed to allay the fear. The wooden handrail was grasped with a moist hand; the ascent was frightening. There was no going back, as a continuous stream of children brought up the rear. The wooden steps seemed never-ending. Here and there was a landing, before mounting yet more steps. At a point when the sides of the structure narrowed leaving insufficient room to ascend further, a nervous figure still clutching his mat emerged into blinding sunshine. A hasty look over the balcony speeded the resolve to return to terra firma as quickly as possible.

The descent on a cantilevered shoot that grimly clung to the wooden structure at such a steep angle whirled body and mat in ever-increasing circles at an ever-increasing speed. The horizon was no longer static and seconds seemed like hours. When everything seemed out of control, two strong hands appeared as if by magic and lifted me into an upright position, although my legs did not immediately function in the traditional manner.

The model railway with its miniature steam engine and tiny passenger wagons with hard wooden seats, the steam roundabout with its gleaming brass and white horses and the rows of swing-boats, almost defying gravity as the occupants pulled at the ropes, were no subsititute for the helter-skelter. In retrospect, Woodside's fame was largely centred on this tower and is the one thing when the memory fails that is best remembered.

Woodside was the original but not the only permanent fairground. In an effort to emulate the success of the Gray brothers, R B Christmas, a speculative builder who acquired part of Black Boy Wood, built his own more sophisticated leisure grounds near the railway. His venture, started in about 1920, included a boating lake and a maze, in addition to many other attractions.

Unfortunately changing times and changing circumstances, largely economic, eventually forced the closure of both enterprises between 1929 and 1930. Bricket Wood became a shadow of its former self, reverting to the sleepy backwood area it once was. Visitors did not entirely forsake the woods and the common, but there was no longer the incentive for special excursions from London. Gradually its fame and fortunes declined and only prospective builders and their bungalows saved the village from its ultimate fate. The station, which was enlarged in 1890 and again in 1910, was once famous for its well-kept gardens but it too ran out of steam.

Bricket Wood has changed almost beyond recognition. With its old rail link with Watford just surviving and a convenient access to the M1, this village has survived from the Roman times. Fragments of its past beauty remain, but the noise of hundreds of excited children alighting from the special trains and walking through the shady lanes to Woodside is now just a treasured memory of the temperance days of the '20s.

60   The Park of Memories

Those of us who have spent all or most of our lives in Watford will have fond and sometimes traumatic memories of Cassiobury Park from our earliest days to the present. Our first visit to the park, if memory permitted, would have been from the confines of a black coach-built pram pushed by a mother, in all probability, wearing a lace-trimmed straw hat and voluminous skirt, a legacy from Victorian and Edwardian days. The focal point of the park, having passed the gates and flowerbeds, was the river and the canal. No walk would be complete without crossing the River Gade and standing on the hump-backed Navigation Bridge to watch the long boats go by.

Navigation Bridge, 1938.

In my early years I was a constant visitor. Firm hands grasped my waist as I was hoisted above the level of the worn brickwork to watch the horse-drawn boats making their apparently casual way towards the locks immediately below. The boats provided an endless source of fascination, especially the cabin area in the stern. Despite the dirty, dusty cargoes covered by tarpaulin, the brasswork gleamed in the sunlight. Stylised roses, daisies and castles adorned the sloping sides. The water cans, dippers and jugs scattered on the flat roof were decorated in the same manner. The origin of the artwork peculiar to long boats remains a mystery. Some experts claim that the traditional daisy is a tansy, a flower found in southern Europe and attributed to the bargees who visually romanticised their long-lost gypsy origin. The children, like their parents, were dark-skinned and casually dressed, and resented any attempt to inspect their spotless floating homes.

With dexterous movements, paddles were raised and lowered, balance arms swung in and out and in a few minutes the lock was successfully negotiated. The knowing horse took the strain of the tow rope and gently moved the craft without disturbing the placid water.

Then came the more adventurous days of jam jars and fishing nets but still accompanied by anxious parents, more often than not equipped with a towel and a change of clothing "just in case". The shallow stony river then became the major attraction. Shoes and socks were carelessly abandoned. The cold clear water offered little cover to the vulnerable tiddlers. Soon, half a dozen fish found themselves divorced from their natural habitat. Then our piscatorial enthusiasm waned and we would watch the watercress gatherer wading through the shallow beds. We envied him his freedom, little realising the arthritic nature of his task. We did not question the purity of the water; the curse of pollution had yet to come.

The next vivid introduction to the wilder areas of Cassiobury Park and Whippendell Woods was strictly to order. The winter terms at Watford Grammar School for Boys brought the cold and muddy reality of the seasonal sports of rugby and cross-country running. The former was played at New Field, bordering the canal, or in the fields beyond the limits of the Cassiobury estate development and almost in the shadow of Cassiobury House stables, all that remained of the house after demolition in 1927.

Sunday afternoons were spent in the park listening to the band outside the perimeter hedge. 'Tuppence' (2d) for a hard-slatted seat was an extravagance we could ill afford. We enjoyed those days of sunshine, military bands, gleaming brass instruments and receptive audiences. They were the days of nostalgia.

I will pass on to the courting days when Cassiobury Park offered a range of secluded arbours permitting traditional but innocent courtship procedures. There were times when the young lady's parents invited themselves on one of our walks. We were not of an independent nature and we accepted their guardian-like presence with dignity and disappointment. Thus we adopted the role of two young people apparently more concerned with the flora and fauna and the pleasure of just walking, rather than illicit but exciting embraces behind the nearest tree. On such occasions we took the reasonably straight and narrow towpath; the artful psychological undertones probably fooled no one.

The walk south with shafts of sunlight sparkling on the water and on the passing long boats with their distinctive odour of thudding diesel engines still charges the emotions with nostalgia. At Cassio Bridge we passed the Halfway House which was as convenient to the water folk as the passing motorists. Beyond the sweeping bend was Croxley Moor and the mills of John Dickinson. Chapman's Farm was a little further, then the bridge and locks of Rickmansworth. Another 200 or 300 yards brought us opposite Frogmore Wharf.

Halfway House at Cassio Bridge with Mrs Colebrook Snr, 1902.*

Once upon a time, Rickmansworth could be described as a boat building town. In the mid-'30s the yard of W H Walker and Bros was a hive of industry; seasoned elm and oak from South West Hertfordshire and Buckinghamshire were carefully stacked ready for use. The elm, used for the sides of long boats, was cut to a thickness of 2 inches and the oak, used on the bottom, to 3 inches. The sound of circular rack bench saws, band mills and horizontal frame saws almost rent the air as they cut and shaped through the English hardwoods.

To the preformed ribs, 40-foot long beams were nailed into position. The process by which various timbers could be bent into the shape of the bow, keel or stern was relatively simple. The timbers were first placed into a long steam oven, after which they could be shaped without difficulty. On completion of the hull, the boat was caulked and then completely tarred from bow to stern. The single cylinder 18 hp diesel engine was located within the hull. Electricity was supplied for lighting and the painter applied the traditional decorations beloved by the bargees.

There were no public figures present that day and no champagne, only a few employees responsible for releasing the boat from its berth sideways into the canal. We joined onlookers on the tow path, bemused by the sight of a 71-foot long boat gently slipping into the water. For a few seconds it disappeared in the spray caused by the impact and for a fleeting moment it seemed as if it had hit the bottom of the canal and stayed there. But suddenly it bobbed up as the spray receded. Without ceremony, it was about to begin a long career as a working boat for the Grand Union Canal Carrying Company.

In 1935 Walker Brothers had as many as nine pairs of boats under construction or on order and the yard was still busy for some years to come. The days of commercial carrying on the canal were numbered, but we did not appreciate the hard facts of life in those far-off days.

61   The Silver Jubilee – 1935

The Royal family were no strangers to South West Hertfordshire. The London Orphan School and the Masonic Schools of Bushey and Rickmansworth frequently enjoyed their presence. King George V once visited Watford under a veil of strict secrecy when he inspected the Watford Munition Works during the First World War. There was no prior publicity in the press; not even an official welcome on his arrival, in compliance with wartime regulations. Queen Mary was present at the opening of the Girls' Masonic School in Rickmansworth in 1934. The Prince of Wales toured the area in 1926 and the Princess Royal had distributed prizes at the London Orphan School, the foundation stone of which had been laid by King Edward when he was Prince of Wales. She paid her second visit to Watford when she formally opened the new Peace Memorial Hospital. In earlier years Queen Victoria and Prince Albert had been given a rapturous welcome on their arrival in Watford.

Two years later, Queens Road looking to Watford High Street, at coronation of King George VI and Queen Elizabeth, 12 May 1937.*

For months in advance the Borough of Watford, in anticipation of the Silver Jubilee, was planning the form the official celebrations would take. They would cost the ratepayers 1d in the £, but there were no complaints and virtually no opposition. The Mayor was appointed Chairman of the Executive Committee, supported by Mrs Wheelwright and Mr W S Mountain as Joint Honorary Secretaries. Sub-Committees were formed to organise catering, amusements, entertainment, music and school displays, as well as an open air thanksgiving service. In a philanthropic mood, the town council, with a reputation the envy of Scrooge, voted £75 towards the carnival procession.

George Bolton, Borough Librarian, was commissioned to compile a souvenir edition recalling the momentous events that occured during the reign of King George and an account of the development of Watford. The book was bound in silver and its free distribution included every school child in the borough.

The unemployed were not forgotten. Vouchers to the value of 5s were distributed to married men and 2s 6d to single men, which were redeemable at any shop in Watford. Mrs Walker of the Empire Cinema generously made available to the Silver Jubilee Committee 500 pairs of tickets for matinee performances for distribution to the unemployed. From my point of view, the most enlightened edict was the decision to make 6 and 7 May school holidays. But in view of the involvement of so many children in the celebrations, perhaps it was not such a generous gesture.

The old mill, Cassiobury Park, 1910.*

Realisation that the Jubilee arrangements were rather special came with the floodlighting of the old mill in Cassiobury Park, the Peace Memorial Hospital and, beyond the borough limits, Bushey Parish Church and the Royal Masonic School – not by electricity as you would imagine, but by the Watford & St Albans Gas Company.

By the weekend, houses and shops in Watford were resplendent with bunting and flags. There was a detectable air of excitement. On Sunday morning every church bell was ringing out a message of thanksgiving.

127

In the afternoon a procession formed in Cassiobury Drive. Supporting the Mayor, Councillor H J Bridges, aldermen and councillors, the local Territorial unit, British Legion, Friendly Societies, Scouts, Guides, Boys' Brigade and Sunday school children marched to the bandstand in Cassiobury Park to the strains of the British Legion and Watford Silver Prize bands. A record-breaking number of people joined in the thanksgiving service.

On Monday those taking part in the carnival procession assembled in Cassiobury Drive. The fire brigade proudly displayed its very latest engine made by Scammell, appropriately named 'Silver Jubilee'. In contrast, Watford's 18th century fire pump was pulled by firemen in the traditional dress of that period. The procession was one of the finest ever seen by the thousands lining the old route via St Albans Road, Station Road, Woodford Road, Queens Road, High Street, Market Street and Cassio Road.

Flanagan's fun fair got off to an early start as the crowds dispersed and moved into the park. At one o'clock the Mayor waited at the Park Gates to receive members of the Cyclists' Touring Club to add his signature to the greetings being conveyed to Buckingham Palace.

In the early afternoon the entertainments programme gathered momentum. There were two platforms. On the first, acrobatic and musical clowns kept children happy until 6pm when Peggy Perkins' Pippins, the pick of Watford's dancing children, went through their well-rehearsed dance routines. On the second, larger platform the May Queen festival, arranged by the local Head Teachers' Association, was enacted by children of Alexandra School, accompanied by the Carnival Queens of 1933 and 1934. This was followed by a physical training display, first by the junior boys of Callowland, Chater, Field and Parkgate Schools, then the senior girls of Leggatt's Way and Victoria, and finally the senior boys of Alexandra, Leggatt's Way and Victoria.

Scholars of Beechen Grove, Garston, Oxhey and other Watford schools gave displays of folk dancing, which were well received and the Watford Silver Prize Band played at the bandstand during the afternoon in competition with two Punch and Judy shows. As evening approached, the King's speech was relayed to thousands of silent people. Dancing at the bandstand continued until 9pm, when a wonderful display of Brock's fireworks thrilled the now weary onlookers.

Beginning at Bushey, the local Scout troops organised a chain of beacons as far as Tring. As a finale, Arthur Caiger persuaded the remaining crowds to join in community singing, in which many First World War songs were rendered with undisguised sadness by ex-servicemen.

The celebrations continued with a service at St Mary's Church, attended by the Mayor, aldermen and councillors. That same evening at the Plaza, which had been showing as its feature film 'King's Jubilee', the last of a series of concerts was peformed. Conducted by Sir Henry Wood, the orchestra of 75 musicians, largely recruited from Watford School of Music, and a chorus of 200 from local church choirs, responded lustily to the magic baton of Sir Henry. Significantly, the festival concerts were devoted to works by Holst, Elgar and Delius, who had all died the previous year.

Those joyous days, I am sure, will be remembered by all of us who were involved or witnessed Watford's Silver Jubilee celebrations, at which loyalty and patriotism were taken for granted. In recognition of the Mayor's dedication to public service, King George awarded Councillor Bridges with a special Jubilee medal. George Bolton also received a medal, along with Norman Smith, Sub-Postmaster at Callowland and Mr F D Coward, a postman with 45 years' service.

Some 15,000 - 20,000 people went to Cassiobury Park on that memorable occasion and if that is not a yardstick of success, I do not know what is. For once, the Borough of Watford exceeded its brief in giving value for the 1d in the £ rate increase to pay for it all.

62   Famous Visitors to Watford

One night in early April 1935 the Watford Amateur Players presented the evergreen play 'The Farmer's Wife' at St John's Hall. It was, and still is, a favourite with audiences and drama groups. The doors were opened and the small queue that had gathered outside filed in one by one. Meanwhile, a gleaming Rolls Royce nosed its way from the High Street through back streets to the hall.

Parking was not a problem and the limousine glided to a halt near the entrance doors, much to the surprise of people passing by. Cars were still uncommon in that part of Watford and a Rolls Royce was unique. A frail but distinguished man alighted from the car; his hair almost white and his suit dark and well tailored. Although the area was not familiar to him, his lined face showed no sign of anxiety. Without hesitation he entered the hall, paid the entry fee and received a programme. He occupied a vacant chair in the third row and patiently waited for the curtain to go up.

Despite its popularity, 'The Farmer's Wife' demanded a high standard of acting ability and convincing West Country accents. Under astute direction, the Watford Amateur Players successfully overcame the traps into which such groups usually fall. The distinguished man in the third row was even more attentive than the hushed audience. His name was George Arliss. In 1930 he had received an Oscar from the Academy of Motion Pictures, Arts & Sciences for best actor in Warner's 'Disraeli' opposite Joan Bennett. He was the first British actor to receive the award.

George Arliss (Augustus George Andrews) as the Duke of Wellington on the set of 'The Iron Duke', 1934, © National Portrait Gallery, London.

George Arliss was born in London in 1868; his father was William Arliss Andrews, a printer and publisher. In 1899 he married Florence Montgomery at Harrow Weald. As a quiet but dedicated young man, he formed his own amateur dramatic society. In later years he became known to London audiences when he teamed up with Mrs Patrick Campbell. An American producer spotted them and invited the pair on a four-month tour of the United States. The emerging movie industry, in their perpetual search for new talent, persuaded him to become a film actor.

In 1921 he made his film debut in the silent movie 'Disraeli'. As a typical aristocratic Englishman beloved by Hollywood he joined Warner Bros, moving to Darryl F Zanuck's fledgling 20th Century Pictures in 1933. George Arliss appeared in many films, including 'The Man Who Played God' (1932), with Bette Davis as his fiancée in her first leading role. His last acting role was in 'Dr Syn' (1936).

So what attracted George Arliss to the inhospitable St John's Hall to see a play which he probably knew word for word? Completely without their knowledge, he had come to see his brother and his niece on the stage. Whether he was impressed by their performances we will never know, but you can imagine the shock he caused when the curtain came down and he made his presence known. No one was more surprised than Cuthbert and Ursula Andrews. His visit was a well-kept secret and we are left to guess what happened at their reunion.

Watford had another famous visitor that same year. She was the daughter of a well-known local architect who lived at Burvale, on the corner of Cassio Road and Rickmansworth Road. Her name was Ruby M Ayres. Her books, George Bolton the Watford Borough Librarian admitted, were in constant demand and never found their way back onto the shelves. She was a highly successful authoress of romantic

Ruby Mildred Ayres by Howard Coster, 1935, © National Portrait Gallery, London.

stories. The record sales of her works must have been the envy of more skilled and less prolific writers.

Her name will be known to many, but few will know that she was born in Watford, then a country town. With a vidid imagination, she was less than an ideal scholar. Her daydreaming reveries and lack of attention to the subject matter finally drove her teachers to distraction. Guilty of being "too romantic", she was expelled from her Watford school. Despite her ultimate success, she never disclosed the name of the school she attended in order not to embarrass either the teachers or the headmistress. Being 'sent down' was usually the prerogative of unruly boys and the expulsion of a young lady of a St Trinian's disposition was something of a disgrace to the family, especially since children were still expected to be seen and not heard.

She became a compulsive writer at an early age and one of her first successes came with the acceptance of a short story by an unsususpecting editor. She had entered a competition which appeared in a boys' magazine belonging to her brother. To avoid a technical if not automatic rejection of her entry, she sent it off under a boy's name. She won a prize of a half-guinea and an enlargement of a photograph of the successful author. Carrying on the deception, she forwarded a photograph of her brother!

Fictional romance gave way to reality when she was married at St John's Church by the Rev Reginald James. After her marriage she started to write in earnest. She sent a short story to 'Pearson's Weekly' which was accepted and published. The editor of the old 'Daily Chronicle' read the story and was sufficiently impressed to offer her the opportunity of writing a serial. Despite her unfamiliarity with serial stories, the impetuous Miss Ayres accepted the challenge and promptly wrote the first chapter. Her story was published over a six-week period. For many years she contributed to women's magazines, wrote numerous romantic novels and supplied the American press with articles. The recalcitrant schoolgirl became a household name.

When she returned to Watford in 1935, it was to address the ladies at a Watford Rotary Club luncheon. As guest speaker she revealed the secrets of a locally-born novelist who, in her own words, never allowed the storyline "to go beyond the bedroom door". In this day and age, the door is all too frequently open. Conversely, she was not tainted with the moral outlook of the Victorian era. "I cannot approve the tendency to write risqué books" she added, with sadness rather than disdain.

Ruby Ayres had been away from Watford for 25 years and in that time she must have been dismayed at the changes that had taken place. Watford Football Club had moved from the South West Hertfordshire ground to Vicarage Road; Cassiobury House, along with the vast estates of the Earl of Essex, had virtually disappeared; and the northern end of the town was slowly being developed. The return to the town of her birth would have been something of a shock and perhaps the visit inspired yet another story in, of course, a romantic vein.

In a recent article I recalled the Silver Jubilee of 1935 when the residents of Watford celebrated in no uncertain manner the 25th anniversary of the ascension to the throne of King George V. The thought occurred to me that it would be an interesting exercise to briefly review the period between 1910 and 1935, the years that determined the social and economic future of Watford.

The proclamation was made outside the old council offices on 12 May 1910 by Sir Alfred Reynolds, High Sheriff of the County of Hertford. Platforms had been erected behind the wall to the left of the entrance to accommodate members of the council and in front of the offices for representatives of public bodies and other prominent citizens. Onlookers were marshalled on the opposite side of the road to allow the entrance of the High Sheriff's carriage which stopped in juxtaposition to the guard of honour. The sun and blue skies were acknowledged as a good omen for the future, but within four years the country would be at war with Germany.

Troops were billeted locally as various regiments arrived and departed. As men and youths joined the colours, so the women of Watford took their places in shops, factories and offices. The council cancelled or postponed all projects and confined their efforts and attention to the essential matters of maintaining the services for which it was responsible. When war broke out, the population was about 40,000. During hostilities the number was decimated. Those left at home were committed to an all-out war effort rather than being directly involved in the conflict. War in the air was something quite new. There was no official blackout, but on 23 occasions all lights were extinguished because of the possibility of air raids. None, as far as I am able to determine, involved damage or loss of life but the fear of being bombed

was no less real. The bomb was an entirely new military weapon and civilians were unaware of its lethal potential. The dreaded Zeppelin was seen in the north west of the district and it was claimed an enemy aircraft was spotted on a moonlit night! An explosion and fire at the munition works, however, did cause a certain amount of panic.

Troops entering Market Place, 1914.

Watford was then a market town surrounded by farms and estates, although development had taken place during the latter part of the reigns of Queen Victoria and King Edward at Oxhey, and west and north Watford. Nevertheless, the incursion of freehold properties on land largely acquired from the Earl of Essex had not changed the essential ingredients of the town. Buses were still horsedrawn and their services were only as good as the weather. Shires pulling coal carts and pantechnicons were a common sight, but constituted little danger to the pedestrian crossing the road. On the other hand, the trotting horses of delivery vans and the whistling errand boy were natural hazards.

Elmcote, eastern side of the Parade. Home of John Sedgwick, husband of landscape painter Emma Oliver, 1908.

The Elms, Little Cassiobury, The Platts and Monmouth House were still private residences, as were the other houses in the vicinity of the Cross Roads and the Pond, where horses were still being watered. Even so, 200 or 300 yards to the south commerce, which had absorbed Dudley's Corner, was gradually encroaching on the last vestiges of rural Watford High Street.

Lower High Street, 1957. Henry William Lloyd at No 262 was a corn, coal, coke, manure and salt merchant. Photo by Denise Mangles.

Lower High Street looking north, 1957. Photo by Denise Mangles.

Lower High Street, A E & D M Perry, antique shop, No 237; to right 237A, Miss E Crane's refreshment rooms, 1957. Photo by Denise Mangles.

Lower down, the shopping centre was relatively quiet except on Tuesdays and Saturdays when the open air market attracted almost every housewife to the town centre. The noise of competitive stall holders was a familiar sound, just as the accumulating rubbish in the gutters was a familiar (and therefore acceptable) sight.

Lower High Street looking north, 1957. Photo by Denise Mangles.

A bustling Watford High Street, 1927.

The shops with their mahogany-framed windows and glass-protected gold-leaf lettering above were inviting and personal. The eye-catching window display was still to become a profession in its own right. Butchers hung their fresh meat on rails outside their shops to attract custom. They were the days when housewives knew their cuts of meat and flies were tolerated, if not ignored, by the straw-hatted and aproned butchers.

Goddard's sold furniture and Wright's sold glassware and china. The Essex Arms Hotel, the Rose & Crown and the Green Man offered hotel accommodation and restaurant facilities, while dozens of pubs and alehouses supplied liquid refreshment. Kingham's, the grocers, sold their special brands of tea as well as every conceivable item of grocery. No prepackaged cheese, ham, eggs, bacon or butter and very few imported foods. Their freshness was more than a substitute for a greater choice of inert frozen contents in attractively printed packages.

For entertainment, the Palace Theatre offered variety shows and the cinemas of later vintage showed their silent epics. Orchestras accompanied the films and teas were served during the intervals. Oh, happy days for those who can remember an era from which we are now totally divorced.

After the First World War, when 828 citizens had died on active service, life was never quite the same. Lorries and motor buses still rumbled through the streets, although the traditional coal cart carried on undisturbed by the internal combustion engine. Nevertheless, the wind of change was already blowing.

Watford's population growth was roughly 1,000 per annum. From 1850 to 1894 the Local Board had administered the affairs of the very rural town. Until 1922 an Urban District Council, with greater powers than the Local Board, was responsible for our welfare and progress. Such consistent growth prompted many forward thinking citizens, individually and collectively, to advocate that an application should be made to the Privy Council for borough status. The application was successful and the Earl of Clarendon became our first Mayor in 1922. Tired of parochial administration, residents expected and without doubt got a new and enlightened era of local government which set the seal on Watford's planned growth.

In empathy, it seemed, the fragmented estate and mansion of the Earl of Essex came under the hammer. Cassiobury House, of Tudor origin, was offered in its entirety but divorced from its estate to a depressed market. A decaying asset was not an attractive investment and attempts to save the building failed. In 1927 it was razed to the ground, but the old lodges survived along with the stables which, in more recent times, became an old people's home. In earlier years much of the park, with its gated entrance to the old estate, had been purchased by the council. In 1935 the town acquired Whippendell Woods with monetary assistance for £15,000. With active housing development on the Cassiobury estate, the seat of the Earls of Essex was physically eliminated from all but the history books.

The new Borough Council of 1922 was faced with many post-war problems, not least the traumatic transition from urban to borough status. Its ambitious programmes were thwarted by lack of finance at a time when central government expected local authorities to be virtually self-sufficient. Loans provided for capital expenditure had to be carefully budgeted in line with a modest rates income. In 1910 that income was only £170,000.

The influence of the church upon our lives was significant and sites had been acquired for St Luke's on the Cassiobury Park estate and for a methodist church in North Watford. In place of a temporary building in Clarendon Road, a new Presbyterian church was completed.

The Anchor; the Hit or Miss on extreme left, 1928. Note poster advertising sale of Coldharbour Farm, Bushey.

Watford Field Place, 1978.

The Lower High Street had changed very little over the centuries. The original Wheatsheaf stood in near isolation, without its orchards and theatre. The gas works had expanded considerably and with it the gaseous by-products disgorged into the atmosphere. The many cottages by the river bridge were frequently flooded, including the Anglers, Hit or Miss, the Anchor and East's, the corn merchants. With the exception of the Wheatsheaf, which was rebuilt in the early '30s, Lower High Street remained intact. The Angel Inn was pulled down in 1910, close to Mr Newbery's house, Brookland, which was acquired by Mr George Ausden the well-known scrap metal merchant to cope with a successful and rapidly expanding business. The once prosperous Watford mill was destroyed by fire in 1924 and the shell of the building remained until the '60s. Local Board Road opposite, lined with cottages once occupied by workers at the Pump House, was an undistinguished entrance to Watford Field Place, a house of no great antiquity which was demolished around 1980. In 1835 it was occupied by Josiah Condor and in a letter to his son he has been quoted as saying "This most gay, hospitable, social, refined, enlightened Watford".

Group of workers outside Benskins, 1910. Tall chimney in distance marks the Railway Tavern.

I am not sure if all Watford's residents of those days would have described the town in such glowing terms.

Then there was Dumbelton's the butcher opposite Farthing Lane where, for so many years, Miss Grover sat in the small pay desk at the back of the shop. She retired to King Edward Road as a little white-haired old lady. The Gospel Mission was still active, tucked away in a courtyard close to the original 17th century Swan Inn. Above this celebrated house, which once brewed its own ale, were old houses bordering the pavement, each with their own stone steps to the front door. Across the road was Sedgwick's Brewery with its red brick walls, ornate entrances and dignified mansion already absorbed by Benskins, Watford's major brewery, with its familiar aroma of hops, malt and bubbling oats.

Watford High Street Station, 1978. Wilkinson's, Ford dealer, to right; the White Hart and Steabben's have been demolished.

The Railway Tavern; Watford High Street Station to right, late 1920s.

Then we come to Watford High Street Station. Once just a hole in the wall down a short ramp for trains to Rickmansworth, it was completely rebuilt when the electric train service was introduced in 1922 to London, Rickmansworth and Croxley Green. Next door was another red brick building which once housed the Liberal Club, later demolished to make way for a garage and showrooms which many will remember as Wilkinson's, the Ford dealer and agent. Nearby was the White Hart, a pub of Jacobean origin, and Steabben's, gentlemen's outfitters. Both premises survived into the late 1970s when they were demolished to make way for the road linking Beechen Grove and Exchange Road. In fact in 1935 the lower part of the town was still recognisable – even by 1910 standards. The pubs were not quite as numerous as in the early years, but drunkenness was certainly not as evident as it had once been. The action taken by the local branches of the temperance societies in prompting social consciences over many years was becoming apparent.

Perhaps the home was where the greatest changes were to be found. The social structure was slowly shifting. The country girls who came to Watford before the First World War to be 'in service' found more remunerative employment during the war years. The tradition of employing servants was slowly breaking down, due largely to the increasing cost of their labour. Labour-saving devices created by post-war industry offered the only, but not always acceptable, substitutes.

The Ragged School and the Adult School offered further education for those who had left school in their early years. Versed in the three 'Rs', their educational standards were meagre and there was a tremendous demand for additional tuition which such night schools provided. A new social era was gradually emerging. The bath in front of the fire, the weekly norm for many Watford residents living in terraced houses and cottages, was coming to an end.

Of all the changes that occurred in Watford during this period, none was greater than in the retail business sector. Some family businesses that were familiar to shoppers at the beginning of the century are still with us today, in name at least. Others fell by the wayside in more recent times. Henry Kingham & Sons, established during the 19th century, is a good example.

From small beginnings, Kingham's became a highly successful wholesale and retail business. The shop, I am sure you will remember, bordered Market Place and achieved fame on a number of counts. Who could forget their hams, which were cured on the premises? The very thought makes my mouth water. Another commodity for which they became very well known was tea. It was blended and packaged on the premises. Needless to say, it complemented the local water drawn from local wells. Another speciality was cheese, properly matured cheese which an assistant at the counter cut freshly within half an ounce of the weight required.

Trewins, Cawdells and Clements were all established well before 1910, although they began trading as drapers. Mr Arthur Trewin opened his shop in Queens Road in 1880 and Mr Albert Clements established his business in 1898. Mr James Cawdell was a relative latecomer, arriving in 1905. Mrs Goodson's Bazaar was another well-known and popular emporium as well as an employment agency. Woolworth's appeared on the scene in 1918 and sold 'nothing over 6d'. Other familiar names introduced themselves and set up in competition with indigenous family enterprises, including Liptons, Home and Colonial, International and, of course, Sainsbury's.

Looking south below Harlequin entrance, 1979.

The Penny Bazaar, almost opposite King Street and now (1983) occupied by Brentford Nylons[55], was acquired in 1928 by Marks & Spencer, with little indication that they would become legendary in one generation. In 1935 a new site was found to accommodate the rapidly expanding store, which necessitated the demolition of the George Hotel and Mrs Goodson's Bazaar. Marks & Spencer duly transferred to a new, traditionally-styled red brick building which has since been substantially enlarged.

We must not forget the Co-operative Society with its base in St Albans Road and with branches including Queens Road and Oxhey, whose golden years were between the two World Wars. Sadly, they could not successfully compete with the sophistication of the nationals and the change of our post-war shopping habits.

Another name already familiar to Watford in 1910 was Phillip Buck's confectionery shop at 48 High Street. Over the years the business had expanded to include the adjacent properties of 50 and 52 High Street and a ballroom was eventually built over the shop and restaurant. Bucks then became an ideal venue for wedding receptions, lunches and afternoon teas, enjoying tremendous popularity when its service was extended to outside catering. By 1952 parking had become a problem and the ballroom was sold and turned into a billiard saloon. In 1961 the firm, which grew its own vegetables, moved to new premises in Upton Road next door to Elliott's, whose premises in Queens Road had been acquired by Standard Range.

The name Morse has always been synonymous with clocks, watches and jewellery. In fact, Mr B S Morse had not always traded in Watford. He opened his first shop in Pinner High Street in 1876 before transferring his business to Queens Road. Before the turn of the century he moved to 136 High Street.

How many readers, I wonder, are wearing their engagement and wedding rings or carefully preserving their silver hunters? In 1926 Mr Morse celebrated his half-century trading in Watford by giving customers ashtrays bearing an illustration of 'Cassio House'. I wonder if any survived. The founder died in 1932, but the story does not end there. In 1935 the late Mr Morse's grand-daughter married Mr Dan Jackson and the business carried on until 1954. In that year the old shop closed and the name Jackson transferred to one of Watford's oldest timber-framed buildings which somehow survived the act of architectural genocide directed towards buildings that were part of our heritage. Thanks to the Department of the Environment, Jackson Jewellers is accommodated in a listed building with, it is said, its very own ghost.

Fisher's is surely another name you will easily recall. The premises were in the middle of the Market Place, close to the old Rose & Crown and on the corner of New Road, in company with the notorious Ballard's Buildings. They were butchers of high repute and long standing. In 1926 Mr Percy Fisher and Mr William Keen Fisher, members of the large Fisher family, established an allied industry in the heart of Watford by the name of Keens (Watford) Ltd to manufacture 'preserved provisions', to quote a description of their trade printed on an old Ford delivery van. Perhaps we will better remember their new premises in Exchange Road and their famous pies and sausages.

Marlborough Road towards Keen's and what is now the one-way system, 1940s.

Few houses were built in Watford with materials which did not come from the merchants known to everyone as Pratts. Mr James A Pratt started business in a yard next to his house in Woodford Road. In 1880 he bought a hardware business and small foundry run by Mr Grant in Queens Road which allowed him to sell cooking ranges, boilers, baths and ironmongery. He retired at the turn of the century and his three sons, James Alfred, Henry and Frank succeeded him. They incorporated two companies – J Alfred Pratt & Co Ltd and Standard Range and Foundry Co Ltd. Local authorities, government departments, engineers and architects could be included in their list of wholesale customers.

Such esteemed and valuable connections brought Standard Range many contracts during the years of the First World War, when they supplied the Armed Forces with metal fabricated products and narrow gauge railway turntables, points and crossings. The latter were also used extensively in army camps and on the Western Front to facilitate the carriage of equipment, arms and ammunition to the static mud-bound forces.

In 1928 the three brothers retired and the firm went public. The site of James A Pratt's house and yard were extended to accommodate the new company, selling virtually all the materials required by the building industry. During the First World War their services were utilised by the Emergency Services Organisation to facilitate the availability of materials to rehabilitate factories and houses and repair bomb damage. Paradoxically, the two kindred firms were reunited in 1962 and became Pratt Standard Range Ltd.

Between 1910 and 1935 Watford Fire Station had hardly changed in appearance. The fire fighting machines with their steaming bodies pulled by fit responsive horses had given way to the primitive petrol engine. Now there were two gleaming monsters, resplendent in spotless red paint and gleaming brass. Both had been made by the local firm Scammells, one in 1930 and the other in 1935, which proudly bore the topical name 'Silver Jubilee'.

Next door, the council offices were hidden rather than protected by a red brick wall. The thoughts that the offices were inadequate had occurred to local government officers, aldermen and councillors. In 1935 plans were already being considered to develop The Elms site, part of which had been occupied by the new municipal swimming and slipper baths. Many years of procrastination had given the Five Arches bathing place a stay of execution.

Cross Roads. Large house in distance is The Limes, 1909.

The Cross Roads had barely changed since the early days, but now the roads to St Albans, Hemel Hempstead and Rickmansworth were adequately paved. However, a new phrase was echoing through the corridors of the corporate offices. That phrase was to augur more than the ides of March. In fact, it was still unfamiliar to the man in the street, but he was soon to find out the implication and meaning of 'town planning'. The country town image would be phased out. The first exercise was to plan the conversion of the cross roads into a roundabout, although at that time it could not be justified for the volume of traffic[56]. In retrospect, I am sure the intention was solely to complement the new town hall, as and when it was built.

We grew accustomed to the vicissitudes and risks of the new roundabout in later years and, when the corporation planted and carefully tended flower beds, even the most conservative residents had to agree that it was an improvement to the northern entrance to the town. Many picture postcards were sold in pre- and post-war days illustrating the colourful roundabout replete with another new idea – belisha beacons. The motoring fraternity had just become familiar with traffic lights which had been installed at Queens Road, King Street and St Albans Road at the intersection of Station Road and Langley Road.

Looking south towards the Pond and the Plaza (later the Odeon), mid-1930s.

Once upon a time a motorist was a relatively free agent, provided he obeyed many different speed restrictions and the policeman on point duty. Now new motorists had to pass a driving test and know the Highway Code. Life was becoming more sophisticated and traffic an increasing problem.

The franchise of the centuries-old street market was purchased by the corporation in 1926 for £19,500 and two years later Red Lion Yard, a mixture of inhabited and derelict medieval buildings, was cleared and paved. The 18th century silk mill, one of three in Watford, was demolished with many other contemporary buildings. Market customers disliked the new venue, but now they were no longer at risk from passing vehicles. The cobble stones were removed and replaced with concrete and tarmac, so the town acquired its first one-way system at the cost of the end of a 700-year-old tradition.

Cassio Hamlet, 1908.

The Public Library and the main Post Office in Queens Road were Victorian contributions to an expanding town. Few could have forseen that both institutions would prove inadequate in a few years. A new Public Library, adjacent to Cassio Hamlet, was completed in 1928. In 1910, approximately 400,000 volumes were issued annually. Today (1983), over 735,000 books are borrowed including, of course, North Watford and the mobile libraries.

In the early '30s, the Post Office moved to new premises in Market Street and the vacated building was converted to a social and working centre for Watford's unemployed during the period of recession.

Watford Cottage Hospital in Vicarage Road was acquired by the Poor Law Authority when the Peace Memorial Hospital opened in 1925, with money raised by public subscription.

The Grammar Schools for Boys and Girls in Derby Road was vacated by the girls in 1907 when they moved to The Crescent. The boys moved out in 1912 to Rickmansworth Road and in the ensuing years what was once the Endowed Schools became Watford Central School. The first new school to be built for 31 years was Garston Elementary School, closely followed by Leggatt's Way in 1934. The National School in old Church Street was closed in 1922 and Almond Wick became the office of the Registrar of Births and Deaths[57]. The infants' school in the High Street closed in 1920 because of the increasing noise from traffic and pedestrians.

The cost of providing schools was largely the responsibility of the borough, but the expense may be equated with the rapidly increasing number of houses which, apart from council developments, now included 800 on the Bradshaw and Tudor estates, 400 at Cassiobury, 500 at Garston and 150 in old Oxhey. In restitution, the rateable value of the borough had increased from £170,000 in 1910 to £550,000 in 1935.

By the same token, the need for new public transport received the attention of more than a dozen operators. Many traffic problems were precipitated by the lack of co-ordination between the services and the corporation. In an effort to control the situation, which by 1926 was getting out of hand, the first licences were issued for a service from the town centre to Harebreaks. Lewis served the Rickmansworth area and National operated via Hempstead Road to outlying villages. London General ran its Harrow and Kilburn services to Watford Junction. Feuding between the operators and crews was not uncommon.

The High Street was rapidly becoming saturated with public transport and the council endeavoured to control services by inducing operators to serve less remunerative routes. The Transport Act and the formation of the London Transport Board solved the problem. All the local bus companies were absorbed and order was brought out of chaos, although the travelling public's temper was sorely tried in the process.

There have been many shortcomings and omissions in my brief survey of the momentous years between 1910 and 1935, but if I have conveyed the social and economic changes of those years and reminded you of the good years of youth or stirred latent memories, I will be well content.

67 A Guided Walking Tour of Watford – Part 1

One of the most surprising developments of tourism has been the increasing popularity of guided walking tours in the metropolis in areas of architectural and historical interest. The day has still to come when an entrepreneur with knowledge of the history of Watford and of good voice decides to emulate the London guides. Until that volunteer is forthcoming, I thought we could take a quiet walk around the town and see for ourselves the remnants left of our heritage that have escaped the ravages of time or the eagle eye of the Town Hall[58].

Before we set out on our journey, we should remember that the town itself was once a tourist attraction, for no other reason than its rustic beauty. Until the coming of the London and Birmingham Railway (1837), carriages, stage coaches, wagons, in fact anything that could be pulled by a horse, brought weekend Londoners by their hundreds to enjoy the fruits of an idyllic rural scene. The epitome of that ideal was to be found at the bottom of Chalk Hill, at the intersection of Pinner and Eastbury Roads and Town End Bridge (Bushey Arches). The attractions were many, not least the River Colne meandering through a pretty wooded valley and the Wheatsheaf inn with its orchards and theatre. The river attracted anglers and lovers, and the inn provided refreshment for those whose prime interests were drinking and eating. The theatre offered the excitement of melodrama to complete the day's outing.

Bushey & Oxhey station, 1915.

What better place to start our walk than Bushey Station. Its cobble-stoned forecourt is now covered in tarmac and the once attractive weathervane surmounting the clock tower no longer responds to the wind. The station clock, after many timeless years, is now working but its accuracy is suspect. The first question which can be reasonably anticipated is why it is called Bushey Station when it is surely in Oxhey. Well, much of old Oxhey was once called New Bushey so, in 1841, it made sense. When Oxhey became a parish in its own right and an increasing number of commuters lived there, the name was changed to Bushey and Oxhey which, too, made sense. However, British Rail thought otherwise and in 1974, as an economy measure, Oxhey was deleted from the title.

St Matthew's Church, Oxhey, 1909.

We leave the silent coalyards of Glenister's, Wilson's and others which have long been converted into a car park and take the subway passage through the station to Eastbury Road. To our left are steps leading to Kingsfield Road by an alley which was once roughly in line with an old disused subway linking the fast and slow platforms. It was filled in during the '60s and came to light again at the time of the rail accident in 1981.

In front of us an isolated detached house,

like a Norman keep, commands the forecourt and in its day housed many Stationmasters. Perhaps you will remember the distinguished dark blue uniforms and peaked caps with gold braid. In those days it was a position of seniority and authority. A Stationmaster's presence on the platform was respected, not just noted by the station staff who would follow the correct procedures to the letter. Instinctively, the Stationmaster would take out a silver watch on a silver chain and check the time between the arrival of the train and its departure. The station garden was colourful with flowers and the mahogany table and leather-covered horsehair seats in the waiting room glowed in the light of the coal fire. The cork linoleum floor covering was equally immaculate.

Flt Sub Lt Warneford's Morane-Saulnier attacking German Zeppelin LZ 37 on 7 June 1915. Sketch by Ted Parrish.

We leave the now deserted and unkempt yard behind us and turn left into Eastbury Road in the shadow of St Matthew's Church. There is one name on the war memorial consecrated to those who died in the First World War that should take our eye: R A J Warneford. His name may not be familiar to us now but during the First World War he was a national hero. Flt Sub Lt Reginald Warneford was a Morane pilot in No 1 Squadron of the RNAS (which became 201 Squadron of the RAF in 1918).

During a patrol on 7 June 1915 he sighted Zeppelin LZ 37. Flying his single-seater above the airship, he dropped small bombs onto its vulnerable fabric. The airship exploded in mid-air and the force of the blast caused his engine to stall. He was compelled to glide back to earth and made a successful forced landing in the dark. He carried out repairs to his aircraft, took off, and finally returned to base nine-and-a-half hours later. For that heroic and successful deed, he earned the highest award the country could bestow: the Victoria Cross. The VC is only given for the most conspicuous bravery, a daring or pre-eminent act of valour or self-sacrifice, or extreme devotion to duty. He was concurrently awarded the Cross of the Legion of Honour by France for the same deed. He later died in a flying accident.

Reginald Warneford, although closely associated with Watford, was born in India. However, many of his service leaves were spent with relatives who lived in Kingsfield Road and Oxhey Avenue, in the Parish of St Matthew's. He was given a hero's welcome when he returned with his VC to Watford. His name is perpetuated in the street name Warneford Place in Oxhey.

Our attention is drawn to the view through the trees of Oxhey Park, which was once the seat of the local Deacon family. We look across the ambling river, where rowing boats and swans were once abundant, to the playing fields beyond, beneath which chalk was once precipitated in filter beds by the pumping station at Watford Fields. The view of Watford Fields is obscured by the man-made embankment which carries the Watford – Euston electric service, started in 1914 and not completed until 1922, to connect with the old Watford – Rickmansworth line opened in 1862 and Croxley Green.

Above the embankment we see the concentration of Watford to the west of the High Street, with St Mary's no longer dominating the skyline. Back in the 1840s that part of Watford virtually terminated at the Parish Church. Here West Watford Fields offered grazing rights to commoners, such as are still enjoyed at Croxley Moor. Once corn was grown right up to Three Crowns Yard, when Mr H Catlin was tenant of the arable areas owned by Jonathan King.

In 1855 the Lammas Rights were rescinded and the land enclosed, except for a small portion which was expropriated for use as a public recreation ground "for ever". Watford Fields is one of the few areas left in the town which may be traced directly back to medieval times.

In part one our walk ended at Eastbury Road, overlooking Oxhey Park. We had walked no more than 200 – 300 yards from Bushey Station. Our progress had been delayed by the excellent view of the west side of Watford, which had prompted us to view the scene as it may have been before the arrival of the railway. It is a distressing thought that what little is left of the Lammas land on the far side of the Colne and which is currently a playing field will, in the foreseeable future, accommodate a new road when the Southern Junction road system is completed. The semi-rural aspect which is still enjoyable if not attractive, by which we may identify this area with medieval times, will be lost forever.

Watford from Oxhey Park, park-keeper's lodge on left; Benskins dominates the skyline. Early 1960s.

We will forgo the pleasure of walking down the steep slopes of Oxhey Park, if only to avoid the site of a once charming lodge to the Wiggenhall estate in which the park-keeper lived until the early '70s, when the Town Hall sneaked in and pulled it down without regard for the environment or their citizens. Instead we will walk down 'Tommy' Deacon's Hill, which some older residents will still remember as a steep winding path. Only recently, I was talking to one of them and he recalled the excitement of sliding down the path on a tin tray.

The story is told that one of the Tommy Deacons (the eldest son was always named Thomas) rode down the hill on horseback for a wager and broke his neck in a fall. He was buried near the top of the hill and it is claimed his grave is always dry in the wettest of weathers.

Wiggenhall was acquired by the Urban District Council in 1920 as a site on which to build housing. It was undoubtedly handed by Offa to the Abbot of St Albans in 790 and farmed by the monks who built fences to keep out the oxen, from which Oxhey derived its name (Oxangehaege).

Tommy Deacon's Hill, 1910.

The path then joined a track which crossed a neglected wooden bridge over the Colne, in much the same spot as the present bridge. Apart from Wiggen Hall, there were no houses to be seen. The silk mill dominated the westerly aspect of the river, hiding a cluster of tiny workers' cottages and the proprietor's house. Now council houses line Riverside Road, built in the '20s to accommodate those evicted from slum properties being demolished around the High Street. The derelict mill was acquired by the Watford Steam Laundry in 1883, but the age-old name of the Rookery lives on.

Before we cross the bridge, we notice the waterside path that emerges from Oxhey Park. Many believe that the path, or rather what is left of it, followed the course of the river, presumably connecting the mills of Watford and Hamper, and was in use in medieval times. The land on the Watford side of the river is low lying and was once probably marsh and water meadows. However, one very surprising feature emerged when Watford & South West Hertfordshire Archaeological Society excavated the site of the Anglers, south of the entrance to the old bus depot which is now occupied by Ind Coope[59]. It seems that no flooding occurred in Lower High Street until the infamous Ballard built his embankment for the London and Birmingham Railway between Bushey Arches and Five Arches. After 1837, the natural drainage of the area was disturbed and, from then to the present, floods have become a feature of this part of the High Street.

Watford Fields and Benskins, 1961, photo by Ted Parrish.

The Cricketers pub and Benskins from Watford Fields, 1965, photo by Denise Mangles.

We turn right into Watford Fields, the origin of which I mentioned in the last article. I have always assumed that the high concentration of terraced houses attracted many of Benskin's employees. By virtue of the electric railway on one side and Lammas land on the other, the size of the Victorian estate was prescribed from the beginning. The area has changed little since it was built. It remains an isolated community, divorced from the more extreme changes occurring on its perimeter. It had its own shops, now reduced to one, its own church abandoned some years ago and its own school which is still flourishing.

The once familiar sight, sound and smell of the Benskins Brewery complex with its own railway yard are gone but, whatever happens in the future, I am sure Watford Fields will retain the same unique identity and spirit of independence .

We retrace our steps back to Wiggenhall Road and climb the artificial slope over the railway bridge under which trains to Croxley Green still pass. On our right, as we climb the hill, we pass Watford Grammar School for Girls, opened in 1907 although its origin may be traced back to Dame Fuller's Endowed School established in St Mary's Churchyard.

Benskins prior to demolition, late 1970s.

Crossing Vicarage Road, a few yards away from the old Cottage Hospital, we arrive in Merton Road. The name Merton perpetuates the former owners of the land: Merton College, Oxford. The land was sold to Mr F Fisher; in all probability only the fourth owner. The first was the Abbot of St Albans, the second was the Crown (Henry VIII) and then Merton College.

Apart from that historical connection, there is little of architectural interest to hinder our progress except the Empire cinema which first opened its doors to the public in 1913 and celebrates its 70th anniversary this year (1983). From Merton Road we enter Cassio Road, distinguished by much larger houses overlooking the South West Hertfordshire ground that was once the home of Watford Football Club.

With some exceptions, early planning and development were influenced by bridle paths and other rights of way. The story is told that a path to Shepherd's Lodge crossed Cassio Road and was once called Monks Folley. It is a name which frequently occurs in monastic towns and cities and is invariably given to a path along which monks regularly walked. 'Folley', we are told, is a corruption of 'fore-ley', a 'meadow in the fore', so the name implies there was once a monastery in Watford and, if we are to believe the legend, it was at Wiggenhall. In fact this belief still persists although no trace of such a building, to my knowledge, has ever been found.

Perhaps one day it will be proved one way or the other but I must admit the heights of Wiggenhall with the river below and four mills to care for, as well as a large area of cultivated monastic land, suggests that St Albans may have delegated their authority to a monastery on such a site.

143

The second stage of our walk brought us to the end of Cassio Road and the decision must now be made whether to turn left or make our way back to the Upper High Street, as it used to be called. Now that the Park Gates, the small group of almshouses bordering Rickmansworth Road and Shepherds Lodge on the corner of Shepherds Road, once one of the lodges to Cassiobury House, were all demolished in post-war years, there is little to attract us historically or architecturally. The Grammar School for Boys, built in 1912, is now listed by the Department of the Environment and is an exception to my comments.

Shepherds Lodge on Shepherds Road corner, 1914.

We turn, therefore, to the right and pick our way along the tedious route back to the Town Hall passing, but not having convenient access to, one of the most beautiful and certainly the most nostalgic building in Watford: the Peace Memorial Hospital. It is interesting to note that although it was built only 13 years after the Grammar School, it was omitted in the recent spate of buildings listed by the Department. I wonder whether we are left to draw our own conclusions?

We must not pass the seat of local government without viewing Mary Bromet's 'Peace Memorial', which the Town Hall still incorrectly regards is the official war memorial. There were three ponds in the vicinity of the old Cross Roads, only one of which remains today. There was one near The Elms, which was demolished to make way for the Town Hall and the other was in Cassio Hamlet, not far from the dower house, Little Cassiobury. The bandstand cannot be ignored, if only for the reason that it stands out like a sore thumb surrounded by alien paving stones alongside Watford Central Library, instead of its natural habitat – the grass and trees of Cassiobury Park.

It is difficult to even guess where the island site of Cross Roads once stood; probably in the middle of the underpass. Here a drinking fountain and a signpost once denoted 'Town End', the name given to The Elms by local residents. Here the AA man often stood, saluting drivers of cars bearing the chromium-plated yellow AA badge. Not everyone will recall the inscribed stone indicating the end of the Sparrows Herne Turnpike. The inevitable question arises: Whatever happened to these field monuments and did they suffer the same fate as Watford Heath's drinking fountain? Before the

Cross Roads, 1930s.

roundabout was built, you may remember the relatively small area of grass that was a feature of the top of the town. Like Watford Fields, it was a remnant of common pasturage where the grazing of animals was an age-old sight.

Unfortunately the Pond received the attention of our local planners and the disastrous treatment given to this once-attractive feature with its green cast-iron balustrade and single fountain has gained little respect from the community at large. We pass the Prudential building, erected on the site of the old council offices[60] and the Fire Station, and stop to admire Monmouth House. The original house was built in the 17th century by the Earl of Monmouth of Moor Park and in later years was split into two residences. An enlightened architect restored the original Monmouth House but rebuilt Platts, thereby providing us with an outstanding example of how one of Watford's older properties could be revitalised to serve a useful purpose in the 20th century. The outstanding success of this project has been ignored by every serving councillor from that day to this.

To our left is Clements, built on the site of Watford House with yet another pond and then Clarendon Road, once the home of Watford's elite, built in fields between the High Street and Watford Junction. The Drill Hall has disappeared to make way for one-way systems and Charter Place became a concrete white elephant before it was even opened by Prince Charles. An oasis in an architectural desert is Jackson Jewellers in its ancient timber-framed building.

We remember the last of the limes that were butchered annually on Dudley's Corner. Like 'Tommy' Deacon's Hill, the name still survives and reminds us of his farm house which once bordered the High Street, before Clarendon Road was cut through to the Junction. The rick yard was said to be located on the site of the Drill Hall. Its last tenant was in all probability Mr Clutterbuck's baliff who farmed the fields at the rear. If you raise your eyes above the building on Dudley's Corner, where Clarendon Road meets the High Street, you will see the old premises of Watford's Conservative Association before its transfer to Halsey House.

As we approach W H Smith[61], passing the site of Lime Tree Commercial Temperance Hotel near Clarendon Road, we walk over the tunnel which undoubtedly existed between the original Green Man and the mausoleum behind the Palace Theatre. If we are to believe legend, it connected to other local houses as an escape route. As Dick Turpin and others are said to have operated locally, need I say more.

High Street looking north. Bucks on left; temperance hotel by lime trees on right, 1910.

Lime Tree Commercial Temperance Hotel, 1910.

Approaching Market Street and the Compasses, now Peter Lord[62], we try to imagine the time when a butcher's shop straddled the entrance to Market Street between the Rose & Crown and the pub. Under the wagonway, there was access to a path to Shepherds Lodge called Monks Folley, about which I have written. In the process of demolishing the butcher's shop to make way for Market Street, a small 15th century window of two cinque-foiled lights was exposed and Benskins thoughtfully built it into the wall of the new Compasses.

If we had turned into Market Street, it would have been for only one reason: to see Holy Rood Church, the often quoted miniature cathedral designed by John Bentley, architect of Westminster Cathedral. Staying in the High Street, we pass through the Market Place, once the setting of our 700-year-old market. The Essex and the George Hotels are only memories, conjuring up the days of the stage coach. On our right was the Spread Eagle and further down the High Street, at No 156, is The One Crown which is now listed. Ignoring its renovated elevations, it is the oldest structure in Watford and that includes the Bedford Almshouses in George Street which were erected in 1580.

One Crown pub, late 1920s.

Our guided tour of the town, by coincidence rather than design, left us at The One Crown, which can claim the rare distinction of being Watford's oldest building, pre-dating the Bedford (Essex) Almshouses.

The shops on the island site fronting St Mary's Parish Church are of many different dates. My earliest recollection of a new building was in 1927 when Lilley & Skinner, now Saxone, moved into their new premises which blended in with the older properties; although the absence of windows on the first floor elevation prompted many adverse comments at the time. In more recent post-war years, the corner block bordering the Market Place was rebuilt. A modern wagonway gives access to the church, car park and Vicarage Road.

This area was once the very heart of the town. Here, the hand-cranked Braithwaite pump supplied water from a very deep well, delinquents were placed in an iron cage or, for instant but rough justice, locked in the stocks. Here, too, stood the Market House which features in many early illustrations of Watford. It was destroyed in a disastrous fire in 1853.

Fires were a perpetual hazard. In the 1830s Sutton's Candle Factory, probably on the site of Fisher's old premises, caught fire and caused the destruction of the King's Head to the chagrin of its regulars. At this point New Street begins. It once fronted the Market Place and joined up with George Street. Here, Ballard's buildings were demolished in 1926. Many years earlier it was part of the estate of the original Watford Place which has been dated at 1500 and was rebuilt about 1620.

It is on record that in 1613 Dame Mary Morrison leased the house to accommodate the church lecturer and four almswomen. Of that estate, only the almshouses remain. Dame Elizabeth Fuller lived there when she opened her Free School in 1704. You will no doubt remember the stonemason's yard behind iron railings and the remnants of a Tudor House at the rear, all of which disappeared in the name of municipal improvements. In one stroke, this once attractive and historic area of New Street and Church Street was effectively eliminated.

Watford Place from George Street, 1979.

King's Arms, on corner of High Street/King Street, late 1920s.

Now Watford Place is to be found in King Street and is skirted by the one-way road system. Built in 1790, access to the house was once gained via the High Street by passing through attractive gates protected by a lodge. When King Street was created in 1852, access was by means of a wagonway under auction rooms. These were subsequently demolished and the lodge became the King's Arms beer house.

There is some historical confusion about George Healey's bewery in King Street. It was already established in 1862 and Watford Pale Ale and Primrose Ale were among its better known brews. By 1898 it had become part of the Benskins empire and it continued in business until new brewery buildings in the High Street took over production. Virtually all traces of the original site have disappeared.

The Parish Church was originally built in the 12th century, but very little remains by which this period may be identified. In 1871 it was restored, which was perhaps just as well as the foundations were giving way. During the renovations a wall and ceiling collapsed and a number of workmen escaped injury. The outside walls were faced with flint and the churchyard was lowered some 3-4 feet. During excavations at the base of the tower, parts of a Norman font were found buried in the wall. They were pieced together and the font was used at St James' Church, Watford Fields.

It is difficult to imagine that St Mary's has been a parish church for 800 years. In that period of time, much of Watford's history may be found within and without its walls. Such names as Morrison, Essex, Heydon and Clutterbuck have become an intrinsic part of our local history. Both Williams (1884) and Saunders (1931) in their respective histories of Watford have written comprehensive accounts of the origin and the changing fortunes of this historic church.

Woolworth's, 1937.*

Old Watford Vicarage, demolished 1914.

We walk along King Street and back into the High Street. We remember Boots on the corner of Queens Road, often called Queen Street in the early days, and their move to new premises on the site of the Rose & Crown. On our left is the new Woolworth's, which store was erected on the site of the original vicarage.

The end of our journey is now in sight as we enter Lower High Street and pass shop fronts which belie the true ages of an assortment of quaint buildings on the east and west sides. We pass the junction of Water Lane where Gibsons once made and sold their well-known brand of pork sausages which deservedly became famous. In our mind's eye we have passed the Penny Bazaar and are now in the vicinity of Smart's, Cox and Percy Wilson's, shops with which we were once so familiar.

Now it is a wilderness of roads, crossings and traffic lights exposed to the east and west winds. Familiar landmarks are few; the station, Benskins mansion and the little houses known as 200 and 200a, which are listed but neglected and are rapidly deteriorating. As we make for Town End Bridge, we see before us the Colne Valley. On our left, in the late 1970s, Westons Fish Restaurant; Swann's, the original Police Station of 1860; and Stapleton's (15th century) were familiar sights and represented what was left of our architectural heritage. Now that has all gone and we are subjected to a view of car lots, hoardings and isolated properties divorced from their natural environment.

Westons Fish Restaurant, left, at 189 High Street;
JWS at 191; and Swann's at 193, 1978.

The demolition of the evil-smelling gas works and showrooms with the arrival of North Sea gas was one of the few benefits derived from modern technology, although the gasholders still dominate the scene and dwarf Frogmore House. The hope persists that one day, despite the advent of the Southern Junction road scheme, some effort will be made to restore the River Colne to its former glory.

71   Watford's Politicians – Part 1

In my experience and, I am sure, in the experience of virtually all ex-service men and women during the war years, there was an unwritten law that religion and politics were two subjects not to be discussed within the confines of a barrack room. They were and always have been inflammatory topics which discussion and argument only served to divide rather than consolidate. With these obvious dangers in mind I will try, as objectively as possible, to recall something of the political history of Watford, upon which foundation our present political system was built.

A little over a century ago, only three county members represented the whole of Hertfordshire – although in earlier years there had been five. Watford and its people were not represented, except as part of the county. From the 18th century there was one surname that was synonymous with public and parliamentary service: the Halseys of Gaddesden.

The Halsey family was traditionally involved and as far back as 1768 a Halsey represented the county. His son, Thomas P Halsey, also stood for the county in 1847 and 1852. However, his life and political career came to an abrupt end when, in 1854, with his wife and second son, the boat in which they were cruising in the Mediterranean capsized and they were all drowned. The first son, Thomas F Halsey, was only 16 years of age when disaster struck.

Like his father and fathers before him, he entered the political arena and, at the age of 36, was returned as one of the members for the county. In those early days the franchise was not universal and only a minority were eligible to vote. Since the electorate was confined to the few and Parliament was dissolved at the drop of a hat, the now familiar hustings were not part of the political scene. However, the age of enlightenment, if not participation, was dawning and six years later he was again returned for Hertfordshire, but now an element of heckling and rowdyism was creeping into the hustings and candidates were becoming familiar with a new kind of politics that had to be fought and argued.

At the General Election of 1885 fresh factors emerged. The new franchise for voters gave the vote to every householder and, of equal significance, the county was divided into four divisions, each with a representative number. One of the new divisions was South West Hertfordshire and Watford was its political centre.

Halsey's rival was George Faudel-Phillips representing the Liberals and the result was closer than one would imagine. Halsey won the seat by a small majority of 320. Parliament only survived another year and he was returned unopposed. The next election took place in 1892 and this time he defeated his Liberal opponent by over 1,000 votes. In 1895 and 1900 he was again returned unopposed and in 1901 became a Privy Councillor.

Nathaniel Micklem came from Hoddesdon and became a Queen's Councillor in 1900. In 1906, as a Liberal, he challenged the old established Halsey territory of South West Hertfordshire and won a decisive victory over his opponent who had given 32 years of his life as a member of the House of Commons. The loss of his seat precipitated Halsey's retirement from the political scene, although he remained Deputy Chairman of the Hertfordshire Quarter Sessions and Chairman of the Hertfordshire County Council. In later years he was honoured with a knighthood for his services.

Liberal meeting at the Clarendon Hall, 1906.

Between the years of 1906 and 1910, when Lloyd George was Chancellor of the Exchequer, the Liberal government introduced measures which even by today's standards could be called revolutionary in concept and ramification. His new budget introduced or increased duty and tax in areas that had been deemed sacrosanct: death estates, land, mining royalties, income, cars, petrol, spirits and tobacco! Not surprisingly, the measures were welcomed in some quarters and deplored in others. The government lasted until the beginning of 1910. Its downfall was anticipated and rival political campaigns in Watford and district were quick to get underway. At the Clarendon Hall, two major demonstrations were broken up as fists and tempers flared.

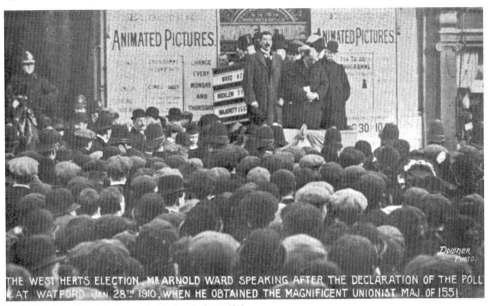

Arnold Ward giving his post-election speech at the Corn Exchange, 1910.

Mr Nathaniel Micklem QC stood for the Liberal Party again and a newcomer represented the Conservatives. His name was Arnold Ward, a name which was familiar to the electorate of South West Hertfordshire. His mother was Mrs Humphry Ward, the best-selling novelist who lived at Stocks, Aldbury; he was the great-grandson of Dr Arnold of Rugby and great-nephew of Matthew Arnold. As a Special Correspondent of 'The Times', Arnold Ward had covered events in India, Sudan and Egypt at the turn of the century and was called to the Bar in 1903.

In 1910 Arnold Ward won the seat for the Conservatives by a majority of 1,551 votes over Micklem. Nationally the Liberal Unionists had been returned to power and, by the year-end, Parliament was again dissolved and Ward was returned, but with his majority halved.

Within four years, the Great War of 1914 was declared and politics were put aside during the period of hostilities. Of all the politicians of those days, none was regarded with more affection than Nathaniel Micklem. In my canvassing days of the early '60s, the old folk invariably mentioned his name, recalling his relatively short term of office and long life. He died in 1953 at over 100 years of age.

After the costly victory, the survivors of the First World War came home from the trenches, the Middle East and the Far East. They returned in triumph and hope; hope for the future in a country fit for heroes. But the country they had left was not the country to which they returned. The celebrations confirmed their triumph, but their hope for a better life was not realised. A coalition government had failed to guide the country back to prosperity. Unemployment, strikes and hunger marches became a familiar feature of the immediate post-war period. For many, the prospect of migration to Canada, Australia and New Zealand offered the only hope of work.

By 1922 the mood of the disenchanted electorate indicated a change in government was long overdue and that a return to the traditional party system was their only salvation. During these turbulent times, Dennis Herbert was the Member of Parliament for the Watford Division. As Chairman of the Incorporation Committee, he had successfully applied for and received Borough Status for Watford. Meanwhile, Liberal Lloyd George had resigned the premiership and was succeeded by Conservative Bonar Law as leader of the Coalition Government.

The position became intolerable, as all three parties brought pressure to bear to end the unsatisfactory state of affairs and bring order out of chaos. Three candidates were adopted by our local parties: Robert Bateman, Liberal; J J Mallon, Labour; and Dennis Herbert, Conservative. Each man promised his dedication to the improvement of trade, pensions, rehabilitation and welfare. Surprisingly, the political climate was relatively quiet with little excitement generated at meetings throughout the town.

The General Election was held on 15 November 1922 and Watford Division returned Dennis Herbert with a majority of nearly 3,500. The result was correctly anticipated locally and nationally. Then Bonar Law resigned leadership and Parliament was dissolved to give Baldwin a new mandate. Dennis Herbert was returned with a majority of 3,001. Despite another Conservative Government, the problem of unemployment remained, but in Watford it was far less than the national average and one of the lowest in the country.

Meanwhile a Knighthood was conferred on Dennis Herbert before Parliament was once more dissolved. In 1931 Sir Dennis Herbert was returned as Conservative candidate to a National Government under Ramsay MacDonald by a majority of nearly 25,000. In 1928 Sir Dennis was elected Deputy Chairman of Ways and Means. In the General Election of 1935 he was returned with a decreased majority of 13,000 in a straight fight against his Labour opponent. He resigned in 1943 as deputy speaker of the house due to poor health, but his service to the nation did not go unrewarded when he took the title Baron Hemingford of Watford and retired to the House of Lords.

A by-election followed and the new candidates were Gp Capt Helmore, National Government; the Hon Douglas-Home, Independent; and Raymond Blackburn, Commonwealth. Gp Capt Helmore was returned on a small poll and a small majority of 2,000. He served from 1943 until 1945, when the National Government had safely guided the country through another major conflict.

The older generation will remember the days when Churchill was rejected and Major John Freeman for Labour was elected with a majority of just over 2,000. However, 1950 brought further changes in representation when a new constituency of South West Hertfordshire was created and Watford Borough was represented by its own Member of Parliament. South West Hertfordshire was contested by Gilbert Longden, Conservative; Lawrence Allaker, Labour; and George Middleton, Liberal; and Watford by John Freeman, Labour; Max Bembose, Conservative; and Brinsley Bush, Liberal.

Watford had become a marginal seat and, in a determined effort to retain it, Premier Clem Attlee and other notable members of the Labour Party came to the town to support Major Freeman. Their efforts on his behalf did not go unrewarded and he was returned with a majority of 1,457, while Gilbert Longden romped home with a thumping majority of over 8,500.

Watford remained a marginal seat when, in 1955, a straight fight with Labour gave Mr Farey-Jones a majority of 1,700 over Ashley Bramall. The Suez crisis and ill health ended the career of Anthony Eden and Mr Harold 'You've Never Had It So Good' Macmillan decided to go to the country in 1959.

The 'First Eleven' Liberal candidates who contested every seat in 1960. Ted Parrish front left in dark suit; to his left Stan Boxall owner of Oakley Studios in Clarendon Road. Next to him Bunny Hensby, Oxhey Village Environment Group founder; Fred Rance with bow tie behind; Ian Steers facing Bunny and John Jacques behind. Others in the photo are: Walter Lang, Ford Longman, George Crowther, Frank Holman and Alfred Hunt

At the General Election the Liberals re-emerged with a new candidate – Mr Ian Steers; Mrs Renee Short was adopted by Labour; and Mr Farey-Jones stood again for the Conservatives. It was a tough three-cornered fight and none came tougher than Mrs Short who took on all-comers at her impromptu meetings at the Pond. However the electorate asserted its right to elect the man it knew and Farey-Jones was returned with a majority of 2,901.

The local political scene of more recent years will be known to you, but I hope that my review of the background of our representation in Parliament during the emergence of Watford from an agrarian to a commercial and industrial economy will bring back memories.

73   Christianity in Watford

We are so often inclined to take the present for granted and the past as something to be found in a local history book. We seldom give thought to the intermediate period; the grey area covering the last two or three generations when the roots of our society were established. Our religious background is a good example.

When Henry VIII decided to disassociate himself and his people from the Church of Rome and assume religious independence as head of the church, one of his final acts after the Dissolution was to order the Great Bible to be placed in every church. What did not change was the nature of the doctrine. The combination of these two events may well have sown the seed of dissension. As early as 1574 Nicholas Colborne of the parish of Watford was named as a man whose beliefs and views failed to conform to official observance and teachings of the church. Perhaps there were others, but he was the first local dissenter to go on record.

By 1662 even some of the clergy, harrassed by the Act of Uniformity of 1594, began to express doubts about the veracity of the prayer book. Philip Goodwin, then Vicar of Watford, became a dissenting cleric and was duly ejected for his personal convictions and puritanical attitude. Others were of the same opinion and the Abbey of St Albans has on record an entry made by the Archdeacon that Anabaptist meetings were being held at the home of a Watford carpenter, Mr J Crawley.

Prior to this date, separatists from the Church of England met at Hemel Hempstead where a Baptist chapel had already been established. Their numbers in Watford increased and by 1707 were sufficient in number to form their own local group with a common form of worship. By 1721 they were strong enough to raise funds for a new meeting house to be built in the northern end of an alley which connected Watford High Street with the fields and farmland behind the main thoroughfare.

But over the years the meeting house became too small to accommodate an ever-increasing congregation and in about 1840 a larger chapel was built on the same site. Without a place of worship while building was in progress, a barn at 'Colney Bath' was acquired. The barn has been described as "a bay, partly filled with corn on either side of the space appropriated to the congregation, the roof covered with tiles admitting wind in every direction which, setting in motion innumerable cobwebs hanging from the roof, not infrequently caused some of immense size to fall on the heads of the congregation". Rats and sparrows added to the diversion. "Rakes, scythes, sieves and other worn-out agricultural implements" were lying around, abandoned and forgotten.

The new chapel was built by Mr Mitchell of Watford, but within 40 years it was again too small to accommodate an ever-increasing congregation. Amongst them were many new families that had moved to the town, attracted by the presence of the London and Birmingham Railway as employees or commuters. Mr J W Chapman, architect, was commissioned to design the new church in a Romanesque style and Waterman Brothers of Watford were appointed building contractors.

Beechen Grove Church, 1905.

152

The design of Beechen Grove Church was and still is unique. It is ironic that the church authorities were denied the necessary permission to pull it down as dwindling congregations and increasing repair costs make it difficult to maintain.

The Wesleyans were relative latecomers in the town. They established themselves in 1808 in converted premises in Hedge's Yard, which became their first chapel. Hedge's Yard was once used as an additional entrance to Woolworth's original store and has since been absorbed into their new building[63]. From there, a move was made to Water Lane and then to new premises in Farthing Lane, which we remember as the town or gospel mission almost behind the Swan in Lower High Street and now occupied by Dan Perkins, the Datsun dealers[64]. At the turn of the century a new stone chapel was built in Queens Road, which subsequently became a victim of the one-way system. Demolished in the last 20 years, the site is now occupied by Allied Carpets[65].

The origins of our Congregational and Presbyterian churches are obscure and less well documented. The Beulah Baptists originally met in a building in Loates Lane and later moved to a new chapel in Queens Road. The Primitive Methodists worshipped in Carey Place in accommodation which, in the 19th century, housed the Petty Sessions and County Court.

The first Roman Catholic Church was consecrated in Water Lane but, because of the generosity of Mr Stephen Taprell Holland of Otterspool, a new church was built in Market Street. Of "remarkable beauty", it was faced in flint with a tower and spire turret rising to 117 feet. The church was designed by John Bentley and, with Beechen Grove and St Mary's, is listed by the Department of the Environment.

Holy Rood Church and Market Street, 1912.

Of the many changes in Watford during the last 50 years, none has been as great as the change from religion to materialism, a social phenomenon precipitated by the confusion of priorities.

74   Victorian Oxhey

The character of Oxhey may be said to be epitomised in the Madonna-like statue of Queen Victoria in a niche at first floor level above 37 Pinner Road. She gazes beligerently at the ever-increasing volume of traffic that uses a road built ostensibly for the horse and cart as a convenient short cut to Harrow.

Oxhey is as ancient as any area in Watford and has survived the rural obliteration by those Victorian speculative builders who somehow managed to reduce the green fields of the town into terraced roads and streets, prompted by profit rather than any consideration for the environment. Oxhey was fortunate in the sense that many cottages had already been built as smallholdings and nurseries, which prevented total annihilation of its rural heritage.

Oxhey was once part of the kingdom of Mercia. King Offa II, who reputedly founded the Benedictine Abbey of St Albans, conveyed the land Oxangehaege to the Abbey and it was farmed by the monks for the ultimate benefit of the Church. At the time of the Dissolution, the Abbey lands reverted to the Crown and were then conveyed in 1604 to Sir James Altham who built the first Oxhey Place in 1612. The original family chapel survived the building of two houses on the same site and it may still be seen today with its Jacobean railings which were returned in the 1970s.

During the 1800s the estate was fragmented, of which Jonathan King, a local builder, acquired a considerable area for development. The London and Birmingham Railway opened Bushey Station in 1841 and the fate of Oxhey was sealed in common with many other areas of Watford. Before the turn of the century, development began in earnest and, with the humble beginnings of a hamlet, Oxhey became a district in its own right, although not before some of it was at first regarded as New Bushey.

The Rev Newton Price, chaplain of Oxhey Chapel, changed all that. He correctly envisaged the development of Oxhey and New Bushey and argued that the area considered to be under the jurisdiction of St Mary's Parish Church should become an independent parish. The Vicar of Watford, the Rev Richard Lee James, also ex-chaplain of Oxhey Chapel, vehemently opposed the declaration of independence, but the Rev Newton Price was not to be moved.

Jonathan King generously presented the new authority with an acre of land and many benefactors contributed to the cost of a new church and vicarage after Queen Victoria had given her assent to a new parish of Oxhey, of which the boundaries were clearly defined.

The parish boundary markers were placed in position in 1879 and some are still in existence. They were numbered and provided with the prefix OD, meaning Oxhey District. Now they are known as field monuments and Tony Rawlings, Chairman of Watford & South West Hertfordshire Archaeological Society, has to be thanked for his work in compiling records of these and other monuments which include, of course, the London Coal Duty boundary markers. The remaining OD boundary markers may be found outside 61 Aldenham Road (No 4) and Jewell's Ford Leasing Depot at 68 Chalk Hill (No 3), at the junction with Vale Road[66]. Miss Marjorie Bray, a local historian, was instrumental in saving for posterity the boundary marker outside the garage. During alterations, which included the rebuilding of the old front wall in which the post was embedded, Miss Bray realised its fate was in jeopardy and made the necessary protestations about the need for its preservation. Jewell's and the contractors gave her the fullest co-operation and now it is resplendent in a new coat of paint for all to see. Way back in 1922, the motor car colonnade bearing the charter giving Watford borough status stopped at this very spot when it crossed the border into Watford.

Miss Bray, in her book 'Oxhey, The History of a Parish', tells of one located in Merry Hill at the point where the footpath from Oxhey emerges at the kissing gate and yet another by a small bridge about 100 yards away in Attenborough's fields. Both are now missing, as she correctly points out. I have good news for Miss Bray. Always curious about the disappearance of the marker near the bridge in Attenborough's fields, the presence of which I remember as a boy, I have never stopped making enquiries about this unsolved mystery. I can confirm that in 1977 it was still there. That anyone would steal it for scrap had never occurred to me. It must have weighed a couple of hundredweight at least.

The thief was, I am told, caught in the act and the iron boundary marker was retrieved. Fate decreed that the marker was recovered in the Metropolitan Police District and, not knowing its significance, the story goes that it found its way to a special museum at Bow Street. I volunteered this information to Watford Museum and a letter is now on its way to London to verify whether the marker is there and, if so, asking for it to be returned to Watford. Since two local authorities have been accused of its abduction and their denials have never been taken seriously, I am hopeful they will both be cleared of any connection with its disappearance.

Beating the Bounds. Rev Peter Palmer and members of St Matthew's Church, Oxhey, Bushey Station, 7 June 1980.

A 'bumping' at the then-missing boundary marker, Attenborough's fields, 7 June 1980. Oxhey historian Miss Marjorie Bray on extreme left.

OD marker No 2 restored to its original position, Attenboroughs' fields, 9 Sept 1986.

In 1980 the Vicar of St Matthews, the Rev P Palmer and many of his parishioners beat the parish bounds after many years. By the small bridge in Attenborough's fields, the point where the post should have been, one youngster was 'bumped' in the traditional manner. When the ceremony is next performed, and if the field monument has been restored to its rightful site in Attenborough's fields, there should be a good reason to celebrate with at least one extra bump[67].

75   Watford's Traders of a Century Ago – Part 1

One hundred years ago, when the railway system had been established over 50 years, its presence brought prosperity, expansion and not a few problems by way of utilities, sewerage and street maintenance. Watford's traders were never slow in fulfilling local needs and new industries went hand in hand with those established centuries before.

There were at least three aerated water manufacturers whose products were marketed in those fascinating bottles with glass balls encapsulated in the neck and which required not a little dexterity to consume its contents. The enterprising manufacturers included Jas Dorrell of 1 Sotheron Road; Smith & Co, to be found in the yard of the original Wheatsheaf at Bushey Arches; and the Watford Steam Mineral Water Co in Nascot Street, managed by Mr J Smith. Of the soft drinks, none was more popular than the proverbial ginger beer. Perhaps you remember ginger beer making a comeback in the late '40s and early '50s, when the ginger beer 'plant' was passed secretively from household to household and the occasional casualties of exploding bottles!

Agricultural implements and machinery were sold by Mr T C Grant in the High Street and Mr W Horton, an active agent, was to be found at the George Inn. The biggest, most prosperous and sophisticated of them all was undoubtedly Rogers Bros. They concerned themselves with almost all facets of farming implements, including repairs and new machined parts. Rogers' sawmills and planemills were one of the biggest in Watford, located behind Meeting Alley, and their major competitor was Mr Thos Turner of Cassiobridge, who also manufactured coaches and carriages. Of the same fraternity were a number of names which may be familiar to you: Christmas, Tucker, and Walker & Lovejoy, some of whom survived the coming age of mechanical transport.

Estate agents and auctioneers were then few and far between. Of the former, Mr J C Binyon maintained two offices, one in Pinner Road, Oxhey, and the other in Queens Road. Humbert & Sons of Lincoln's Inn Fields were represented in Watford. Messrs Didsbury, Lavender (also an architect), and Rodell Son each had premises in the High Street, together with Sedgwick Son & Weall who offered additional services as architects, appraisers and valuers. Mr W S Weller conducted his business at 86 Estcourt Road. A list of estate agents operating in Watford today would fill several pages.

Advertisement for The Ladies' Bakery, Oxhey, 1909.

To fulfil our everyday needs, there were many local bakers who baked on their premises. Few, if any, have survived into the 1980s. They were Mr Wand of Villiers Road, H Alsford of Fearnley Street, Bowler of Beechen Grove, W Downer of Chalk Hill, W Gibbons of Langley Road, D Hawkins of Watford Heath, F T Hill of King Street, H Lambert of Sotheron Road, and G T Sear of 38 Estcourt Road. In Watford High Street there was a high concentration: Barton, Griggs, Gristwood, Grove, Munday, Phillips, Simmons, and Uezzell. In Queens Road there were Beckley, Cordery, and Webb. The most famous name of all was Bucks, established in 1868.

In the days when the man in the street would have been wealthy if he had a few pounds in his Post Office savings account, just two banks served the community: the Bucks & Oxon and the London & County. The premises of the latter institution at 63–65 High Street, later Lloyds and located opposite Market Street, are presently (1983) being rebuilt. Although the building was listed, no objections were raised subject to the retention of the charming front elevation which will be faithfully preserved.

There were at least three basket makers: Mr E Norman of Albert Street; Mr Ludgate; and Gibbs & Son, both of the High Street. Gibbs & Son were located at 103 High Street, now occupied by Littlewoods store[68], but their interests extended well beyond the manufacture of baskets as they were well-established coopers. The firm specialised in wooden products including trunks, boxes, picture frames, hen coops and beehives. They made 'plain and fancy' doormats, sieves of every description, wicker garden furniture and repaired, or rather re-bottomed chairs in wicker, rush or cane. They were one of Watford's first sports shops, selling cricket bats, wicket keeping leg guards, batting gloves, nets, scoring boards, long bows, foils, rugby and soccer balls, carpet croquet and puzzle money boxes!

Mr J Harrington of 112 High Street and R Tucker of King Street were manufacturers and retailers of bicycles, which occupation reminds us once again of Watford's light industrial past; a feature that has so often saved the town from mass unemployment.

One hundred years ago, two taxidermists were kept busy mounting the heads of foxes killed by local hunts and record-breaking fish caught in the pure waters of the River Colne, such as a Neuchatel trout weighing 9¾ lbs caught by Mr C H Thomas of Colnebrook in 1883. Both taxidermists traded in the High Street. I wonder if the work of Bowers or Tyler is still gracing some ancient mahogany sideboard in one of Watford's massive Victorian houses.

In one of Watford's 19th century trade directories, 21 boot and shoemakers are listed, of which at least 10 traded in the High Street. It is interesting to note that we were then a nation of shopkeepers. Mr C Atkins cobbled in Weymouth Street; Mr Geo Busby in Southeron Road; Mr Geo Hayes in Paddock Road, Oxhey; Mr W Hayes in Aldenham Road; and Mr William Hayes in Cassio Hamlet. In Queens Road you will surely remember Geo Sturman, although who will recall Benjamn Tiner in Prince Street or J Shaw in Estcourt Road?

I have already written about some of the trades and traders of Watford a century ago and, with your indulgence, I will continue the search for names with which we are still familiar.

The foundry of Cassell, Clowes & Co, called the Colne Valley Iron Works of Lower High Street, has long since disappeared in common with the brick and tile manufacturers. One proprietor was Mr Jos Coote of Woodford Road and the other, Mr W T Stone of Oxhey Lane. Mr Stone worked his clay pits and fired his products in local kilns until the '30s. Evidence of his hand-made and fired bricks may still be found in Oxhey and one easily identifiable house in Kingsfield Road was built entirely with his bricks. There is no uniformity in their appearance and each is different in colour and texture. They were built with bricks of character and their everlasting qualities reflect the self-sufficiency of a country town capable of producing its own building materials.

There were many local builders; at least 20 in 1883. The Bonnetts of Grosvenor Road and Queens Road; Jas Pratt of Woodford Road; Clifford & Gough of Estcourt Road; T Kempster of St Albans Road; J Longman of Smith Street; and J & G Waterman in the High Street. I am sure many of them will strike past and present chords.

To my knowledge, only one of the old butchers has survived: W Dumbelton of the High Street, about whom I have already written[69]. There were Epgrave of Chalk Hill; Horace Tipple of Southeron Road; Mrs Fenn; and Mr F Fisher of the High Street, as well as many others whose names and addresses are now an enigma. However, I would add a rider to my reference to Dumbelton. I recently received a letter from Mr Henry Williams of Bushey who told me that when Dumbleton's displayed its merchandise outside the shop, straw was laid on the road surface, presumably to overcome the problems of mud or dust, as dictated by the season. George Dumbleton, he adds, succeeded his father in the butcher's business.

Dumbelton's, 231 Lower High Street, 1965, photo by Denise Mangles.

"Then my father and I", wrote Mr Williams, "bought the business from George Dumbelton just before the First World War. We carried on the high-class family trade with four ponies and carts for daily deliveries in the area and as far as Kings Langley, Chipperfield, Croxley Green, Pinner, Hatch End and Wealdstone. There were quite a few titled families on our books, also such well-known names as Mr Peter Cadbury, the Dunhill tobacco magnate at Stanmore and the Blackwell farming family at Oxhey, from whom we bought most of our animals for slaughter. Also, we were purveyors of poultry and meat to the Officers' Mess at Bentley Priory". Distance was no object in those days.

Mr Henry Williams reluctantly retired in the late '70s and passed on the business to "a good tradesman who kept the name as a good trademark". He in turn retired and sold the business to another "good tradesman who will keep the old name surviving, the premises now being in Bushey Hall Road where I moved from the High Street when they cleared the area". Mr Williams believes he is the last survivor of the "old Dumbelton saga" and recalls those great days with not a little sadness and pride.

Such personal recollections are invaluable to the historian, since the impersonal documented evidence of those far-off days fails to capture even part of the everyday life of a local resident and tradesman, whose objective, in this case, was to live up to the name of Dumbelton; a name synonomous with the best meat and butchery service in the town.

Cabinet making and carpentry were well patronised trades. Of the elite woodworking fraternity, Mr Geo Capell had his workshop at 214 High Street along with Mr Timms, also in the High Street, and Mr A Wilson of Duke Street. The choice of carpenters was a little more difficult. Their names included Clifford & Gough; George Dowse of Pinner Road; Mr Goodwin of Stamford Road; T Kempster of St Albans Road; J Longman of Smith Street; and T Tennant of Langley Road. Many of these names will be familiar to you, I am sure. It would be remiss of me not to add that Clifford & Gough also specalised in masonry, bricklaying, slating, plastering, plumbing, painting, glazing, gas fitting and bell hanging!

Cabs were used less frequently than they are today, since few could afford the fares and walking to one's destination was by far the most common and least expensive means of transport. Mr C Ash held the franchise at Watford Junction and J Lonnon at Bushey Station, while G Luckett had his stables at Bushey Arches and W Large transported his fares from the Clarendon Hotel[70].

Horse-drawn carriages at Clarendon Hotel, now The Flag, 1908.

A century ago, Watford was very much a country town and cattle dealing was an important contribution to the way of life.
The Fowlers of Little Bushey and St Albans Road were respected and well-known cattle dealers. It is not so long ago that Mr Bone, a rag and bone merchant by trade, kept his pony and cart in Oxhey. On his death, the old wooden stable behind Wilcot Avenue was demolished and council lock-up garages were built on the site. Once in isolation, the area is now part of a newly-developed area called Field End Close; a name that is difficult to relate to, since the site was once the Wilcot Avenue allotments.

In the days long before the National Health Service, chemists and druggists were not afraid to prescribe for common ailments, since not everyone could afford to visit a doctor. We may remember Chater's at 129 High Street, although Cottell's of St Albans Road or Parrott's of the High Street and Queens Road are probably forgotten.

Before the days of electricity but not of gas, the most popular household fuel was coal, brought in from the coalfields of the midlands and the north via the new railway. Depots were logically established at local stations. Bushey Station was

The piggeries and allotments beyond; now Field End Close, Oxhey, 1980.

then and remained until more recent times an important coal yard, not only for the distribution of domestic coal, but also as the unloading point for Watford's gas and coke works which were established just before the arrival of the railway. The gas works were built in 1834 and the railway arrived in 1837.

Lower High Street would never have been chosen if it had been realised that coal trains could have been brought directly to the works via sidings from the main line. That three-year disparity sealed the fate of the area that was once a beauy spot.

In my last article I made reference to Bushey Station as the depot for the coal processed at the gas works. Now I will tell you about the means by which coal was transported to the Lower High Street.

Local coal carters, 1910.

How many horses and carts were in use at any one time I do not know, but a continuous procession of carts trundled up and down the cobbled Pinner Road, which must surely have been one of the tasks of Hercules. The coal wagons were drawn into the sidings and a gang equipped only with shovels transferred the coal to the waiting cart. As soon as it was full, horse and driver pulled out of the yard. A metal block on a metal chain was unhooked from the cart and placed under one of the wheels. The friction of metal on cobbles effectively acted as a brake down the rather steep incline to Bushey Arches. The horse was quite capable of finding its own way to and from the works, but the driver was also a labourer and he worked from morning until night to maintain the coal mountain at the gas works. Drivers literally spent their whole working lives shifting coal from one place to another because the gas works arrived in Watford before the railway.

Coal, our staple form of heating, and coke for the boiler produced many by-products which collected in the domestic chimney. After the winter season and before the rites of spring cleaning were performed, it was customary to call the sweep. It was a love-hate relationship. Before his arrival, every old sheet was brought into use and every horizontal surface was covered after the removal of ornaments, trinkets, vases and clocks. Old newspapers were brought into service to cover the linoleum and the rugs miraculously disappeared. The ritual completed, the arrival of the sweep would be nervously awaited.

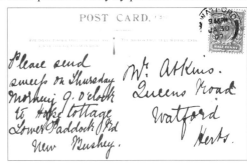

Request for Mr Atkins, the sweep, 1907.

A century ago there were at least three sweeps in Watford: J Northwood at Red Lion Yard (now under Charter Place); W Chance at Meeting Alley; and D Atkins of Queens Road. By coincidence, I remember another Mr Atkins who may well have followed in his father's footsteps. He would arrive in a Morris van of doubtful vintage that was as dirty as his trade and long before the MOT inspection was ever introduced, otherwise he would have had to walk with his brushes. Of slight build but as tough as nails, he would placate the householder in reassuring terms as dust flew before he had even completed his preparation. Up went a grimy black canvas screen covering the fireplace and in went the brush through a centre slit. Another cane was screwed on and another until the brush made a brief appearance outside the chimney. Ominous thuds could be heard behind the screen as a mixture of mortar and soot obeyed gravity and clouds of near-invisible soot radiated from the fireplace.

The offending pile was hastily bagged and 6d changed hands, then Mr Atkins was once more on his round of chimneys. The aftermath almost defies description. The insidious smell of soot pervaded the room and spread throughout the house. Sheets and newspapers were gathered together and shaken outside. The smell persisted as the fine soot was dusted off unprotected surfaces such as the tops of doors. A new fire was laid and as the newspaper ignited the wood and the wood ignited the coal, the fire drew well. There was a sense of satisfaction that the operation had been carried out successfully.

The coffee tavern was at 87 High Street, a limited company managed by W B Cosham. It was the brainchild of the richer element of the temperance fraternity to offer meeting place facilities without the necessity of visiting a public or ale house. The new promotion was a great success for the sponsors, including the Hon Reginald Capel and the temperance members. By 1883 the tavern was enlarged with the addition of bedrooms and other rooms, as well as a new temperance hall at the rear big enough to accommodate some 200 pledged Blue Ribbons.

Whether G Downer of Woodford Road; C M Hosier of St Albans Road; J Squire of Estcourt Road; or E Roberts of the High Street earned a doubtful living in the capacity of rent and debt collectors, we shall probably never know. Recalling those sometimes callous days, I expect they were instrumental in evicting families and possessing their furniture. The bad debtor, albeit in a minority, has always been part of our social system in any age.

Of a more agrarian flavour, Lambert & Reeves of Sotheron and Escourt Roads were dealers in corn and flour, manufactured in the town by East, Hudson, King and Rowse Brothers, all located in the High Street. If you needed the services of a dairyman or cow keeper, there was no problem as the choice of names was considerable. Five of them could be found living in the High Steeet, including Mrs Tookey at No 185. Mr Birch lived in Princes Street; Mr Gilbert in Nascot Road; H Taylor in Sotheron Road; and Mr Mendham in Beechen Grove.

Pursuing our country heritage, two curriers (leather dressers) and leather sellers worked in the High Street, giving some credence to the presence of the popular Leather Sellers' Arms that was located at 235 High Street. The occupation of hurdle maker was not, as far as I know, perpetuated in the name of a pub but, nevertheless, Mr C Lovett of 30 High Street was an expert in this long-forgotten country craft. The same may be said of Mrs Unwin, who was probably the town's last woolstapler. She too lived and worked in the High Street and, with her death, came the end of an industry which could be traced back to medieval times.

78   The End of the Clarendon Connection

The post-war years of the First World War precipitated many social changes. The era of cheap labour upon which Victorian industrialists capitalised was coming to an end. But the period of transition and adjustment was not without problems, especially for the aristocracy whose age-old lifestyle was in jeopardy as a result of the new social and economic order with the transfer of labour to more remunerative jobs and greater personal freedom.

Prior to 1935 there had been a number of casualties as the vast estates surrounding Watford came under the auctioneers' hammers or were sold privately. Moor Park, the home of the Eburys, is one example. Here once lived George Neville, brother of Warwick, labelled in history as the Kingmaker; Cardinal Wolsey; and the Duke of Monmouth, who literally lost his head in 1685.

Nearer home the Blackwell family lived at Oxhey Place, bounded by 1,000 acres of beautiful countryside including Oxhey Woods. The estate, or rather part of it, became a golf course at which the Prince of Wales frequently played. Within a quarter of a century and another World War, part of the post-war rebuilding programme included the purchase of the golf course and the building of a new estate primarily for Londoners, which we now call South Oxhey.

Cassiobury House, to which I have so often referred, was demolished in 1927 and broken up for housing and recreation. The family seat of the Earls of Essex was destroyed almost without trace. There were compensations, which we are inclined to overlook. The vast estate, already whittled down in the 19th and 20th centuries by piecemeal sales, had restricted the growth of Watford. Its slow decline and ultimate sale served to allow the growth of the town. The loss of the historic connection with the Earls of Essex is virtually forgotten.

It was in such a climate that the dissolution of Watford's last historic estate was the subject of rumour and speculation. All eyes centred on The Grove, the family seat of the Clarendons. The Earl of Clarendon had not lived there since 1925 and the inevitable announcement, which came in mid-1935, that the estate would go up for auction should have come as no great surprise. In fact, the shock of

The Grove and Watford's original coat of arms, 1910.

losing the last aristocratic family and the foreseeable fragmention of the estate was considerable and fear was expressed as the fate of Cassiobury House was still fresh in the public's mind.

The Grove did not enjoy the same architectural antiquity as Cassiobury House since it was built in the 18th century, but the close association of the family with Watford during the period of its emergence from an agrarian to an industrial society shocked the largely static population whose reverence for the nobility was still very much an association of the past. The Earl's inevitable decision was received with regret, as the final bastion of the town's elite fell victim to the economic changes brought about by the war.

Royalty was no stranger at The Grove. An enterprising diarist recorded the following event. His name was Robert Fulke Greville, equerry to King George III. He tells of the occasion in 1789 when the King suddenly decided to pay a surprise visit to the Earl of Clarendon, although one cannot help suspecting that George III was more interested in Lady Clarendon, if not her husband's wealth. He hurriedly assembled an entourage and set off at an early hour to Watford with Queen Charlotte and members of his family.

They passed quietly through the estate of the Earl of Essex without making contact with the Earl, for fear word would be passed on to the unsuspecting Earl of Clarendon. Their unheralded arrival at The Grove created the desired effect. No reference is made to the presence of the Earl, but we are told his wife rushed to her rooms and quickly appeared in a dark green silk gown, in all probability from silk made at one of Watford's mills. Her exaggerated curtsying and theatrical smiles must have reassured the King that his secret had been well guarded.

Another Royal visit - King Edward VII enters The Grove, 17 July 1909.

As the horses were being stabled, he requested to be shown around the house and Lady Clarendon obediently conducted the Royal Party acting as a guide, much to the amusement no doubt of George III. Then it was suggested that perhaps they may care to inspect the grounds and the idea appealed to the King who may not have appreciated the ruse to give the staff time to prepare a meal for the Royal party.

Lady Clarendon ordered her phaeton, a low four-wheeled carriage covered with a white net and drawn by a small fat pony. Lady Charlotte Villiers drove the Princess Royal in a two-wheeled chaise drawn by one horse, followed by Princess Augusta and Lady Egremont in a post-chaise. The Prince of Wales accompanied his father on horseback. During the tour of the estate, the party visited the farm and the piggery. One can imagine the panic within The Grove as the staff hastily prepared a breakfast fit for a King. Someone had the forethought to alert a neighbouring village and gathered together a band of handbell ringers who assembled near the house and played for the unexpected guest.

The Royal party, having been well fed, watered and entertained, expressed their thanks and bid their farewells at about 1pm and by 3.15pm they had safely arrived at Windsor, a distance of 23 miles, having changed horses at Chalfont St Giles.

In 1935, by the order of his Excellency the Right Hon Earl of Clarendon, The Grove was offered for sale by auction. The agent's notice stated that the estate fronted the main Hempstead Road and was about 17 miles from central London via the Watford by-pass. The sale included valuable freehold building land, the mansion, farms, residences, the mill and cottages "embracing about 296 acres, eminently suitable for developing as a building estate".

The auction was to be held on 15 July 1935 at the London Auction Mart, offering the estate as one lot. The disposal of The Grove captured the imagination of the public. Some feared that Watford, like Topsy, would grow and grow without limit; that the countryside to the north would become another Cassiobury Park Estate and the town would lose its identity. But The Grove is still preserved almost in its entirety. London Transport acquired the estate and, in later years, ownership was transferred to British Rail as an executive management training establishment[71]. The redeeming feature was that Watford's expansion in the northwest was at last contained and the countryside was preserved for future generations to enjoy to the full.

79   The Big Spenders

The pattern of Watford as I lovingly remember it began to take shape in the '20s and '30s. The late lamented Cassiobury Park Gates were synonomous with the care and attention which had been given to the preservation of the town with its country origins and friendly population. In the mid-'30s traffic problems, or anticipated traffic problems, were destined to change the face of the town. Traffic lights at King Street and at St Albans Road junction with Station Road replaced the familiar policeman on point duty.

In 1935 the fate of the old Cross Roads was sealed when approval was given for a new roundabout north of the Pond. Implementing the scheme, delayed 12 months because of lack of funds, would cost £12,000, of which the corporation would only have to contribute 20%.

At Cassio Bridge, rebuilt after the First World War, a number of accidents on the hump-back bridge prompted its widening in 1935. At the same time, the Metropolitan railway announced the electrification of the lines between Rickmansworth and Amersham and the addition of two lines between Harrow and Rickmansworth, which would necessitate widening the existing tracks. By coincidence, the Duke of Bedford followed the action of the Earl of Clarendon and planned to put 106 picturesque acres of Chorleywood to auction as prime building land.

It seemed at the time that the country was pulling itself out of the moribund economy and financial restraints were being lifted, giving public authorities the opportunity to become 'big spenders'. Watford was no exception. The Public Baths and the new Central Library were jointly sufficient indication that The Elms site would one day be fully developed and accommodate a new town hall complex.

The site had been acquired as far back as 1919 when the house and a large tract of land were acquired for £7,500! In the days of the Urban Council, just after the First World War, the restrictions on local authorities were lifted and they could resume their normal function. To this end, the visionary councillors purchased The Elms which had once been a private house and later became a hotel. But funds were not made available for large municipal projects and, like the Public Baths, the good intentions did not materialise.

The Borough had purchased 162 acres of Whippendell Woods for £15,725 with a little help from Hertfordshire County Council and, surprisingly, the old London County Council, in the sums of £2,500 and £2,000 respectively. In addition, £92,000 was required for a new water scheme, £10,000 for improved lighting, as well as a new branch library at North Watford, and necessary extensions of the sewerage system to accommodate new housing developments. A further £25,000 was needed to widen St Albans Road at Garston.

On another front, the decision had been made to acquire 118 acres of agricultural land at Leavesden Green for £23,500 for playing fields. You may well ask yourself whatever happened to the playing fields. Well that is another story which I will recount as a separate article. But the big spenders were still not content and although one project had already been turned down at government level they persisted in planning a new town hall, arguing that the sale of the Urban District Council offices in the High Street

View from the Pond, 1937, The Elms on left.

would go a long way to financing the development of The Elms, where the financial departments were then temporarily accommodated.

Same view from the Pond, 1939, Town Hall on left.

Notwithstanding these commitments, nothing could stop Watford Borough from going ahead with their proposals. It became obvious that the proposed roundabout at the Cross Roads was intended to complement the new building. An assessor had been appointed by the Borough and under his jurisdiction six architects were given the opportunity of offering competitive designs for a town hall. Considerable criticism from inside and ouside the council chamber was provoked by restricting the competition to six named architects. The question was asked why Watford's own resident architects were not invited to compete, but the assessor remained unmoved and the rules remained unchanged.

In June 1935 the results of the competition were announced and the submission of Charles Cowles-Voysey was chosen as the most functional, aesthetically pleasing and competent design for Watford's new municipal buildings. The next step was an application to the Ministry of Health for the necessary loan and many government officers, aldermen and councillors anxiously awaited the ministerial decision whether Watford could have its town hall.

At that very moment, the council had received a plea from Lady Verulam to save The Grove from the speculative builder and purchase the house and estate for the community. Her fears were well founded, as new developments of detached houses and semis were gaining momentum, and the town's farmland was being swallowed up at an alarming rate. Lady Verulam no doubt lobbied Sir Joseph Priestly KC, Chairman of Hertfordshire County Council, voicing her fears for the future of the historic Grove.

Sir Joseph was obviously moved and wrote to the Borough suggesting that if the council decided to purchase the mansion and the estate that county would do its best to offer financial assistance. On receipt of his letter, the Mayor suggested that the matter be referred to the Finance Committee. He was paying lip-service to both parties, as the town was now totally committed to so many projects that it could hardly entertain a further drain on its resources to purchase an estate it did not really want.

Rates had already suffered regular annual increases and there was a limit to which the rate payer could continue to underwrite the extravagances of a big spending council. Whether the Earl of Clarendon had privately offered the estate to Watford we will never probably know, but in their over-extended position and, in the final anaysis, in their respect for the ratepayers who were earning probably an average of less than £5 a week, the purchase was never seriously contemplated.

As it happened, Lady Verulam and Sir Joseph need not have worried. We lost the family seat of the Clarendons, but we gained the benefit of countryside which has changed little since the unannounced arrival of George III at The Grove. In this particular instance, we may count ourselves lucky.

The changes taking place in Watford during 1935, which have been the subject of my last two articles, were not confined solely to the activities of the Borough Council or the sale of ancient estates. Not to be outdone, the Parochial Church Council authorised a number of major changes to the interior of St Mary's, Watford's Parish Church.

St Mary's Parish Church and churchyard, 1914.

Mr M T Bevan had been the organist for over 50 years and when he died he left the church a substantial legacy to meet the cost of rebuilding the organ. Mr Geoffrey Shaw, an authority on church music and Mr Harold Gibbons, an ecclesiastical architect, were consulted. They realised that the organ was inclined to drown the choir and suggested that the removal of the instrument from its existing location would permit more daylight to enter the church, while the seating capacity could be increased to accommodate an additional 50 to 100 people.

Their recommendations were accepted and, at a cost of £2,600, new vestries for the clergy and choir were erected in the north transept with an organ loft. G & J Waterman contracted to do the necessary work in just four months. During the alterations a coloured board bearing the Royal Arms dated 1736, which had hung almost forgotten over the chancel arch, was relocated above the entrance to the Essex Chapel.

Now let us walk some 200 yards north and enter the world of telecommunications. Just a few months ago, in October 1981, the Post Office discontinued its telegraph service and so ended an era in which the receipt of a telegram was traditionally regarded as an omen of bad news. We must remind ourselves that very few families could afford a telephone in the mid-'30s and often the humble telegram was the only means of speedy communication. It was also true that fewer people were availing themselves of the facility, partly for economic reasons and partly because an excellent postal service invariably delivered a letter the following day.

To popularise the telegram, the Postmaster General introduced a new cheap rate at a cost of nine words for 6d. The event was celebrated nationwide and, as an important communication centre, Watford became involved in a unique ceremony at the new Post Office in Market Street. In the absence of the Mayor, Councillor Mrs Bridger, in the capacity of Mayoress, arrived at the front entrance of the new building (now bricked up) and was received by Mr S Stubbs, Watford's Postmaster, and taken to his office on the first floor, accompanied by members of the corporation and heads of department of the Post Office. There Mr Stubbs made a short speech explaining that the introduction of the cheap telegram was in response to the wishes of the public, to whom the cost had been regarded as exorbitant. "It is the practice of His Majesty's Government", continued Mr Stubbs "on the occasion of the King's Silver Jubilee to introduce some concession". That concession was to reduce the cost of the telegram.

It was really a public relations exercise, since the telegraph business had declined by 50% between 1897 and 1935. To create the necessary publicity, the Prince of Wales agreed to attend the Central Telegraph Office in London and officially inaugurated the new service by sending the first telegram to the King. Then it was the turn of chosen towns and cities to send telegrams to the Prince of Wales.

A silver pen was handed to the Mayoress by the Postmaster, with which she wrote the following message on the appropriate form: "I have the honour to address to your Royal Highness the first telegram from Watford at the new rate of nine words for 6d. Mary Ellen Bridger, Mayoress".

The Mayoress was conducted to the main office, after being presented with the pen and a bouquet, and handed her telegram across the counter to the Post Office clerk. Then she handed new armlets to six telegraph messenger boys who were presented to her. The party returned upstairs, by which time a reply had been received from the Prince of Wales. Addressed to the Mayoress, Watford, the message read: "To the inaugress – much appreciate Watford's inaugural telegram. Edward P".

Perhaps it was the red-coloured envelopes which used to contain the telegram that gave it a reputation as the harbinger of bad news. Striving for a new image, the old envelope was discarded in favour of a yellow one. The age-old service was discontinued 48 years later, so the occasion and the concession can be regarded as a long-term success.

81   Here Comes the Sun

In the early morning hours of Saturday 20 July 1935 all the roads in Watford seemed to lead to the Junction. Householders in Woodford Road, Clarendon Road and St Albans Road who were light sleepers heard the hushed voices of groups of people making their way to Station Road. The forecourt of Watford Junction Station gradually filled up as more and more people arrived. The first party had assembled on the cobbles as early as 1.30am and they were joined by a constant stream coming from all directions.

Under the guidance of station manager Mr B Bunker, the railway staff tried to control the large numbers; they had been well briefed, but were only just able to cope with an event which barely conformed to normal patterns.

To celebrate the King's Silver Jubilee, at the invitation of the chairman and directors of the Sun Engraving Company, the staff were invited to take a day trip to Blackpool. They dutifully responded, despite the early and staggered hours of departure of a series of special trains. The first train departed at 3.58am, full to capacity. As soon as the platform was clear, the second party was conducted from the forecourt to await the next train. The second train left at 4.15am and the third at 5.38am. The last train steamed in at 6am, having started its journey from Euston. On board were employees of the Milford House operation. The train made a courtesy stop and no doubt collected a few stragglers who had missed the earlier trains. In front of the engine's boiler a board had been securely mounted on which had been painted "Here comes the Sun."

The directors of the Sun had preceded the Saturday trains by leaving Euston in a special saloon coach attached to the Fyld Coast Express. Mr H E Roberts, District Manager of the LMS Railway, made sure that they were satisfied with their accommodation before the departure of the train. Sun's employees from the Nottingham and Leicester works had also left on Friday night to make their cross-country journey.

The movement of all Sun's employees to Blackpool had been arranged by Mr H A Yates with the same precision as the LMS. The four trains ran on schedule. Breakfast was served to the hungry passengers, many of whom had nodded off to sleep, induced by the rhythmic 'clackety clack' – a sound with which we are now not so familiar with the advent of continuous welded track.

Once at Blackpool the employees assembled at the Winter Gardens and by the time the last train arrived everyone was ready for an early lunch. That too had been arranged. The Spanish, Indian and Baronial halls were prepared to receive the new arrivals. Some guests would have been content to find themselves a deck chair on the beach or paddle in the sea, but those in the Spanish Hall found themselves involved in the anticipated formalities of speech making. They were not disappointed.

Edward Hunter, Sun's Chairman, paid tribute to Mr Summerfield, father of his chapel for over 20 years. Mr Summerfield responded with a toast to the success of the Sun Engraving Company and said with meaning and sincerity: "the failure of the firm would cause an immense amount of suffering to us all". Despite his words of warning, he was confident of the Sun's future.

Mr Hunter responded by reminding his directors and staff that it was still a family business. He recalled that the present company was founded in 1898 when he and Mr Hughes had each borrowed £300, together with a third person whom he did not name of a less than adventurous nature. After the first year's trading they declared a profit of £46, whereupon the third person asked for his money back! Then he recalled how the Sun acquired its name. It was his elder brother who first came up with the title of the Sun Engraving Company, but a printer in the City of London had already registered his company in that name. At the beginning they had called themselves André and Sleigh and Anglo Engraving, but in their expansion programme the printing enterprise in London was acquired and with it the title they had always wanted.

David Greenhill, one of Watford's personalities, proposed a toast to trade unionism, stressing that he had been a union member since the age of 20. He recalled working a 54-hour week with an additional 45 hours' overtime, agreeing that there should be a limitation on hours of work. The speeches continued, including a jovial response from Geo Isaacs, General Secretary of NATSOPA (National Society of Operative Printers and Assistants), but formalities did not end with the last toast and last response. Now it was time for presentations.

A book signed by all the members of the Sun and its subsidiaries and a silver ink stand were presented to Edward Hunter by Miss Hamblin and Miss Sheldrake on behalf of the girls at the Watford works. Then Mr A G Symmon, Watford's Managing Director, presented a model horse and cart to their oldest employee, Mr G Wright, who was 85-years-old. As a material bonus, the cart was loaded with silver coins, one for each year of his service.

In retrospect, perhaps the organised day out at Blackpool was a demonstration of unity, if not loyalty. The magazine 'Passing Show', an Odhams publication, was then printed by the Sun. Odhams were interested in a site in Watford and the day was foreseeable that the contract would be lost. Commercial rivalry was already rearing its ugly head. The first cloud had appeared on the horizon, but there was plenty of sunshine in the middle distance.

We do not have to cast our minds back many years to recall the tiled building in what was and is still called the Market Place. The name emblazoned above the shop front was Cawdells. To the extreme left was a glass-roofed arcade between the store and its nearest neighbour, Timothy Whites. Like most arcades it had the usual window displays, but it also served a secondary purpose by giving access to the market in Red Lion Yard. The market and Cawdells store were sacrificed to make way for Charter Place. With the demolition of one of the town's landmarks, the name James Cawdell is still remembered. It was a store in the traditional sense, selling everything from china and glass in the basement to fancy goods and haberdashery on the ground floor and ladies fashions on the first floor. By today's standards the restaurant was modest, not in terms of its culinary standards, but in its size, décor and prices.

Cawdells was a friendly store where the staff were mature and experienced, some having spent much of their lives serving one master. Their selection of high-class reasonably priced china made the store justly famous. In fashions, they were up to date and fashion parades were a frequent event enjoyed by young and old. Chairs were always to be found on the fashion floor where husbands could sit and patiently wait for their wives to make up their minds; a courtesy that has largely fallen by the wayside.

Today the old Cawdells site is an open space of bleak paving stones and steps open to the wind and weather. The arcade too has disappeared, but not without a trace. Short stubs of the old girder work supporting the roof, respectably covered in cement, still bear witness to the arcade as they protrude above Timothy Whites' side windows[72]. It would not surprise me if the ghost of James Cawdell walked this now barren area; his life's work destroyed for a town planner's dream and a shoppers' nightmare.

James Cawdell served his apprenticeship as a young lad with Hitchcock, Williams & Co in the City of London and, in true Victorian tradition, worked very long hours. He 'lived in' and his wages amounted to £20 a year. For this meagre sum he worked from the early morning to late at night. For recreation, he often walked to the Embankment after a staple diet of 'bully beef'. There were few perks for a boy learning his trade. After walking along the bustling riverside, he would prepare himself for yet another day.

After a number of years he decided to leave his employers and start up on his own. He was told that Mr George Longley, a highly respected citizen of Watford and a well-known trader with a shop in the Market Place, wished to dispose of his premises. James Cawdell made enquiries and discovered that Mr Longley was involved in local public service and, although well liked, had given less attention to increasing his business turnover. In 1904 James acquired the draper's shop and its fourteen assistants. He and his wife lived over the shop, which was still customary in those far-off days.

He was not content with just carrying on a good business in the manner of Mr Longley. At that time the Market Place still accommodated the cattle market and, of course, the street market. He capitalised on their presence with new lines and the latest fashions. The shop soon earned itself an enviable reputation and by 1924 he had increased the turnover sixfold and the staff to 50. When reminiscing, James Cawdell recalled the excitement of those times when a wayward flock of sheep entered the shop and the occasional bullock purposefully strayed, with ultimate escape in mind.

His success was founded on hard work, which he expected from his staff. He was not prepared to rest on his laurels and, with the foresight upon which some men thrive, he looked for alternative premises as a means of expansion. There were no premises available but, undeterred, he looked longingly at the Essex Arms, whose fortunes were never quite the same after the demise of the stage coach. The site, he considered, was ideal for his purpose and he made an offer that could not be refused.

When the sale was completed, Mr Cawdell automatically became the licensee of the Essex Arms, one of the most historic of Watford's early buildings. But he expressed no sentiment for its historical associations and architectural interest as the demolition crew moved in and reduced the inn and the Corn Exchange to a heap of rubble.

To cope with his change of fortune, the new enterprise was given a new title on the recruitment to the board of David Greenhill who was appointed chairman. James Cawdell became managing director. In 1935 he retired in that capacity and a luncheon was given by three fellow directors and the staff to mark the occasion. Like the plot of the best soap operas, he retained a seat on the board so the occasion was a matter of saying 'au revoir' rather than goodbye. Mr Greenhill presided and present were members of the Cawdell family, representatives of London business houses and his faithful staff. On behalf of the board he was presented with a silver salver and, from the staff, he received a far more practical gift: a leather case carrying a set of bowls, a game to which he was always partial.

Essex Arms Hotel, on the site of which James Cawdell later built Cawdells, 1905.

Cawdells in the original draper's shop. Essex Arms Hotel to left, Market Place, 1910 (see later photo of Cawdells on p 185.)

As a private company, the firm prospered in its new tiled building. When the street market moved to the Red Lion area the public still passed by his shop windows, so his market day trade was not lost. Here the success of one man's efforts was encapsulated in a white tiled building which contrasted with the brick frontages of other shops; in its day, it was the most modern store in the town. Times unfortunately change and we are now deprived of yet another little bit of Watford's more recent history.

83   The Bushey Jamborette

My dictionary defines "jamboree" as "a large rally of boy Scouts". The word "jamborette" does not appear, but take my word for it that it means a "small rally of boy Scouts". Let me explain in greater detail.

Bushey House and lake, 1910.

Who inspired the county Scouting movement to hold a jamborette in Bushey I do not know, but the decision was made after Lord Bethell had offered the grounds of Bushey House as a venue. Alan Chapman, known better for his Scouting association in Buckinghamshire, was commissioned to devise a pageant which would take into account the natural arena and public vantage points presented by the undulating countryside behind the mansion. Many groups were to be involved and each unit rehearsed its own episode in the traditional club hut. A week before the event a full dress rehearsal was planned, but the weather in 1935 was just as indifferent towards outdoor events. It rained so hard that the rehearsal had to be cancelled.

On the next Wednesday as many as possible attended an ordinary rehearsal and that had to suffice as the only time in which the groups got together. Our contrary weather half a century ago almost reverted to heatwave conditions, so the scene was set for a record attendance and a pageant without a dress rehearsal. Scouts fortunately thrive on adversity.

That afternoon in late June brought thousands of people to Bushey. The audience was accommodated on a gentle slope facing rising ground lined with trees. Using nature's backcloth, 1,000 Scouts presented their 'Quest for Peace through the Ages' after a short opening ceremony conducted by Lord Hampden, Lord Lieutenant of Hertfordshire, in the presence of Lady Hampden; Sir Percy Everett, County Commissioner; Sir Dennis Herbert MP and Lady Herbert; and the Mayor and Mayoress of Watford, Alderman H J Bridger and Councillor Mrs Bridger.

The theme conceived by the author required Mother Earth to be accompanied by her four daughters, Europe, Asia, Africa and America. Scouts in drag were not acceptable in those days of pseudo respectability, so they were played by Pat Woodhead, Nina Shaw, Ella Walker and Ursula Andrews.

You may remember Miss Andrews was related to George Arliss. Mother Earth sat on her throne with a symbol of a gold-coloured sun as a background. The young ladies entered the arena and grouped themselves around the throne to watch the re-enactment of an edited version of the earth's history.

A cohort of Roman foot soldiers marched into the arena led by a centurion and were set upon by an unruly band of barbarians. The Britons were duly captured, without apparent bloodshed, and marched off as prisoners by the jubilant Roman soldiers, to become slaves. The battle over, the soldiers and captives disappeared into the trees and we witnessed a lone centurion taking pity on a beggar shivering with cold (on the hottest day of the year) by tearing his scarlet cloak in two and giving one half to the beggar. Next we witnessed a pagan festival, much enjoyed by the participants, until a band of uncouth Picts decided the moment was opportune to mix it. Once more, the Romans were victorious and a captured boy had to dig his own grave before execution. But who should arrive and save the situation (and, of course, the boy) but a Roman general.

Then we were transported to the Middle Ages and witnessed the investiture of a figure in shining armour and it occurred to us that this was the dawn of chivalry. The new knight, imbued with the spirit of the age, fought off two robbers who were beating up an old and weary traveller. Times do not seem to change.

Another scene change and an 18th century sailor told Mother Earth of the exploits of her children in the brave New World. That was a cue for the entry of a covered wagon moving west, while the inevitable tribe of Red Indians entered from the east for a confrontation. Firewater was bartered for furs; the Indians got plastered and massacred the innocent settlers.

More episodes, as we moved to Africa, David Livingstone, the Matebele Rising orchestrated by Chief Lobengula, and the foreseeable arrival of Cecil Rhodes who negotiated a peaceful settlement. In our innocence, I think we all subscribed to the 'send in the river gun-boat' philosophy as being a sure cure for all social and political ills. We were still the greatest empire the world had ever known and, to prove it, most countries on the world map were still painted red.

Now came the finale as a 1910 Scout troop in their elaborate uniforms accompanied by a bugle band marched into the empty arena, followed by Mars, God of War, heading a platoon of steel-helmeted khaki-clothed soldiers. In the best tradition of patriotism, a Scoutmaster answered the call to arms, leaving his troop in charge of another. The message was loud and clear but who, apart from the visionaries, would ever have believed that that was how it really was to be. The Scout pennant and the Jack were unfurled, the camp fire burned brightly as the Scouts formed a circle round the focal point of their creed and the koodoo horn was sounded as a call to the world's Scouts. On cue, hundreds emerged carrying the flags of all the nations that had then adopted the Scouting movement. For the life of me, I cannot recall seeing the German flag.

Taking part in this tremendous achievement and colourful pagant were the 1st, 2/1st, 28th, 30th, 31st, 32nd, 33rd, 36th, 41st and 43rd groups, including Bushey and Oxhey, Merchant Taylors and the Watford Grammar School. The magnitude of the production was of Ralph Reader proportion. Many Scoutmasters and leaders gave their all to ensure the success of their Jamborette. The pageant master was A J Emery and the producer was G A M Goodfellow. They were supported by A J Conquest, K H B Willks, J T Sayers, S J Wright, H Riggs, A Barton-Smith and H J Collins. I doubt if Bushey has ever presented a greater spectacle.

That evening, the thousands who attended were invited to a Scout camp with demonstrations, games and life-saving by 1st Chorleywood Sea Scouts. It was a magnificent presentation and I wonder if many were tempted to join up that evening.

One of the first air crashes in Watford occurred early in January 1927 when a de Havilland Moth, piloted by T Salway of the Royal Air Force Reserve, was forced to make an emergency landing in the grounds of Stanboroughs at Garston. The incident prompted curiosity rather than fear that the light aircraft could have crashed into one of the many local houses. Few realised the potential danger of such an incident. The aircraft was wrecked and the pilot injured.

British aviator Grahame White flying over Watford in a 'Daily Mail' London to Manchester race. Frenchman Louis Paulhan beat White into first place, 1910.

After the First World War, the topic of flying captured the imagination of young and old alike. Air circuses regularly visited the farms of Watford, charging 5s a flight in old-fashioned but airworthy aircraft. The pilots were invariably some of the few veteran airmen who had survived the war but could not find job satisfaction in any other field. Comics, annuals and books exploited the subject to the full and children thrilled to the astounding and sometimes bizarre adventures of their flying heroes.

Inevitably, a local flying club was formed called the Watford Light Aeroplane Club. Information on its activities is so hard to come by that I cannot say from which fields they operated. Some weeks ago I mentioned that in May 1932 an application had been received by Watford Corporation to build film studios at Leavesden[73]. I did not mention that at the same time a letter was received from the Watford Light Aeroplane Club suggesting that the site for the proposed film studios could be better and more fruitfully utilised as an airfield. Why cannot the corporation purchase the land and create its own aerodrome, they asked.

The film company immediately protested that the Borough should ignore the proposal and claimed that in the ensuing six weeks, work with an initial expenditure of £100,000 was commencing and, spread over a three-year period, expenditure in excess of £250,000 was planned.

Such contrary views were prompted by the availability of land owned by Mr Henry Lloyd who was endeavouring to sell 'One Mile Field' at Hunters Lane. By the following July, the Borough had taken sufficient interest in the suggestion made by the Watford Light Aeroplane Club to arrange a preliminary survey to cost the project. Purchase of the land and preparation of the site was estimated at £28,000 and the capital cost of developing the airport was another £59,400. The estimates looked very attractive on paper, but the concept was reluctantly shelved. The council decided to take no action at that time or, at least until it was known whether the film company was going ahead with the building programme.

Although I have attributed the sowing of the seed of the idea to the Watford flyers, the influence of Lady Cobham (wife of the well-known aviator Sir Alan Cobham) when she met officials of the club in May 1932, was more than coincidental. She had ostensibly visited Watford to discuss a proposed visit of her husband's famous air show in the coming autumn. She was met at a pre-arranged venue on the by-pass by chairman, Reg Kilby; secretary R Landon; and treasurer E Corless. Together they inspected Mr Lloyd's field, which was then farmed by Mr Green of Hunton Bridge. It was bounded by Russell Lane on one side and the footpath from the bridge at Gypsy Lane to Leavesden on the other. The part of the field in which they expressed interest was approximately 800 yards by 400 yards, a total of 80 acres.

The land was beng cultivated at the time and it was agreed with Mr Green that the field could be used after the harvest and before the sowing of the new season's crop. Sir Alan's air fleet at that time comprised 12 aircraft. Lady Cobham was so impressed after her short but meticulous appraisal that she was prompted to say it was ideally suited as an airport for planes travelling north, as there were no other airfield facilities in the area except Hatfield that offered landing facilities for private aircraft owners. Credit in part or in full must be given to Lady Cobham for her accurate evaluation of the potential offered by Mr Lloyd's 'One Mile Field'.

The officers of the Watford Light Aeroplane Club were duly impressed by her assessment, which confirmed their own views. They had good grounds for recommending that Watford should invest in a municipal airport. The proposal was well received at council level and brought aldermen and councillors closer together in savouring the prospect of putting Watford on the air map as one of the country's most progressive local authorities. In the next article I will tell you what happened to this grandiose scheme.

85　　Watford's Light Aeroplane Club – Part 2

Mindful of the municipal deliberations triggered off by the Watford Light Aeroplane Club's proposal that Mr Lloyd's 'One Mile Field' be acquired as a municipal airport, let us recall the fate of Aldenham House, once the home of the Hon Vicary Gibbs. After his death, the house remained empty for a year until one day a member of the '30s equivalent of our jet set spotted the mature property nestling among the trees, surrounded by relatively flat fields in otherwise undulating country. He reported his find to his rich friends and together they acquired the property, which they promptly converted into an exclusive club. Deep in the attractive countryside, it was readily accessible by the newly completed by-pass (A41). The new proprietors, mindful of the latest craze of flying, soon converted the fields into a small landing strip and planned hangers to accommodate the fragile fabric-covered aircraft. In January 1934 the country club was opened.

Meanwhile at Watford, our aldermen and councillors were excited at the prospect of a municipal aerodrome at Leavesden. Few local authorities were given such an opportunity and they quietly hoped the film studio project would fall by the wayside. In December 1934 the Finance Committee were able to report that the Deputy Mayor had been in communication with Mr Lloyd's estate agents and that the District Valuer would again be approached.

The news that Watford was becoming aeronautically minded travelled far and fast. Within the space of a few weeks, a letter reached the council offices from a firm wishing to establish a new flying school that it was interested in the Watford project. Another company offered to negotiate terms by which it would be prepared to offer workshop facilities for the repair and manufacture of aircraft, or involve itself in the organisation of an airport.

Mattters moved quickly. The Finance Committee recommended to the town council to pass a resolution to purchase the whole area of 118 acres from Mr Lloyd of Langleybury, the asking price for which was £25,000, expressly for the purpose of setting up a municipal aerodrome subject to contract and the sanction of the Ministry of Health and any other sanctions.

The recommendation was referred back to the Finance Committee, largely due to Councillor Williams who pointed out what everyone already knew: that within the next year there would be major expenditures in the areas of water and the public health service. The cost to Watford would be £212 an acre and the interest on the loan would amount to an annual figure of around £900. Could Watford afford to make the purchase, he asked. The Finance Committee's enthusiasm was rejected and a full report was called for.

One month later, the matter was put to the vote. Some of the supporters of the scheme relented and the result was 14 votes for and 14 votes against. The Mayor, Alderman H J Bridger, a known opponent of the project, did not register his casting vote. The Borough was heavily committed to expenditures amounting to £200,000, an enormous sum in those days. The battle had been fought and lost.

In April 1935 the Finance Committee demurred and recommended that Mr Lloyd's agents be asked to sell to the corporation 50 acres rather than the original area of 118 acres, and called for estimates to be submitted for the cost of cricket and football pitches, tennis courts, bowling greens and pavilions. The thought was expressed that Mr Lloyd would not split his land and the matter was again deferred. On 7 May 1935 Watford Council agreed to purchase 118 acres at a cost of £23,500. The resolution to purchase was carried by 22 votes to 7.

The converson of 'One Mile Field' to playing fields rather than an airport appealed to our councillors and aldermen, I suspect as a means of acquiring the land at minimum expense. In July the picture was made clear. A condition of sale was the erection of a fence and road access at a cost of £4,500. The layout was estimated at £15,500. However, Hertfordshire County was prepared to meet 20% of the acquisition cost on the understanding that recreational opportunities were provided for children. The Carnegie Trust offered £800 and the National Playing Fields Association came up with £200. However, the council insisted on the right to sell or develop frontages or roads. The concensus seemed to be that Watford had made a bargain purchase.

Whatever happened to the Watford Light Aeroplane Club is something of a mystery. Perhaps it was abandoned following their failure to convince Watford Borough of the advantages of a local airport. Conveniently, the manager of Aldenham Aerodrome, Major Shield, a veteran war pilot with commercial licence No 10, proposed the formation of an artisan's flying club. If recruitment was successful, he argued that the cost of tuition could be reduced from £3 an hour to 35s for dual instruction and 30s solo. He envisaged an entrance fee of a ½ guinea and a weekly subscription of 1s 6d.

Major Shield further announced that more land had been acquired at Aldenham for new hangars, where a new two-seater cabin aircraft would be constructed of Canadian design, called the Aeronica. The market price was expected to be £375. Ironically, at the time of the announcement, Sir Alan Cobham's flying circus was holding a display at Mill End. There he introduced the Flying Flea, which a DIY man could build for £70.

Had Watford agreed to build an airport, Aldenham or Elstree Aerodrome as we know it now, would probably never have survived. As for the North Watford Playing Fields, time dictated that they were to feature in Watford's contribution to the war effort in the following four years.

86   Return to Prosperity

Although the unemployment centres in Watford still offered training and social amenities, and every encouragement was given to the local unemployed to acquire an allotment, 1935 could be said to be the turning point in Watford's fortunes. Other parts of the country were still suffering, but South West Hertfordshire came out of the recession sooner than most.

Our local postal authorities gave the lead by announcing improved local deliveries. The main feature of their programme was the introduction of an evening postal delivery service beginning at 7pm. It was argued that letters posted in London during the early afternoon would be delivered the same day instead of next morning. Saturday was an exception. A local letter dropped into a box before 5.15pm would be received the same evening, and then it was claimed a letter could be posted and a reply received the same day.

To accomplish this near miracle Watford recruited a considerable number of men, which helped the unemployment problems. When we had once been a nation of shopkeepers, we became a nation of letter writers. The consumer was being spoilt by such an efficient service and, for those who can remember those halcyon days, the Post Office was as good as its word. There were no grounds for complaint and we enjoyed a service which has never been, nor never will be bettered.

House prices were coming down and Bradshaw Estate new houses were put up for sale from £475 up to a maximum of £650, all freehold. The properties were well built by a well-known old established local firm, Charles Brightman & Son.

Furniture, too, was becoming cheaper as the choice improved. Cawdells, in their new arcade, were selling the latest oak cocktail cabinet and solid oak writing desk for £4 15s – and that included six cut glasses and a cocktail shaker! And to further impress the Joneses, an all-electric HMV radiogram in walnut veneer could be purchased for 16 guineas. An oak dining room suite with an extending refectory table, four panel-back chairs and a sideboard with cupboards and hidden drawers came complete at £10 9s 6d. For the bedroom, a veneered burr walnut dressing table with frameless mirrors, a linen chest with drawers and cupboards and a four-foot wardrobe cost £19 10s. If you waited for the sales, J Lewis on The Parade, just north of Bucks Garage, offered an oak bedroom suite at 7½ guineas and a three-piece suite upholstered in "hair and white wool" at 8½ guineas.

At Pearkes, ladies' trimmed velour hats were offered at 12s 11d, English cape gloves at 8s 11d and pure wool velour cloth dressing gowns at 18s 11d. Quality in those days was a foregone conclusion. Wool was wool, and a little printed logo certifying the garment was made of pure wool would have been regarded as an act of lunacy. No man-made fibres and fewer allergies 50 years ago.

Between October and November 1935 the first block of residential flats were built. Until then, a flat was invariably to be found above a shop; no one had thought in terms of custom-built apartments. You will remember them when I tell you the block was called Elm Court. They were constructed on a narrow site which had been a miniature golf course at the rear of the car park to the old Plaza. Elm Court is still bounded by a car park and only just survived the building of the new one-way system as it dips and swings behind the Odeon site and merges at a roundabout by the Town Hall. The flats were once the most modern accommodation in central Watford. They were designed by Max Lock, who was given the unenviable task of overcoming the narrow frontage to Albert Road. In this he succeeded and, with a choice of one or two bedrooms and large lounges, the flats were offered at a rental of £75 to £95 a year.

Other significant changes were also taking place at much the same time. By order of F T Moore, C H Halsey sold by public auction at the Rose & Crown freehold property known as 28 High Street, with two cottages and outbuildings as well as land in Wells Yard.

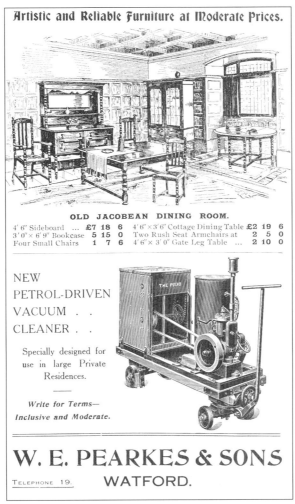

Advertisement for Pearkes, 1910.

The sale of the shop let to E T Simmons started at £2,000 and finished at £5,100, when it was knocked down to Benskins Watford Brewery. The modest frontage of 25 feet represented £200 a foot and Watford's old residents asked themselves what things were coming to. At least for the first-time house buyer, the mortgage interest was a universal 4½% so their weekly repayments over 25 years were not far divorced from rental charged for Victorian terraced properties still equipped with gas lighting, coal for heating and a tin bath for ablutions.

A new era was at last emerging; a new concept of building in pairs instead of terraces, plenty of windows, space and labour-saving devices, of which electricity was the greatest boon. Watford became a boom town and, in the years immediately preceding the last war, the town expanded as never before, especially on the north side. There were surprising ramifications to this unprecedented increase in population, quite apart from the demands made upon the utility services, sewerage and transport. Without any discussion, a proposal was adopted by the town council for the addition of two new wards in North Watford, six more councillors and two aldermen. The town was rapidly moving into a new industrial age.

87   The Shylocks of Hertfordshire County Council

A clash of parents with educational authorities because of financial restraints is a familiar story. To many it may come as something of a surprise to learn that such clashes are not new phenomena. Let me tell you about the attempted take-over by Hertfordshire County of Watford's Grammar Schools in 1935.

The story begins with an innocent request by the Boys' School to the County Council for a modest £18,000 to replace inadequate and out-dated school buildings, which included a wooden dining hall. The application was made by the governors of the Schools through the usual channels and they patiently waited for a favourable response. The response came, but it was not favourable. You can have the grant, County replied, but we will take your Grammar Schools.

These conditions were tantamount to waving a red rag at a bull. The governors were incensed at the devious nature of County's decision. They were the trustees of a then 230-year-old foundation and flatly refused to sacrifice tradition by allowing the transfer of the independent schools to a local authority. County justified their attitude by claiming that uniformity in educational administration and control should be vested in the hand that feeds it. Each side mustered its troops, dug in and declared war.

The thought of Watford losing one of its few connections with the past, relinquishing control of the schools to an alien administration and subscribing to its loss of independence was abhorrent to the town in general and parents in particular. After minor skirmishes, the big guns were placed in position and fire was exchanged at point-blank range.

We claimed County had invested thousands of pounds in the educational system, although they conveniently overlooked the grants forthcoming from the Board of Education. Watford retaliated by pointing out to Hertford that whatever the sum put into the educational pot, the town contributed one sixth of the county rates and therefore helped indirectly towards such grants; besides, what about the income derived from the Fuller and Platt charities which were channelled to County?
County responded, claiming that £92,000 had been "sunk" into the two schools. The Chairman of Hertfordshire Educational Committee, Alderman W Graveson and the Vice-Chairman of the County Council, as well as a Governor of the schools, Alderman D C Rutherford of Bushey Heath, stuck to their guns and their arguments in favour of transfer. The battle continued.

A public meeting was called by the Watford and District Ratepayers' Association later in the year. The venue was the Oddfellows Hall. Councillor W H Beale presided, supported by Sir Dennis Herbert MP and his good lady, as well as County Council aldermen and members and, of course, governors of the schools including Alderman W Bickerton and Councillors Last and Coates.

The hall was filled beyond its capacity, many having to stand around the sides and at the back. Only one invited speaker supported County proposals and that was Mrs A Wheelwright, daughter of J C Benskin; a newly-elected County representative of Queen's Division and a Watford elementary school manager. Apart from this one dissenter, there was little doubt as to the sentiments of the remaining speakers and the audience, which included Mr E Reynolds, Headmaster of the Boys' School and Miss E Fergie, Headmistress of the Girls' School.

Mr Blackwell, representing the Brewers' Company (Platts) told those present that they were there to consider "selling your souls to the possessor of the largest purse." There was the question too of democratic principle, "the recognition of local conditions and the English love of freedom". The applause was almost deafening. To the question "Are you in favour of the County Council taking over the Grammar Schools", only one hand was raised.

The fervour, earnestness, mood and outcome of the meeting surprised few people. The view expressed by Mr J Ginger, Borough Treasurer and an Old Fullerian, perhaps best summed up the situation. "This school originated as a Watford institution and must, therefore, be regarded by the people of this town as a Watford institution. We trust it will remain so and we must see that the government of the school must remain in Watford, by Watford people for Watford".

On a more down-to-earth note, Alderman Bickerton had pointed out that of the £18,000 requested as a grant, three-quarters of that sum would have been funded by Watford anyway. The outcome of the strong feelings apparent in the town forced another meeting at St Albans between the County Council and the governors. There, Mr A Bromet, a County member, secured the removal of the condition that provision of the school's new buildings in Rickmansworth Road would be conditional upon them being handed over to Hertford. Sir Dennis endeavoured to improve the position by an amendment that work should be carried out, but he failed.

The issue finally reached the local council chamber and by 18 votes to 6 the governors of the Grammar Schools were supported in their opposition to the transfer to Hertford. Labour councillors remained neutral for the reason that none was represented on the Board of Governors. And it was a long time before those improvements were made.

In retrospect, the first intimation at local level of the government's long term preparation for a state of war only became apparent long after the actual event. At the time of the Silver Jubilee, George Bolton, our Borough Librarian, was the recipient of King George V's specially minted silver medal presented by the Mayor for "special services outside of his council work in connection with the air defences of the district". Few were familiar with George Bolton's extra mural activities. To many, his name was familiar as the compiler of the very attractive 'Guide to Watford' and the corporation's Silver Jubilee souvenir edition presented to all Watford's school children. His interest in and work for the Royal Observer Corps was less well known.

If one man was doubtful about an everlasting peace, there were thousands who put their trust in the League of Nations by joining the League of Nations Union. Many of our local residents became members of Watford branch. They fervently believed that peace could be made to last and that Mussolini's invasion of Ethopia was a hiccup in the process of maintaining world peace.

Engine of the Royal Scot, class No 6170, the 'British Legion'.

The war to end all wars was still clear in the memory of those who came back and the families of those who did not return. Watford's British Legion branch fulfilled a very necessary task in caring for the bereaved and remembering those who gave their lives. It was well supported by ex-servicemen and women and, in the mid-'30s, was a major force in the town's social and ceremonial life. In November 1935 an engine of the Royal Scot, class No 6170, was nostalgically named 'British Legion'. Its first journey was a historic occasion as the train, hauled by the new steam engine, made its first stop at Watford. On the platform, a contingent of the Watford British Legion greeted the engine with a salute of the colours and Mr Armand Blackley, Chairman of the West Hertfordshire Group, shook hands with the engine driver. Formalities over, the engine steamed proudly out of Watford Junction to pay its next courtesy call.

We could not believe there would be another war. Prayers were said at every church service for a continuing peace. We did not live in fear of war, for we believed that peace was attainable and that was what the League of Nations was all about. Our faith was almost unshakable. After all, we had barely recovered from the last war. However, the government was ever vigilant, as governments should be, and as 1935 ended we were introduced to the never-to-be-forgotten letters ARP (Air Raid Precautions). A national directive had been received at the Municipal Offices via Hertford and a comprehensive report was prepared by Watford's Finance and General Purposes Committee on the treatment of casualties and the decontamination of civilians.

Civic reaction was positive; almost fatalistic in those days. There were no fringe elements prepared to declare Watford a bomb-free zone. The realities of a successful land-grabbing dictator in far-off Africa were enough to spark the fires of caution in the highest echelons. At civilian level the belief in peace was unshakable, but common sense prevailed and Air Raid Precautions became a new phrase in our vocabulary.

The committee's first act was to appoint a sub-committee to deal with this new and complex subject. An experienced officer had to be found to organise and implement the scheme and Watford recommended to Hertfordshire County Council the appointment of Lt Col J S Dunne, who was the county organiser of the British Red Cross. None disputed that he was the ideal man for the job. Approval was also requested that the newly-nominated sub-committee should report on the requirement of and progress in Air Raid Precautions.

The reaction of Watford's residents to this news was reflected in a speech by Alderman Graveson who proposed that the Council should implore the government to utilise instruments of peace rather than war to settle international disputes. He quoted an incident that had happened in the 17th century when the Chairman of the Hertfordshire Quarter Sessions sentenced "seven Quakers to six years' banishment for gathering in silent worship." The case was incomprehensible today, he argued, and by the same token "mankind should rise to a higher conception in international affairs than war".

Such was the mood of Watford's citizens that the Palace Theatre took the precaution, when presenting a play called 'Billeted' with Betty Nelson and Donald B Edwards, of telling the public that it was not a war play. In 1935 'war' was a dirty word.

89   A Cry for Peace

In my last article I touched upon the first impact of Air Raid Precautions on our daily lives. I also mentioned the Watford Branch of the League of Nations Union, as well as our local British Legion. The two latter institutions are the subject of this article, linked by the common thread of the gathering clouds of war and remembrance of those who died in the Great War.

On 11 November 1935 the customary open air service was meticulously planned. The Mayor, Councillor Last; the Mayoress, Mrs Last; the Deputy Mayor and Mayoress; aldermen and councillors attended the service outside the Municipal Offices in the High Street. Also present were two Parliamentary candidates: Sir Dennis Herbert and Mr S W Morgan. In the street below the dais gathered the Mens' and Womens' sections of the British Legion with their standards. The Salvation Army Band accompanied the hymns and the service was conducted by the Mayor's Chaplain, the Rev G H Ruffell Laslett who gave a short address. Rev J B Hardy, President of the Free Church Council, read the prayers and Mr S J Simmons sounded the Last Post, after which the National Anthem was sung. The large crowd, with many men wearing black ties, dispersed, their faces pale and drawn.

The following Sunday morning, members of the British Legion and other veteran organisations gathered outside what was then called the British Legion Club in St Albans Road and marched to the strident tones of the Watford Branch band to Vicarage Road. There wreaths were laid at the base of the Cross of Sacrifice.

In the afternoon, the annual Service of Remembrance was held at Watford Parish Church. The procession to the church was a unique event. Despite an overcast sky and rain showers, crowds stood in silence as they watched the assembly of representatives of the town council and many organisations, as well as the British Legion, Old Comrades Association, Hertfordshire Yeomanry, Watford Detachment 1st Battalion Hertfordshire Regiment TA and the 343rd (Watford) Battery Royal Artillery (TA). They marched to St Mary's Church via the High Street and King Street. The church was packed to capacity and many had to stand.

That same Sunday evening the Carlton Cinema opened its doors, but not for a picture show, as the showing of films on a Sunday was still not permitted. The weather had worsened and kept many people away because of local flooding, but those who attended the annual armistice demonstration arranged by the Watford Branch of the League of Nations Union were all the more determined that the meeting would be a success.

The Mayor and Mayoress, Deputy Mayor and Mayoress, local ministers, the Rotary Club and the Salvation Army were represented. The Mayor addressed the rain-drenched audience with these words: "The whole world at present is seething in unrest and worry, and war has already broken out between two member nations (Italy and Abyssinia). I am sorry to see some members of the League of Nations are saying the League has failed. With this I do not agree. We must not forget the League of Nations was absolutely a new idea or ideal in world politics when it was created and it had, as a new organisation, to learn by experience. At no other time has the League needed greater support".

The demonstration ended with a resolution proposed by Mr T Blackwell and seconded by Mr A E Millett that "the meeting assures His Majesty's Government of its full support of whatever measures might be necessary to enable the present war of aggression against Abyssinia to be brought to a speedy and satisfactory end through the collective action of the members of the League of Nations".

The meeting ended and the audience filed out into the rain. And still the pressure mounted. James Cawdell, better known for his business acumen, joined the moves for peace by donating some of the window space in his new arcade to an exhibition of pictures illustrating the horrors of the First World War. The pictures were officially released by the War Office, some of which were particularly gruesome and not previously released for public consumption. They were intended to shock, and in this the exhibition succeeded.

Cawdells on right; arcade entrance is on left-hand side, late 1940s.

Accompanying the exhibition, the local branch of the League provided an electrically-driven model ingeniously devised to illustrate how money allocated to armaments could be diverted to expand the ailing industrial sector and provide better social services for the civilian population at large.

James Cawdell's decision to stage such an exhibition was a calculated risk. He could so easily have offended if not shocked Watford's citizens by his surprising action, but he realised that the visual impact of the exhibition might help to strengthen the public's resolve to demand peace. In this he succeeded and congratulations were forthcoming from many quarters for his courage in mounting the unique display. That November left no one in doubt that the newly-introduced Air Raid Precautions were alien to a peace-loving society.

90   The King is Dead

Those who may have ventured as far as the Pond in the inclement weather of January 1936 were dismayed to see the elm trees at The Elms being cut down. It was not a case of elm disease. The preliminary clearance exercise was part of the plan to make way for a new town hall and municipal offices. Watford's citizens were not convinced that the changes would be for the better.

Christmas and New Year were celebrated in the traditional manner, but the rapidly deteriorating international situation gave cause for concern. In this climate of diminishing confidence in the ability of the League of Nations to preserve peace, the illness of King George V added to the anxieties of the man in the street. The turn of events seemed beyond his understanding. The economy was picking up, the number of jobless was on the decrease, yet we were all ill at ease.

At 11.55pm on Monday 20 January came the announcement that the King was dead. All local concerts, dances and sales of work were immediately cancelled and the people of Watford mourned his death. The Royal Family had patronised South West Hertfordshire and the Prince of Wales had made an extensive tour of hospitals and orphan schools in this area in 1927, including visits to the Peace Memorial Hospital, London Orphan Asylum, Royal Masonic and Royal Caledonian Schools. At Halsey Hall he had signed the Minute Book.

Flags flew at half mast and we, the people, were sad at the loss of a King who, too, knew the devastation and loss of life brought about by war. Our anchor with the past, the good times and the bad times, was suddenly lost. The King is dead; long live the King.

Watford Town Council held a special meeting on the Tuesday when the Town Clerk read the text of loyal addresses of sympathy and loyalty to the new King, Edward VIII, and the widowed Queen Mary. On the same day a memorial service was held at St Mary's Church attended by the Mayor and corporation to coincide with the service at Westminster Abbey. Representatives and members of Watford's Free

Upton House, offices of Watford Urban District Council. Reading of the Royal Proclamation of Prince Albert as King George V, May 1910.

Churches held a united service at Queens Road Methodist Church, part of which included the relay of a broadcast service from Windsor. That night, the fully muffled bells of St Mary's Church echoed through the deserted streets of the town. Bewildered citizens wondered what the future would bring.

On the Friday, rays of the low winter sun penetrated the bare branches of the trees at Upton House, offices of Watford Urban District Council. A large crowd stretched across and down the High Street from Bucks Garage to Elliots with school children joining in, as many schools had closed at noon. Under the familiar canopy and standing on the dias in the presence of the Mayoress, Deputy Mayor and Mayoress, the Town Clerk with aldermen and councillors gathered in a semi-circle below him, the Mayor read the Royal Proclamation. Many veterans of the last war were present, their faces drawn. The formalities completed with the words "to whom we do acknowledge all faith and constant obedience with all hearty and humble affection, beseeching God, by whom Kings and Queens do reign, to bless the Royal Prince Edward VIII with long and happy years to reign over us". Mr S Edwards of the British Legion, dressed in a Councillor's black robe and a three-cornered hat, sounded a fanfare.

The Mayor led cheers for the new King and from this point everything that could go wrong, went wrong. Apart from Mr Edwards, no bandsmen were present and, to end the ceremony with the National Anthem, someone had the bright idea of using recording equipment. Whether on test the record player, amplifier and loudspeaker worked well, we will probably never know, but when it should have given of its best by playing the National Anthem, accompanied by the voices of many hundreds of local citizens, it failed. Distorted and intermittent, the poor reproduction upset those present and many words of criticism were uttered by the disappointed throng as they made their way home.

It was a nine-year old Brownie of 16th Watford Pack, whose name was Gwendoline Goymer, who expressed the sentiments of Watford's school children by writing to the Mayor and telling him that many children could not send flowers to the Royal Family but that they could raise money for a cot in the childrens' ward at the Peace in memory of the late King George V. The Mayor was so touched by the letter that he requested the Borough Treasurer and Councillor E J Baxter of Oxhey to arrange school collections. The cost, he said, of a cot was £250 or 60,000 pennies, which number more or less represented 1d for every "man, woman and child" now living in the enlarged Borough. From total obscurity, young Miss Goymer emerged as a heroine and her greatest fan was the Mayor of Watford.

91   Body and Soul

One of the aspects of the mid-'30s that we are inclined to forget was the increasing volume of traffic in the Watford area. It is true that maximum speeds and acceleration were of a modest order, but so were the four-wheel brakes on cars and two-wheel brakes on older commercial vehicles. The increase in accidents involving children crossing roads was causing concern and Councillor Mrs Beall, Chairman of Watford Safety First Committee, conceived the idea of utilising the facilities offered by the national organisation of a safety first film. In 1936 schools were not provided with audio and visual aids, so the task of showing a film to 6,000 school children appeared to be insurmountable.

Mrs Beall found a relatively simple but radical solution. She approached the managers of the Plaza and the Coliseum, who agreed to offer their picture houses to accommodate the children. The prospect of missing school lessons was reward enough, but the prospect of going to a cinema in school time thrilled every youngster. Even the presence of the Mayor and Mayoress, Councillor and Mrs Last and, of course, Mrs Beall on stage could not detract from the sheer pleasure of a morning at the pictures.

It was the Mayor who warned the excited audience that although cinema-going was associated with entertainment and amusement, they were there that morning to be instructed. "Many people," he warned "are very concerned about the large number of accidents which occur every week and a large proportion of deaths from accidents occurred to people under 18 years of age". His address continued; children began to fidget.

Mrs Beall thanked everyone for their co-operation, not forgetting Mr G E D Woodman, Manager of the Plaza. When the film began it was almost an anti-climax, but the producers must have taken into account the foreseeable frustrations of the young audience. The adults' love of ceremony and speeches contrasted strangely with the main characters of the film, in the form of Great Danes! The children's imagination was immediately captured and the message came over loud and clear. The slogan "Stop, look and think" said everything and, for that matter, is still good advice, except that the speed of today's traffic requires a few more "looks".

Two shows were given at each of the cinemas and the project was a complete success, although I doubt whether there was a statistical follow-up to determine the long-term effect of the novel use of film as a warning medium. When you watch traffic warnings on commercial television, remember it is by no means an original concept.

If attempts were being made to prevent accidents to children, the Salvation Army was equally intent on saving souls. National headquarters had adopted and implemented a nine-year plan. A number of sites had been purchased so that when sufficient funds were available, church halls could be built.

Between 1935 and 1936, a new Salvation Army Hall had been erected in St Albans Road. In May the Hall was officially opened in the presence of a large gathering of people. It was a day of substitution as Mrs Pratt, wife of the Rev William H Pratt, explained when she conducted the official ceremony by opening the entrance door with a key handed to her by Lt Col Rushton of Salvation Army Headquarters. She explained that Mrs Arthur Kingham was unable to be present and that she was pleased to have the opportunity to deputise for her. She declared the hall open for the worship of God. The delighted gathering broke into spontaneous applause. Accompanying Mrs Pratt were County Alderman D C Rutherford, Mrs Armitage and Councillor A J Eldridge.

The hall, which was designed to accommodate 250 worshippers, was soon filled and the service began with the singing of the hymn 'Thy Presence and Thy Glories, Lord'. Prayers were said by the Rev A H Yates of Leavesden Road Baptist Church and the Rev E D P Kelsey read the scripture.

Alderman Rutherford explained that he too was a substitute as Sir Dennis Herbert should have presided but, as everyone knew, Lady Herbert was recovering from pneumonia. Lt Col Rushton announced the actual cost of the hall was £1,878 of which National Headquarters had paid £920, but there was a mortgage of £500. While £391 had already been raised, there was an outstanding balance. Then the chairman made a magnanimous offer. If nine donors could be found who would contribute £50 each, he would make up the outstanding mortagage. The new Salvation Army Hall never looked back.

92   Legacy of the Past

It could be said of the first half of 1936 that it was a period of dotting i's and crossing t's. After the death of King George V in January, the promise of spring sunshine offered the only ray of hope. Nationally, gloom and doom prevailed but our economic recovery continued – although prosperity, evasive as always, remained just around the corner.

Dalton House, 1906.

Lower High Street, second-hand car lot, 1979.

Many events of that time influenced, if not determined, the future growth pattern of Watford. On 7 March 1936 over 300 guests attended an event which, as a legacy of the past, was destined to change the once prosperous Lower High Street into a new and second-hand car mart. Messrs P R Monkhouse and I F Connell were well known in the production car racing scene and together they purchased part of the grounds of old Dalton House. On the site bordering the High Street, opposite the northern entrance to the Watford & St Albans Gas Company, they built a new garage with the very latest design features and set the trend for petrol stations with which we are now so familiar – except for the self-service aspect.

Devon Filling Station and old oasthouse, 247 High Street. Demolished, now Alamo Car Rental, 1977.

We expected and received service with a smile in those days, at no extra cost.

Behind the large sliding doors of the showrooms, the very latest cars were on display. Immaculately painted Morris cars and MGs attracted the attention of guests as they inspected the latest products of British industry. The exhibit that created most interest was Mr Connell's track model MG painted in 'Monaco' grey, which he had raced at Le Mans. His favourite racing venue inspired the name of the garage.

As the new Monaco Garage opened, another business closed. The George had been part of Watford's history for over 300 years. Some will remember it as an unpretentious building of dirty red brick with five large sash windows on the first floor facing the High Street, and at street level a wagon-way to the left and three sash windows with two steps to a panelled oak doorway, above which a sign was suspended on massive wrought iron brackets.

Among the documents relating to the George, once a Sedgwick house acquired from Benskins Watford Brewery, were deeds dated 1655. Until the mid-1800s, the George was a coaching house. The stables were at the rear of the premises and, with the loss of the coaching trade, they were later converted into a club room. In the early days a balcony spanned the front of the stables and it was said that soldiers were billeted there during the Great Rebellion. It was here that members of the Local Board discussed the town's business over tankards of ale and made their decisions before official meetings. In more recent years, the old club room became the training quarters of the Watford Amateur Boxing Club. In March 1936, the 300-year-old hotel finally closed its doors and, along with Goodson's toy shop, the site was cleared for James Cawdell's new store.

At more or less the same time, the town council finally made up its mind about the Five Arches bathing place. It was opened in 1899 and soon became one of Watford's major leisure attractions. But from time to time complaints were received by the authorities about scum and debris floating downriver into the pool. In 1934 an attendance of 18,000 had been recorded and in 1935 this figure had dropped to 14,000. Another factor emerged. Attendance at the new Municipal Baths was not improving and, reading between the lines, one cannot help but suspect that councillors may have conspired to cause its early demise. To precipitate matters, the Medical Officer of Health was hastily despatched to Five Arches to take samples of the water. The results of his analysis indicated that the water was contaminated. No amount of questioning revealed its true nature, except that it included "sewage and manurial matters".

The anti lobby pointed out that during a summer drought the water level at the Five Arches dropped substantially. At the shallow end the depth of water was 1 foot and only 3 feet at the deep end. It was further pointed out that "hundreds of children" used the river at the corner of Radlett Road and Bushey Mill Lane, over which the authorities had no control.

Although no one could cite an instance that bathers had ever suffered any ill effects from its less than pure water, its fate was sealed. The closure of Five Arches was confirmed with the proviso that consideration would be given to providing a suitable alternative. Few of Watford's dedicated open air bathers believed that alternative baths would ever be found, since an improved attendance of the municipal covered-in baths was of paramount importance. They were correct in their assumption and all we are left with is the memory of those carefree days, which pollution brought to an inevitable end.

93   Watford's New Look – Part 1

The unprecedented growth of Watford's population in the mid-'30s forced our financially reticent councillors into action. For many years they had governed in the most frugal manner and, as I have mentioned in earlier articles, they suddenly became big spenders once loans at low interest rates from government sources became more easily available.

The roundabout near the Pond was built in anticipation of the new town hall and municipal offices. Upton House, adjacent to the Fire Station, became totally inadequate and some departments were transferred to The Elms, where working conditions were less than ideal. This situation became increasingly aggravating to councillors and local government officers alike. You may remember that the design for a new municipal edifice was put out to competition and won by an architect named Charles Cowles-Voysey. Two major problems remained unresolved: the design of the interior of the town hall and how the project was to be financed.

Watford Town Hall, late 1930s.

As early as September 1935 a suggestion was made to the Council that local drama and operatic groups should be consulted with regard to the layout of the stage and accommodation of props and dressing room facilities. It was a logical move, since local amateur dramatic and operatic societies naturally expected to stage their ambitious productions at a custom-designed hall planned to seat 1,500. For reasons that were never made clear, those responsible did not pursue this suggestion or, if they did, the architect was instructed to go ahead and design a concert platform without the advice of interested societies.

At the same time, Watford Borough applied to the Ministry of Health for sanction to borrow £158,000 to meet the cost of the project. An enquiry followed. The Government Inspector, Lt Col L F Wells, was pleased to note that there were no objections to the proposal and his time was largely taken up discussing the terms of the loan. Watford asked that the repayment period of the loan should be 60 years as opposed to a 30-year period proposed in the course of preliminary discussions. It emerged that the rates would suffer an increase of 3½d in the £, taking into account the sale of Upton House and Little

Nascot. Second thoughts suggested that perhaps a long-term lease as opposed to an outright sale would be more appropriate.

The hall, the inspector was told, was not designed for "domestic performance", a point which he quickly picked up on. He detected the friction between those who wished reasonable provision to be made and those, who no doubt handled the purse strings, who did not. He made his position quite clear and proffered the following advice. "If you want dramatic performances afterwards, it will cause you inconvenience to make the necessary arrangements rather than if you had made them at the start". It was a profound, but rather obvious statement.

The indignity of being ignored, plus the prospect of having no stage for show promotions really upset the local amateur groups. A stand-up battle ensued but, as we now know, their pleadings for municipal facilities to accommodate their productions came to naught. As it turned out, the ideal acoustic properties inherent in the hall, by design or good fortune, attracted recording companies and many symphony orchestras have since been recorded there. In retrospect, the action of the Council appeared quite unjustified and we are left to imagine the internal wranglings of a Council burdened by a large capital programme.

In July 1936, influenced no doubt by the practice adopted by the Borough, a design for a new Police Station in Clarendon Road was put out to competition. The land had already been purchased at a cost of £10,000. You will recall that Watford then had two Police Stations, one in King Street and the other in St Albans Road.

Watford's first Police Station was established in the 1860s in a private house, which you may remember as Swann's near Woodman's Yard. The building was demolished to make way for the new ring road joining Beechen Grove and Exchange Road at the point where it crossed our medieval High Street. Here a modest force of one superintendent and a constable originally kept the peace in a more disciplined fashion than the night watchmen whom they succeeded. The cellars below the house were said to be used to accommodate prisoners. The constable was known to all Watford's inhabitants and was affectionately called 'Ducky'. The nickname was derived from his use of white trousers, which were part of his 'uniform'. As the force expanded, a move was made to Estcourt Road into a building that still exists.

The problems of the uneconomic duplication of administration and communication prompted the centralisation of the two Police Stations and plans were made to update Watford's constabulary. The King Street Police Station was built in 1888 when the population was 15,000. In 1936 the number had increased to 63,000, but in those days we could be said to be more law abiding.

Last week I touched upon the many changes that occurred during the '30s as a result of the town's unprecedented growth. As the population increased, so greater demands were made on all the supporting services that had been relatively dormant for so many years. The population explosion in Watford may best be illustrated by quoting the census figures for the northern wards in 1931 as 20,000, or one third of the Borough's total population. Following the development of Kingswood, Bradshaw and Bushey Mill Lane, five years later the population had increased to 40,000. Now, two-thirds of Watford's residents lived in North Watford.

The new semis were supplied with electricity from the corporation and gas from the Watford & St Albans Gas Company. The all-electric house was becoming a sales gimmick and gas looked as if it was likely to become a back number. To capture new custom the decision was made to open a showroom on the corner of North Western Avenue and St Albans Road, since the showrooms at Lower High Street and the Pond were too far away from the new estates. In 1936 families could choose from a large selection of cookers, washing boilers, heaters and fridges almost on their doorstep. Once upon a time, the new Watford Library at the Cross Roads had commanded a central position in terms of accessibility, but in fewer than 10 years it could no longer conveniently serve those living in North Watford.

Carey Place, 1979.

Taking a leaf out of the Gas Company's book, the Borough decided to build its own branch library at a cost of £11,000. In little more than a half-century, the library service had grown out of all recognition. It started as a voluntary body called the Literary Institute, which occupied an old hall in Carey Place. Such was the demand for books that the building could no longer accommodate the increasing number of borrowers, books and voluntary workers responsible for administration.

A Building Committee was formed to explore the possibility of expanding the hall, but a plot in Queens Road attracted their attention as ideal in size and location. Three thousand pounds was raised by public subscription and a new Library was built on a site now occupied by Sainsbury's supermarket[74]. A schoolmaster was appointed the first Librarian. He attended mornings and afternoons, while volunteers applied themselves to the problems of administration. At first a charge was made of 4d a month or 3s a year, but by 1887 all borrowing charges were abolished.

At a time when many children were illiterate the insititute, which had the overwhelming support of local social reformers, began to accept children and adults for instruction. Money for the project was raised by every means possible and pressure was successfully applied to the Urban District Council, Hertfordshire County Council and

Watford Library, Queens Road, on right, 1903.

the Board of Education to contribute to this good work. The Vicar of Oxhey, the Rev Newton Price and Dr T Brett, the town's Medical Officers, were two of the many workers of those days whose names deserve mention.

In 1884, with newly acquired charity funds, the long-established Endowed School, once Dame Fuller's Free School, was able to build brand new premises in Derby Road for boys and girls. The schools changed their name to Grammar Schools in 1903. In 1907 the girls moved to a new building in The Crescent and in 1912 the boys to Rickmansworth Road. The old Derby Road School was empty.

The standard of general education was then 'elementary' and here was an opportunity to create a new school offering higher elementary standards. Entry into this school was competitive. Children from the local council schools were disappointed if they could not make the grade. The school never pretented to be classed as anything other than academic; teaching on the one hand and good old-fashioned trades on the other. One of the earliest members of staff was Mr Adkins who retired as headmaster in 1935, not of the 'higher elementary' school but the Watford Central School, with a reputation second only to the Grammar Schools. There is no doubt some Centralians would still dispute that comparison.

Mr Adkins grew up with his beloved school. He steered it in the right direction, taking heed of the demands of local industry and training his pupils accordingly. Finally, ill health forced his retirement. When the Old Centralians' Association held its eighth annual dinner at Bucks Restaurant Mr Adkins, then its President, was unable to be present. In his absence, Mr G Viner, Vice-President, proposed the toast of the association and claimed that the school had become "a force to be reckoned with". He proved the point by referring to its latest venture: a new magazine called the 'Centralian Critic'.

Mr Adkins' long term as headmaster promoted stories and anecdotes – all in his praise – for he was the man who had created this much-loved institution in the span of one lifetime. Few other headmasters in Hertfordshire could claim in 1935 that 100% of his students who entered for the School Certificate passed the examination. Sadly, an era was lost on his retirement. Times were changing. Watford was no longer a country town; it was now a commuting town with its own industries, to which printing could be added. Old Centralians could anticipate jobs in print, light engineering or accounting perhaps, for which they were well qualified. Unemployment no longer loomed as a perpetual bogey; the future looked promising. No one wanted war, so why should there be war? The answer seemed as simple as the question.

Only three years of peace remained, but school leavers never gave a thought to the armed services into which they were finally conscripted. Nothing was ever going to be quite the same again.

95   The Boys' Brigade

The chances are that only members or ex-members of the Boys' Brigade could tell you what Jimmy Hill, Cliff Richard, Bill Martin and Sir Neil Cameron (former Marshall of the Royal Air Force) have in common. If you do not already know, the common factor is the Boys' Brigade. Three were once members; Cliff was a Brigade Hon Vice-President.

We have all heard of the Boys' Brigade. You will have seen them marching to the music of their own bands, dressed in dark-coloured jackets and trousers, with leather belts, white sashes and blue forage caps. Others will recall the excellent exhibition mounted at Watford Museum telling the Brigade's 100-year-old story.

On 4 October 1983 the Brigade celebrates its first centenary. Like so many young organisations, its beginning was humble and timely. Humble because one man, William Alexander Smith, embarked on a seemingly impossible dream and timely because he recognised boredom as the motivation of Glasgow's boisterious youth in his Glasgow Sabbath School. He realised the need to give them direction by exercising discipline, tempered with religious instruction and promoting outdoor activities to create a healthy mind in a healthy body. William Smith formed the First Glasgow Company of the Boys' Brigade at the North Woodside Road Mission. Of the 59 boys who initially joined, the number reduced itself to 39 when the lads discovered, in real terms, the strictures of applied discipline.

Then, to the consternation of an inflexible Victorian society, William Smith decided to organise an annual camp; the first ever enjoyed by the Glasgow Company on the Kyles of Bute. Here he proved to his satisfaction that the boys needed orderly adventure to allow them to forget their frustrating poverty stricken world. The idea caught on and spread throughout the United Kingdom.

By the early 1900s, the success of his venture was assured. Throughout the land there were 790 companies, 2,900 officers and 35,000 boys. At Glasgow Central Station on 9 April 1983, a Class 86 electric locomotive No 86243 was officially named the 'Boys' Brigade' and on 24 March 1982 the Post Office's new pictorial issue depicting youth organisations featured the Brigade on the prime inland rate stamp. Official recognition in the centennial year of William Smith's contribution to the youth of this country was outstanding and in 1909 he received a Knighthood in recognition for his services.

I suppose it could be argued that as a society we have completed a full circle and that similar problems (but for different reasons) are emerging. The symptoms are there: restlessness, lack of direction and boredom, but the days are gone when a band of undisciplined children aspired to a camp on the Kyles of Bute. Now they are given opportunities to travel the world to meet their counterparts in far distant countries.

On 27 August 1983 local churches celebrated the centenary with thanksgiving services in Watford, Croxley Green and other active centres in South West Hertfordshire. On Sunday 30 October 1983 the South West Hertfordshire Battalion invited the North Hertfordshire Battalion to join with them in a thanksgiving service at St Albans Abbey.

The South West Hertfordshire Battalion once represented 24 local companies, of which eight were in the Watford area. The 1st Watford Company was formed in 1904 at the Leavesden Road Baptist Church. The 2nd Company, based at the Kingswood Baptist Church, was disbanded several years ago. With the demolition of the Presbyterian Church in Clarendon Road, the same fate befell the 5th Company. The active 3rd Company at Bushey Baptist Church is a good example of weathering a crisis. Today the 1st, 3rd, 4th (Methodist Church, Harebreaks) and 8th Companies (Church of the Nazarene, Woodside) are still active, as is the 1st Oxhey, but the 2nd Company foundered several years ago[75].

1st Watford Boys' Brigade Company on parade with 1st Watford Girls' Brigade, Garfield Street, 1954/55. From 1st Watford Boys' Brigade archives.

How is the Brigade faring in this computer game era? Mr Leslie Smith, Hon President of the South West Hertfordshire Battalion, told me that only a shortage of adult leaders prevents the Brigade from expanding. "We have a full-time leader" he said, "one of whose duties is to encourage recruitment of young and old alike. We look forward to the future with confidence".

96   The End of the Line

Let us borrow H G Wells' time machine and travel back to the beginning of the 1860s. Watford's medieval street plan and timber-framed buildings had changed little over the centuries. Here and there new buildings had been erected or old ones modernised to Victorian standards but, in essence, the town was still "one long street", as Daniel Defoe had described our "genteel market town" in 1724.

Watford Mill used the water of the Colne to power its grinding stones, as it had done since feudal times. The railway had been established for a quarter of a century, during which time the population had doubled to 6,500. The toll gate at Bushey Arches was still manned as coaches, carts and gigs used the busy highway to and from London. The Watford Gas Works had been established for much the same period, spoiling the beauty of the Colne Valley.

Watford's pure spring water attracted London brewers and, over the centuries, brewing had become the town's major industry. In 1852 the local Board of Health had taken over the duties of administration, but there was little sign of improvement in education, highways, drainage or sewerage. Disease was rife and the mortality rate high. There was still no isolation hospital. The courts, yards and alleys obscured from public gaze the poverty of residents forced to live there. To the casual visitor, Watford was a town of plenty.

In the early 1860s there were no local newspapers. County publications were available, but the reporting of local news was minimal. Samuel Peacock, son of John, who founded a local printing and book-binding business in 1823, decided to fill the obvious gap with a newspaper of his own. The venture was not without financial risk. He looked beyond the town to the villages and hamlets to ensure a viable circulation and, in January 1863, launched the 'Watford Observer and General Advertiser' for Watford, Bushey and Rickmansworth. It was priced at three 'ha'pence' (1½d) and was published on Saturdays.

A London agency supplied the four-page newspaper, of which three pages were pre-printed with national and international news attributed to "a London correspondent". The first page had been left blank for completion on a hand-operated flat bed machine in Watford. That orginal Columbian printing press, built in 1820, may be seen at Watford Museum.

Demand for advertising space and a slowly increasing circulation sustained the paper in those early days, until the whole front page was given over to advertising and local news was relegated to the inner pages. The newspaper was sold at places as far away as St Albans and Harrow. Its price was reduced to 1d and by 1865 the flatbed had been replaced by a cylinder machine. By 1880, the year of Samuel Peacock's death, the whole six-page newspaper was printed in Watford.

In September 1887, the 'West Herts Post' challenged the monopoly of the 'Watford Observer' with eight pages of news and advertising, with a circulation spread as far as Chesham, Tring and Hemel Hempstead. Within five years the price was reduced to 1d and within 10 years it became the 'Watford and West Herts Post'. In 1892 its circulation was claimed to "exceed that of all other papers printed in the Watford (Parliamentary) Division combined".

On 17 December 1887, yet another weekly paper appeared: 'The Watford Advertiser and District Free Press', with six pages and many black-and-white illustrations. Its front page was wholly devoted to advertising, now a traditional feature of many newspapers, and its editorial content was inclined towards the man in the street. By the following year the paper had been increased to eight pages without an increase in price. Its success seemed assured but, for some unaccountable reason, publication ceased as far as I can establish in 1892.

Perhaps the introduction of the 'Watford Leader' and 'Bushey and Rickmansworth Gazette' in 1891 hastened its end. It was printed and published by H T Gardiner of 101 High Street, better known for their 'Illustrated Watford Almanac and Year Book' marketed at 1d. The new paper started with a circulation of 4,000. Within six years the eight-page weekly cost ½d and claimed that "the combined sales of 'Herts Leader' and 'Watford Leader' far exceed that of any weekly paper printed in the Parliamentary Division of West Hertfordshire". In July 1897 its name was changed to 'Watford Leader and West Herts News' and, as far as I can determine, it continued until 1915 when shortages of labour and materials presumably dictated its downfall.

Even in those days, editors did not pull their punches. This is the view expressed by the 'Watford Leader': "We take this opportunity of endorsing the remarks of Mr Micklem (Liberal Parliamentary Candidate) in reference to the care which should be exercised over the erection of public buildings and planning of new streets. Watford's onward march cannot be stopped and it behoves them in power to see to it that everything is done to avoid ugliness in buildings and inconvenient and dangerous arrangements of streets..." After nearly a century that advice remains relevant but, unfortunately, went unheeded by successive boards and councils.

The last early 20th century weekly newspaper to be lanched in Watford could well have been the 'Watford Newsletter'. It was printed and published by Curtis Brothers of 8 King Street in 1908. The paper sold for ½d and within a year a circulation of 5,000 was claimed. Despite, or maybe because of its popular journalistic approach, this modest little paper survived the Great War and finally disappeared in 1920. Exactly 50 years later, there was another casualty when, in 1970, the 'Watford Post', successor to the 'Watford & West Herts Post', suddenly ceased publication. The last copy gave no indication that the axe was about to fall. The pleasant little office on The Parade quietly closed its doors and Watford lost one its oldest surviving weekly papers.

Now, in November 1983, we witness the demise of the 'Evening Post- Echo'. It is a sad occasion as the paper passes from the present into the historical past and joins that exclusive band of journals that have served South West Hertfordshire but did not stay the course.

Editors Note: On 26 September 1983 my father received a letter from the Editor of the 'Evening Post-Echo' advising that the newspaper would cease publication by 16 November unless a buyer came forward. Sadly, after a lifespan of only 16 years, it was the end of the line.

LETTERS

Here are a selection of readers' letters received by my father:

"I always read your page with great interest and have just seen your article about Ballard's Buildings. I come from an old Watford family and was born at Wells Yard, which is now called Wellstones. I often heard my elder sisters talking about the old days at Wells Yard and Ballard's Buildings. I understand my grandmother, Mrs. Day – who was always called Granny Day – lived at Ballard's Buildings and had a lodging house, as they were called in those days. She used to hold prayer meetings with friends from the Parish Church in her front room, which was later turned into a barber's shop".

Mrs Rosamund Stanton, (née Day), Third Avenue, Garston

"I was fascinated to read your article about Lord Bethell. Lord and Lady Bethell were my grandparents and I remember the day you wrote about – the NSPCC Golden Jubilee at Bushey House in 1934 – as I have a photograph of myself aged about three presenting Princess Alice with a bouquet of flowers (see chapter 53). *My father succeeded to the title and, on his death, my brother who sadly died. My cousin is the present Lord Bethell.*

Thank you for giving me the fun of reading the article".

The Honourable Mrs Peter Brown, Petworth, Sussex

"I was surprised and delighted to read your article about Dumbelton's, the butchers, when it was located at 231 Lower High Street; the time of the remaking of Watford and subsequent demolition of the very handsome old houses, including the home of Mary Ann Sedgwick, the widow of the founder of the brewery business, later to become Benskins.

I am delighted that you singled out Dumbelton's for comment. May I say how much we enjoy your page. Long may you continue to make our memories more vivid" (see chapter 76).

Henry Williams (born 1905), Bournehall Avenue, Bushey

"It is with much interest and pleasure that I read your memories of Watford. Having lived there for quite a number of years, I can well remember many of the people and places you write about. I am wondering whether you have written a book on your memories. If not, why not?"

Mrs I White, High Street, Kings Langley

"I should like to thank you for your weekly stories. As a person who has lived in Bushey most of her life, I found the article on the Parish Church and Herkomer's 'castle' most interesting. The elm tree and the lych-gate were a great part of Bushey village. On the Saturday before war broke out I was a bridesmaid at the Parish Church and the next day the lych-gate had gone.

During the Second World War, I was in the Women's Land Army and used to appear on the stage at the old Gaumont cinema in Watford during the interval to canvas for new recruits. I am still in contact with some of the Land Girls and every four years we have had reunions at the Royal Albert Hall. This year

(1982) we went to the Royal Festival Hall. There are about 2,000 of us 'girls' and the gathering really is something".

Mrs Gladys Feldman, Bournehall Avenue, Bushey

"I joined Benskins in February 1927 and was initially engaged by Mr John Kilby to be his shorthand typist. At that time he was the leading light in Watford Football Club because of the tie-up with the brewery. As I progressed, I was moved to the same office as Mr T L Simmons, who was Watford Football Club secretary for a good number of years. I had the opportunity to help him with the books and occasionally deputised for him at the football ground on Saturday afternoons.

During my 40-year employment with Benskins, I had custody of all the company's title deeds, from which I gained a good knowledge of its history. When we celebrated 100 years of Thomas Benskin acquiring the brewery, the staff and tenants were issued with an Irish porcelain tankard.

Averting to Watford cinemas, as a youngster I went to a cinema with an entrance in the High Street at the corner of King Street, adjoining Barclays Bank (see footnote 2). *My local was the Coliseum, commonly known as the 'Flea Pit' in St Albans Road. I spent some happy Saturday mornings there, egged on by 'see next week's episode'. I think this must have been the first cinema in Watford to have an organ, because in those far-off days it had a small chamber organ which I enjoyed hearing, long before the days of the mighty Wurlitzer at the Odeon.*

I find your articles most interesting because I was born at Acme Road, a stone's throw from Callowland School, and my bedroom window overlooked the playground. At 11 I gained a scholarship from Alexandra School (Headmaster Mr Owen and teacher Mr Tipler) to Watford Grammar School for Boys. Amongst the teachers there were Messrs Rous, Wood, Cooper, Merrett, Hopkins, Hedderwick, Grundy, Squire, Hulme (woodwork) and Miss Baigent; also the Rev C E McEvoy, who admonished me for train-spotting at Watford Junction when I should have been revising for exams.

Regarding your article on 'The Day of the Semi', when I married 50 years ago I bought a house from a builder named Goss on the Bradshaw estate; the land was formerly Farmer Ayres' potato field. As a schoolboy I went potato picking one Saturday morning and was told off for not working hard enough. Never again! The estate is on the opposite side of Bushey Mill Lane to the Tudor estate and my house backed onto the Watford – St Albans Branch line. During the war I sold the house and moved away from Watford, but in 1947 Benskins granted me the tenancy of Russell Lodge at the junction of St Albans Road and Longspring. I believe it was once a shooting lodge on the Earl of Essex's estate. It was later demolished and the site turned into a car park".

Patrick Brentnall, King Street, Tring

"We read your article about 'The Upright' in the days before television took over with great interest. Miss G Leader, a near neighbour of ours, wishes to be remembered to you, for you brought back happy memories of friends of younger days, in particular Rosie Chilton and Lil Allitt.

You mentioned Gosling Homes and I think you may be interested to know about their foundation. Mr Gosling, my aunt's father, was the town's missionary and had a mission hall in Lower High Street. He visited many old people and came across numerous elderly ladies who were terribly worried about their future accommodation: how they could obtain a room and even pay the rent. I gather that, with the help of several well-disposed local people, Mr Gosling managed to rent first one house and then others so that he could let off single rooms to these unfortunate people. An annual house-to-house collection was started and eventually sufficient money was raised to build the home in Cassio Road, which then gave security to about 22 people, with a resident warden to keep an eye on them.

Mr Gosling's second daughter – one of three – used to collect the nominal rents of 6d a week and call on each lady to enquire how she was. Her husband, my Uncle Charles, was the secretary of the homes and, with the other trustees, organised sales of work and coffee mornings to raise funds. My earliest recollections are of old Mr Gosling visiting us and me sitting on his knee. Later I helped with the house-to-house collections and looked after the bran tubs, etc at the annual sales of work".

Elsie Sutton, Radlett Road, Watford

"I have read with great interest your article on James Cawdell. He was my grandfather. Much of the information in your article was unknown to us. Unfortunately it often transpires that within families such details disappear, unless written down to be handed on to future generations".

Nigel J Chiltern-Hunt, Felden Lane, Hemel Hempstead

"May I express my warm appreciation of Ted Parrish's extremely well-informed articles on old Watford. There must be many of your readers who, like me, look forward to his weekly column. I make a habit of retaining them, but I think they warrant a more permanent record in book form which, I am sure, would find a ready sale. Would you give this your consideration, please?"

Laurence J Watson, Princes Avenue, Watford

"I write to tell you how much I enjoy the series 'Ted Parrish Remembers'. It is, in my opinion, one of the best series you have ever published. The style of writing and research or terrific memory – I've no way of knowing which – makes me wait for the next article with keen anticipation. His story-telling gives us a clear insight into the past and lifts the veil on the history of old Watford in a fascinating way to a comparative newcomer to the area like me. Mr Parrish, in the very best old-fashioned way, I raise my glass to you and say thank you for these nostalgic flights".

V. Allen, Verdure Close, Watford

And a letter from a member of the audience at one of Ted's film shows on old Watford:

"I lived with my family in Lower Paddock Road, my parents having moved there in 1913 from Peterborough. I saw many changes over the years. I used to attend London Road School and took the route every day past Haydon Road and the sweet shop there. Before the houses were built in Wilcot Avenue, there were fields that led onto Watford Heath. The hedges used to be full of dog roses and we took picnics over there. If we were lucky, we saw the odd grass snake in the hedgerow!

My uncle had a farm in Oxhey Lane and I walked there many times with my mother; our return journey was made in my uncle's pony and trap. A highlight of my visit was to collect the eggs, which were laid in various corners of buildings!

The big attraction at Bushey Station for children used to be the beautiful dray horses that were kept in Wilson's coal yard next to the lines. They were beautiful creatures and everyone stopped to watch as *they left the yard and started the rather slippery journey over the cobbles; they carried very heavy loads of coal at that time".*

L. Warren, Milton Keynes, Bucks

In 1978 I was researching the history of Attenborough's fields. As a result of one line of enquiry, I received a very interesting letter from Mary Harford, who was then living in Stafford. As Attenborough's fields were much loved by my father throughout his life and Haydon Hill, the large house adjacent to the fields, was the home of Mary's grandparents, I would like to share Mary's reminiscences. I have used one of my father's photos of Attenborough's fields and Haydon Hill on the front cover of this book. Ed.

Memories of Haydon Hill and its Grounds

"Robert Percy and Laura May Attenborough came as bride and bridegroom to Haydon Hill around 1872; I think Thomas was born and died in infancy in about 1874. They made Haydon Hill their only home. My grandfather died in 1932 and his widow and unmarried daughter continued to live there until the house was taken over by the RAF in 1942.

My own first clear memories of Haydon Hill are from 1916, although it was already familiar to me at that time. I was told that when my grandparents arrived only the central part of the house, including the tower, was in existence. My grandfather built on the kitchen wing, with nursery accommodation above. After about 10 years, as he had six surviving children, he later added the colonnade and billiard room with stage, and bedrooms above. The billiard table was on runners and could be easily moved and stored under the platform – for dances, receptions or parties.

My grandfather farmed the land from Haydon Road and High Street, up as far as his neighbour living in the house called Hillside in Merry Hill Road, now used by the BBC Religious TV Centre, then owned by Sir Harry Peat, father of Henry Peat of Peat, Marwick & Mitchell, Chartered Accountants.

My grandfather kept pure bred Jersey cows and produced his own butter, much of which was given to his family in the 1914-18 War. He also reared beef cattle and sheep and pigs and, of course, poultry, as did all farmers in those days. The large field adjoining the farm buildings and gardens down to the 'moat' was always known to the family as the 'Home Close'.

There was a public footpath with good stiles between the fields running from the Gardener's Lodge in Merry Hill Road through to Oxhey Lane. These fields were known at that time as the 'Brick Fields', as there was a brick kiln in operation bordering on Oxhey Lane. There were also public footpaths running from Haydon Dell in Merry Hill Road to the 'moat' and 'weir', which was crossed by a footbridge and from there both to Oxhey and also Haydon Road. The 'weir', I was told, had something to do with the Colne Valley Water Co supply, and the 'moat' and 'weir' were connected in some way to Bushey House grounds. My grandfather was most insistent that the public should keep strictly to the footpaths on his land and even employed a retired policeman at weekends to patrol the fields to see that this was so. Woe betide anyone who broke the rules!

He was a very rich, fiery tempered man but very just and exceedingly generous if approached for help with any worthy cause. He gave a great deal of money to Bushey, but only on the firm understanding that it should be entirely anonymous in most cases. He was one of the instigators of the Reveley Charity Almshouses, which he endowed very generously by the financial standards of those days. He also bought the land, now the village green in front of St James' Parish Church, on which there were slum cottages. Unfortunately some of the occupants refused to move out and had to be evicted, which I believe caused a furore in the local press of the time. He gave the green to the village in perpetuity upon trust of certain conditions; mainly that it should always remain a green with the low railings and grass maintained by the Council for children to play in safety. Never were there to be public meetings held on the green – religious or political – and no hoardings or notice boards of any kind were to be put there.

This trust was completely honoured in all respects until the 1939-45 War, when the railings were removed to help the war effort and no objection was raised. However, at a later date the council allowed a German Messerschmitt to be placed there with canvas erected all around so that people could view it. A sentry was posted to collect money for the war effort or RAF charity. My grandfather's youngest daughter, Ella May, was so angered at the Council's breaking of the trust that she attacked the unfortunate sentry with her umbrella and had to be forcibly restrained. The plane was forthwith removed but the 'Watford Observer' made a great report of the whole affair. At that time the land now occupied by the RC Church was empty and derelict and highly suitable for this purpose.

One Christmas between 1962 and 1964 the Highways Committee of Bushey Council erected a dismal notice of a woman in widow's weeds with the caption 'Keep death off the roads', thereby blocking the view of the Church notice board showing times of Christmas services. Within an hour of three local inhabitants seeing this eyesore, the Clerk of the Council was inundated with telephone calls and complaints. (I was in his office for that reason myself, so know it is a fact) and it was removed the same day. The Council has since put up concrete bollards to replace the railings, as cars were ruining the green. No objection has ever been raised to the placing of small crosses on the green for Remembrance Sunday".

Mary Harford

FOOTNOTES

1. The mill stream that passed under Lower High Street disappeared in the latter part of the 1980s when the old river course was diverted for Tesco's superstore development.
2. Watford's first purpose-built cinema, the Cinema Palace, opened in 1911 at 134 High Street, but closed four years later.
3. The hall was located in Clarendon Road between Arliss Court and Beechen Grove Baptist Church, now part of the one-way system. In this book it is referred to by the name in use at the period described.
4. The Carlton closed on 12 July 1980 and was demolished in 1982. Arliss Court/Palace Theatre Green Room occupy the site.
5. The Electric Coliseum in St Albans Road opened in 1912 and reopened in 1930 as the New Coliseum. It was renamed the New Plaza in 1936, closed in 1954 and was demolished in 1957. A tyre/exhaust business occupies the site.
6. The Central Hall in King Street reopened as the Regal in 1932 and the Essoldo in 1956. It has been a bingo hall for many years.
7. The Empire in Merton Road reopened as the ABC in 1986 and later that year as the Cannon. Now the Al-Zahra Centre.
8. The Odeon closed in 1963 and was demolished in 1964. Oceana occupies the site.
9. 44 High Street. After WWI it became the Empress Winter Gardens, where the short-lived Bohemian Cinema operated. Now The Moon Under Water.
10. The replacement memorial cross on Watford Heath was dedicated on 8 May 1994.
11. Sedgwick's Brewery was at 223 High Street, now Phoenix Apartments.
12. The Swan Inn fronted the road at 216 High Street. It was rebuilt further back from road in the 1930s and demolished in the 1990s. Watford Jaguar occupies the site.
13. The cobbles and maltings have gone. The walk now passes Tesco and Waterfields Shopping Park before reaching Water Lane.
14. The new Colne Valley Linear Park is near Radlett Road.
15. 23-33 High Street, formerly T J Hughes.
16. Now Halifax Building Society.
17. 60 High Street, now The Entertainer Toy Shop.
18. Beside Stephenson Way (A4008).
19. The remnants of the sluice gates have gone.
20. Falconwood apartments occupy the site.
21. 102-102a High Street, now Caffé Nero.
22. 4-6 Aldenham Road, now flats.
23. The Croxley Rail Link is due to open in 2016, diverting the 'Met' Watford branch services after Croxley Station to Watford Junction via a new section of line on a viaduct above the River Gade and the canal.
24. Tesco petrol station occupies the site of George Stephenson College.
25. Now the Peace Hospice. Only the central building remains, the side wings and rear outbuildings were demolished.
26. 107-115 The Parade, now Yates's.
27. See letter from Elsie Sutton at end of book.
28. A B Cox lived at Monmouth House. A prominent British crime writer, his novels included *Malice Aforethought* which he wrote under the name of Francis Iles. He also used the pseudonyms Anthony Berkeley and A Monmouth Platts.
29. 76 High Street, now Brook Street Bureau.
30. 82 High Street, William Hill occupies the site.
31. Titania's Palace is owned by the LEGO Group, Denmark, and is currently on loan to Egeskov Castle in Denmark where it is displayed in their museum.
32. 312 High Street. The Wheatsheaf was demolished in the mid-1990s. Mercedes-Benz occupies the site.
33. 112-114 The Parade.
34. Now Bushey Academy.
35. 76 Upper Paddock Road, now a private residence.

36. Herkomer's former film studios are at the corner of Bushey High Street/Melbourne Road, now Tryford House.
37. Gartlet Road marks the site of the school, which moved to Baynards, Nascot Wood Road in 1949. Baynards later became Watford School of Music. Now Harmonia Court
38. The Grove is now a hotel, spa and golf resort.
39. The Sun buildings were demolished, now Gateway residential/shopping complex.
40. Watford Trade Union Hall was demolished. The new Watford Trade Unionist & Labour Club is located nearby.
41. The site is adjacent to the pedestrian access to Waterfields Shopping Park.
42. 193-195 High Street is now the car parking area for Woodman's House.
43. 1a Carey Place is of early 16th century timber-framed construction, as is Jackson Jewellers at 16 High Street.
44. Cygnet Films was dissolved in the mid-1980s.
45. Film production finally ceased in 1985.
46. Watford Heath was designated as a Conservation Area in 2001. The designation was not finally adopted until 2008.
47. The historic clock was stolen after the Peace Memorial Hospital fell into disrepair in the late 1980s. It was replaced with a modern copy.
48. Now Ask Italian restaurant.
49. Watford Central Baths were demolished in 2007, now Watford Leisure Centre – CENTRAL.
50. Demolished, site to the rear of Watford Arches Retail Park, Lower High Street.
51. The Royal Caledonian School in Bushey closed in 1996, now the Purcell School.
52. Now part of Watford General Hospital.
53. The Whitsun Carnival was replaced by the Rainbow Festival. The latter was replaced in 2005 by Watford Celebration.
54. Odhams closed in September 1983.
55. 125-127 High Street.
56. The conversion of the Cross Roads into a roundabout took place in 1936.
57. Almond Wick was a yard with two barns, adjacent to the Bedford Almshouses.
58. Themed High Street walking tours are now capably led by Sarah Priestley, Museum & Heritage Manager, Watford Museum. (01923 232297)
59. Both are now under B&Q.
60. The Prudential Building is at 58-68 The Parade.
61. W H Smith was at 39 High Street.
62. 72 High Street, now Moss.
63. Woolworth's original store was at 118-124 High Street. Its replacement store occupied 118-128. Now McDonalds and adjacent small shops.
64. Now Watford Jaguar.
65. Rebuilt, now a residential/retail block at the side of Dreams.
66. 68 Chalk Hill, now Citygate Volkswagen.
67. As a result of Ted Parrish's endeavours, Oxhey District boundary marker No 2 was returned to Attenborough's fields in 1986.
68. Demolished, now Gap.
69. Dumbleton's has gone. See Henry Williams' letter at end of book.
70. Now The Flag, Station Road.
71. The Grove is now a hotel, spa and golf resort.
72. Timothy Whites was at 69 High Street, now the Card Factory.
73. Filmmaking finally came to Leavesden when Leavesden Film Studios were created in 1995. Warner Bros Studios acquired the film and media complex in November 2010.
74. Demolished, several small retail units including Scholls are on the site.
75. There are now eight Boys' Brigade companies in the Hertfordshire battalion, five run junior and below girls' sections. The surviving Watford Company, the 1st Watford Boys' Brigade, established in 1904, runs a Girls' Brigade in tandem.

INDEX